From Mud to Jug

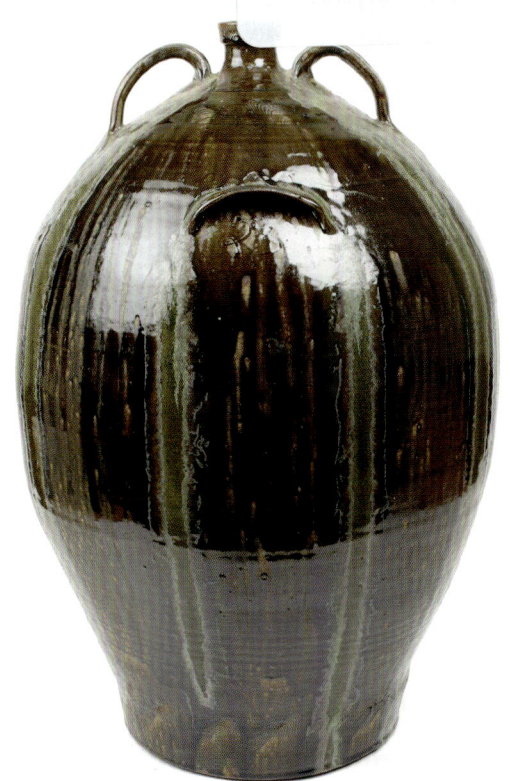

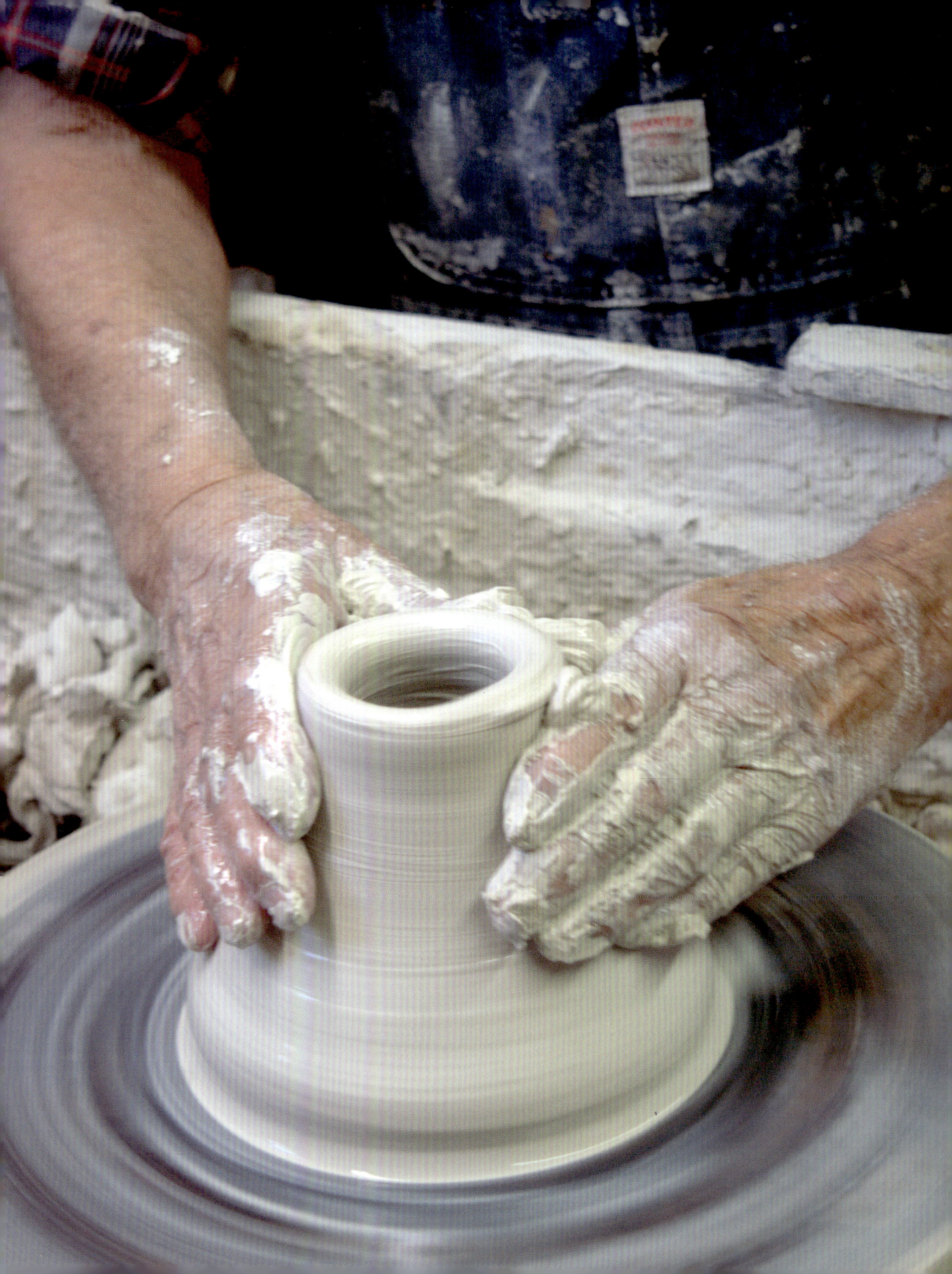

JOHN A. BURRISON

From Mud to Jug

The Folk Potters and Pottery of Northeast Georgia

THE UNIVERSITY OF GEORGIA PRESS | ATHENS AND LONDON

IN COLLABORATION WITH THE FOLK POTTERY MUSEUM OF NORTHEAST GEORGIA

Front-page image: Twenty-five-gallon jug, Michael Crocker, Lula, 2001, ash glaze with melted-glass decoration; photo by David Greear, Folk Pottery Museum collection.
Frontispiece image: Edwin Meaders at the potter's wheel; photo by Emory Jones.

© 2010 by the University of Georgia Press
Athens, Georgia 30602
www.ugapress.org

Designed by Erin Kirk New
Set in Scala
Printed and bound by Kings Time Printing Press, Ltd.

Most University of Georgia Press titles are
available from popular e-book vendors.

The paper in this book meets the guidelines for
permanence and durability of the Committee on
Production Guidelines for Book Longevity of the
Council on Library Resources.

Printed in China

17   16   15   14   13   P   6   5   4   3   2

Library of Congress Cataloging-in-Publication Data

Burrison, John A., 1942–
    From mud to jug : the folk potters and pottery of Northeast Georgia /
John A. Burrison.
    xxii, 161 p. : ill. (some col.), maps ; 26 cm.
    Companion and sequel to: Brothers in clay : the story of Georgia folk pottery.
Athens : University of Georgia Press, 1983.
    Includes bibliographical references and index.
    ISBN-13: 978-0-8203-3325-0 (pbk. : alk. paper)
    ISBN-10: 0-8203-3325-5 (pbk. : alk. paper)
    1. Pottery, American—Georgia. 2. Folk art—Georgia.
I. Burrison, John A., 1942– Brothers in clay.
II. Title. III. Title: Folk potters and pottery of Northeast Georgia.
        NK4025.G4B875 2010
    738.309758—dc22   2009024824

British Library Cataloging-in-Publication Data available

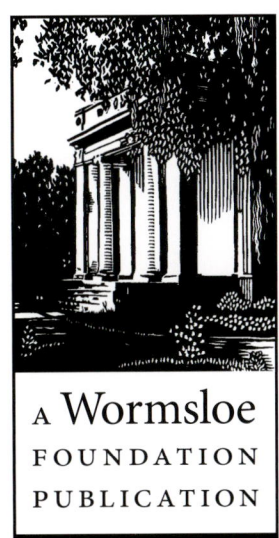

A Wormsloe
FOUNDATION
PUBLICATION

Publication of this book

was also made possible, in part,

by generous gifts from

Lucy Allen

Peggy Galis

Contents

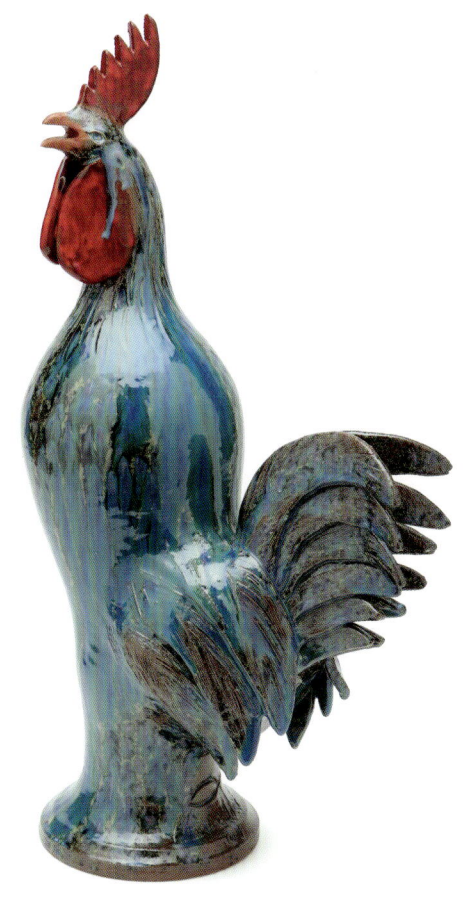

A Foreword in Celebration

Brothers in Clay, published back in 1983, is a masterpiece. In it, John Burrison combined the methods of folklorists and historians to create a comprehensive account of Georgia's ceramic tradition. Now in *From Mud to Jug*, a quarter of a century later, he brings the story up to date. It is an exciting story of sincerity, artistry, and courage—the story of a triumph. A grand tradition, once imperiled, abounds with new life, and John Burrison's scholarly endeavor— his writing, collecting, and work in museums—has proved to be a critical dimension in this tale of a successful artistic revival.

Traditions do not flow of their own momentum. They are picked up and carried on, constantly refigured in new acts by individuals answering the inner need to create. When the entrepreneur John Milton Meaders built his pottery at Mossy Creek, the demand for his ware was deep and wide; farm folk needed his jugs and crocks and churns to sustain their agricultural existence. But when John Milton's youngest son, Cheever, took over the works, the need had drained away. He should have stopped, but he kept at it. Something more than commerce drove him: the hands had their habits, the soul rolled with its creative desires, and Cheever Meaders, in his day, was the one who bravely carried it on. Then, in his day, it was Cheever's son Lanier, who was joined in success by his brothers Reggie and Edwin and their cousin C.J., a man as bright as beaten gold.

Though Lanier and C.J. have gone, the tradition of the Meaders family continues, carried on by C.J.'s son Clete, by Reggie's son

David, and David's wife, Anita. But today Georgia's tradition is anchored at Gillsville, in the skill, spirit, and hearty wit of Chester Hewell. Chester learned from Lanier and served the old master at the end of his life, and he urged into new vitality the tradition of his own family of potters, a line running back to old Nathaniel in the nineteenth century. Chester works with his father, Harold, with his mother, Grace Nell, with his sons, Matthew and Nathaniel, and with his grandchildren, Matthew's kids, Eli and Susannah. Someday, it may be, Eli and Susannah will be the ones to carry it on, but now the Georgia tradition finds its festive focus in the Hewell family's day of Turning and Burning, with Chester's able and delightful wife, Sandra, behind the scenes, gospel music in the tent, bright tractors in rows, and smoke rising from Chester's wood-fired kiln.

Chester Hewell and his family center the energy that swirls around Gillsville. Wayne Hewell, Chester's cousin, and Wayne's son

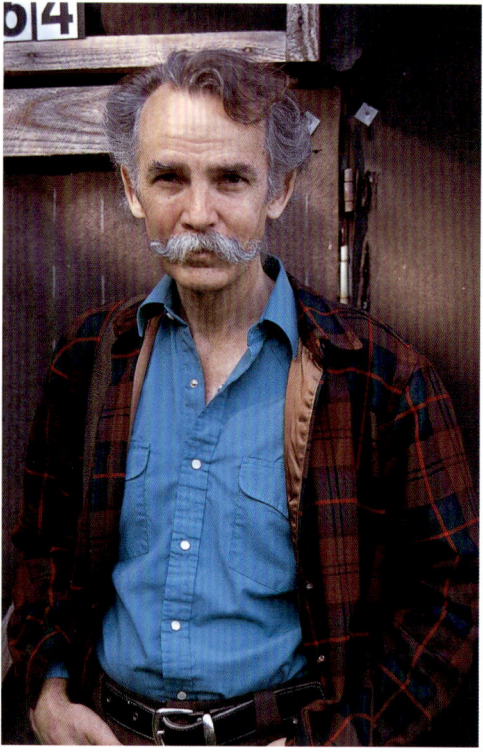

Folklorist Henry Glassie at Meaders Pottery, Mossy Creek, 2000. *Photo: author.*

Kevin, B. R. Holcomb who fires Chester's kiln, Bobby Ferguson's son Stanley, Lin Craven, Chris Holly, and those brothers of refined skill, Michael and Dwayne Crocker—all are working and reworking Georgia's old tradition into new wonders. A massive, exciting revival has taken place. The credit belongs, first of all, to the hardworking potters. But they have not reached this level of achievement alone.

In 1967, Ralph Rinzler, a gifted musician, was tasked to mount the Smithsonian Institution's first Festival of American Folklife on the national mall in Washington, D.C. Ralph had arranged demonstrations of craft to harmonize with the musical performances at the Newport Folk Festival, and he began the search for artisans to bring to Washington. Having read about the Meaders family in Allen Eaton's *Handicrafts of the Southern Highlands*, Ralph went to Mossy Creek, and miraculously, Cheever Meaders was still alive and still at work. Ultimately Ralph Rinzler would coauthor a fine book, *The Meaders Family: North Georgia Potters*; in 1967, he filmed Cheever's process and commissioned him to burn a kiln of ware for sale in Washington. Cheever called his son Lanier to his side. It was Cheever's last act; he turned a pitcher for the camera, fired the kiln, then died. But, in coming to help his father, Lanier had learned from Ralph about a new market, about city folks who did not use pots, who pickled no kraut, churned no butter, but who collected pots as examples of folk art, as emblems of history and skill. Lanier Meaders left the bad jobs with their bad pay, and came back to his heritage, moving onto the old place and concentrating on the face jugs—his father made few; he made thousands—that appealed to the customers in this new market. They snapped up those face jugs because they had been raised to believe that art had to be pictorial, representational, though the heart of the tradition beats in the honorable, calmly beautiful utilitarian ware.

Cheever had passed, Lanier had returned, and he was industriously at work when John Burrison came south from Philadelphia to settle in Atlanta as a professor of English at Georgia State University. Folklore was John's passion, folksongs in particular, but as he began to explore his new state, pottery claimed him. Lanier

Meaders became his teacher, his friend, and Lanier is the hero of *Brothers in Clay*. From Lanier's shop in Mossy Creek, John ventured away, meeting the Hewells and Fergusons, tracing their genealogies, learning their history, and writing his first book. *Brothers in Clay* remains a sterling piece of material culture research, and it has become the bible for collectors of Georgia pottery, old and new. Go to the Hewells' Turning and Burning (and you surely should), and there you will find collectors clutching copies of *Brothers in Clay*, hoping to meet the potters, to buy their pots and have them sign John's book beside their photos or names. An earnest work of scholarship, that is, has become a key component in this artistic revival, a source of encouragement to the artists, and an aid in their financial struggles.

Without Cheever and Lanier and Chester, there would be no pots, but without Ralph and John, this artistic revival, dependent on appreciation of proud forms and lively glazes, might never have happened. The artists and scholars are colleagues, as they should be, joined in the effort to keep alive the noble old arts that—as the wise and talented Matthew Hewell will tell you—serve to bring the past into the present and point a route to a richer future.

The buoyant revival in Georgia is not an isolated phenomenon. It is matched in North Carolina. There, Terry Zug, who was long ago in school with John Burrison and me at the University of Pennsylvania, conducted folkloristic and historical research like John's in Georgia. When Terry wrote *Turners and Burners*, Burlon Craig was his hero, as Lanier Meaders was for John—both were masters of the popular face jug—and Terry's book, like John's, has encouraged the potters and taught the collectors, becoming basic to the robust revival of North Carolina's ceramic tradition, celebrated in *The Potter's Eye* by Mark Hewitt and Nancy Sweezy.

Mark Hewitt is at once a potter and a scholar. Trained by Michael Cardew in the great tradition of Leach and Hamada, he came from England and settled in North Carolina to be part of a vital tradition. Revived and revived again, that tradition thrives in Mark's hands, and in the hands of Ben Owen III, Vernon and Pam Owens, Sid Luck, Kim Ellington, David Stuempfle, Chad Brown, Matt Jones,

Daniel Johnston, Michael Hunt, and Naomi Dalglish. Traditions cannot be confined by merely political boundaries, and the tradition of forms and glazes that developed in South Carolina, then flourished in northern Georgia and western North Carolina, has a modern master in Michel Bayne of Greenville, South Carolina. And in Alabama, Jerry Brown, with family connections back to Georgia and North Carolina, is still at it, as Joey Brackner's *Alabama Folk Pottery* will tell you.

The ceramic tradition of the South is alive and well—old, new, and going strong. The modern potters have their integrity, their books, their collectors, and the revival that *From Mud to Jug* documents for Georgia is part of a worldwide revitalization of the potter's art. You can find the same excitement, the same return to the past to shape a fulfilling future, in the pueblos of the Southwest, in Kvidinge and Raus in Sweden, in Kütahya in Turkey, in Jingdezhen and Pengcheng in China, in Hagi and Seto in Japan, in hundreds of places scattered over the earth. Pull them all together, and you will locate a force that is gathering to counter the technopop, commercialized spread of globalization. Then you can read *From Mud to Jug* as a model instance of productive cooperation between scholarship and art, and you can read it as a sign of a modern movement designed to preserve dedicated handcraft and artistic quality in a troubled old world.

HENRY GLASSIE

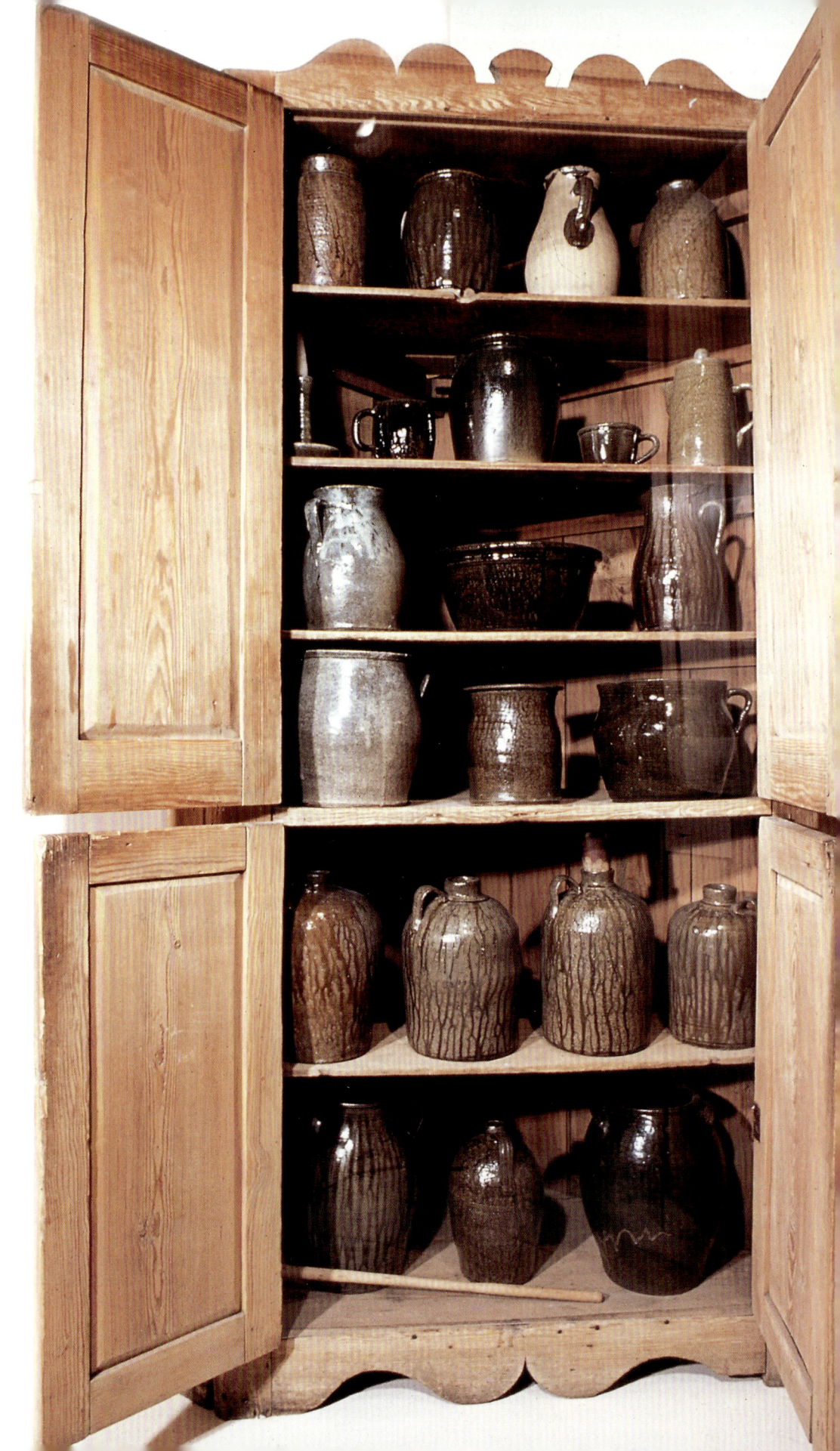

Preface

From Mud to Jug is a companion and sequel to my *Brothers in Clay: The Story of Georgia Folk Pottery*.[1] This book focuses on that part of the state that maintains an active practice of traditional pottery making continuously since the early nineteenth century. For this distinction north Georgia has become nationally recognized: it received a Library of Congress Local Legacies designation for its ceramic heritage in 2000; the Meaders Pottery of Mossy Creek was honored with a Library of Congress event in 1978 with the release of the Smithsonian Institution's documentary film, *The Meaders Family*; and the Hewell family of Gillsville was represented in the Southern Arts Federation's 2008 traveling exhibit, Tradition/Innovation: American Masterpieces of Southern Craft and Traditional Art. The tradition has also been featured in other museum exhibits and in books, magazines, festivals such as the Southern Crossroads Marketplace at the 1996 Olympic Games in Atlanta, and the *Antiques Roadshow* series televised by Public Broadcasting Service.

Purpose and Outline of the Work

My primary goal is to introduce readers to one of the last places in the United States where traditional pottery making still flourishes. To that end, after reviewing the craft's historical development in northeast Georgia, I explore the living tradition there, adding the

Opposite: North Georgia alkaline-glazed stoneware in a cupboard from John Meaders homeplace (in Atlanta History Center exhibit, Tangible Traditions: Folk Crafts of Georgia and Neighboring States, 1984–86). *Photo: author.*

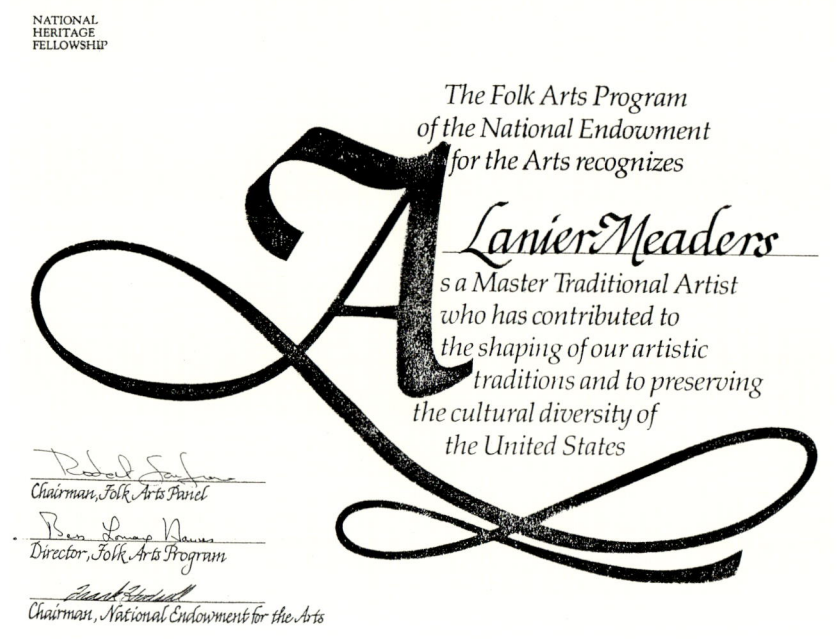

NATIONAL HERITAGE FELLOWSHIP

The Folk Arts Program of the National Endowment for the Arts recognizes

Lanier Meaders

as a Master Traditional Artist who has contributed to the shaping of our artistic traditions and to preserving the cultural diversity of the United States

Chairman, Folk Arts Panel

Director, Folk Arts Program

Chairman, National Endowment for the Arts

latest chapter to this constantly evolving story. Another important mission of this book is to support the Folk Pottery Museum of Northeast Georgia, which opened in 2006 at Sautee Nacoochee Center in the White County hills; royalties from the sale of *From Mud to Jug* will go to the museum. The book largely follows the exhibit scheme I developed as the museum's curator, making it usable as a visit guide or follow-up.

Involvement with the Folk Pottery Museum caused me to return to the subject I'd devoted fifteen years of my early career to studying and writing about, and to explore later developments in the living tradition. The effort exerted to produce *Brothers in Clay* had taken its toll (I estimate that I spent a solid year reading microfilms in the Georgia Archives and Federal Records Center, and I revised the manuscript a dozen times without the aid of a computer), so I was more than ready to move on to other projects after that book was published. I never completely lost touch with the subject and tried to maintain an active research file, but in retrospect I think I was temporarily burned out, and needed to distance myself for what turned out to be nearly two decades! But my love of the pottery and my positive feelings toward the potters never changed, and when I felt that the time was right, I was happy to immerse myself once again in writing about the subject.

From Mud to Jug is intended for a nonspecialist audience, especially readers new to the subject, although researchers and advanced collectors will find fresh information here. As a departure from *Brothers,* this book offers a large selection of new photographs of pots, people, and places—many in color—to enrich the story visually and to contribute to the University of Georgia Press's ongoing series on the state's decorative arts. Further, I offer some sources of north Georgia's stoneware tradition (chapter 3) and describe the Folk Pottery Museum and how it came about (chapter 9).

Of particular interest are a "census" of, and transcripts from recent interviews with, currently active folk potters (chapter 10), some of whom had not yet emerged as such when *Brothers* was

Potters at the Folk Pottery Museum of Northeast Georgia construction site, 2005. L–R: Reggie and Flossie Meaders, Dwayne Crocker, Wayne Hewell, Mike Perdue, Michael Crocker, Jeff Standridge, Dean Swanson (patron), Jamie, Stanley, and Mary Ferguson, Chester and Sandra Hewell, David and Anita Meaders, Roger Corn, Whelchel Meaders, Clint Alderman. *Photo: author.*

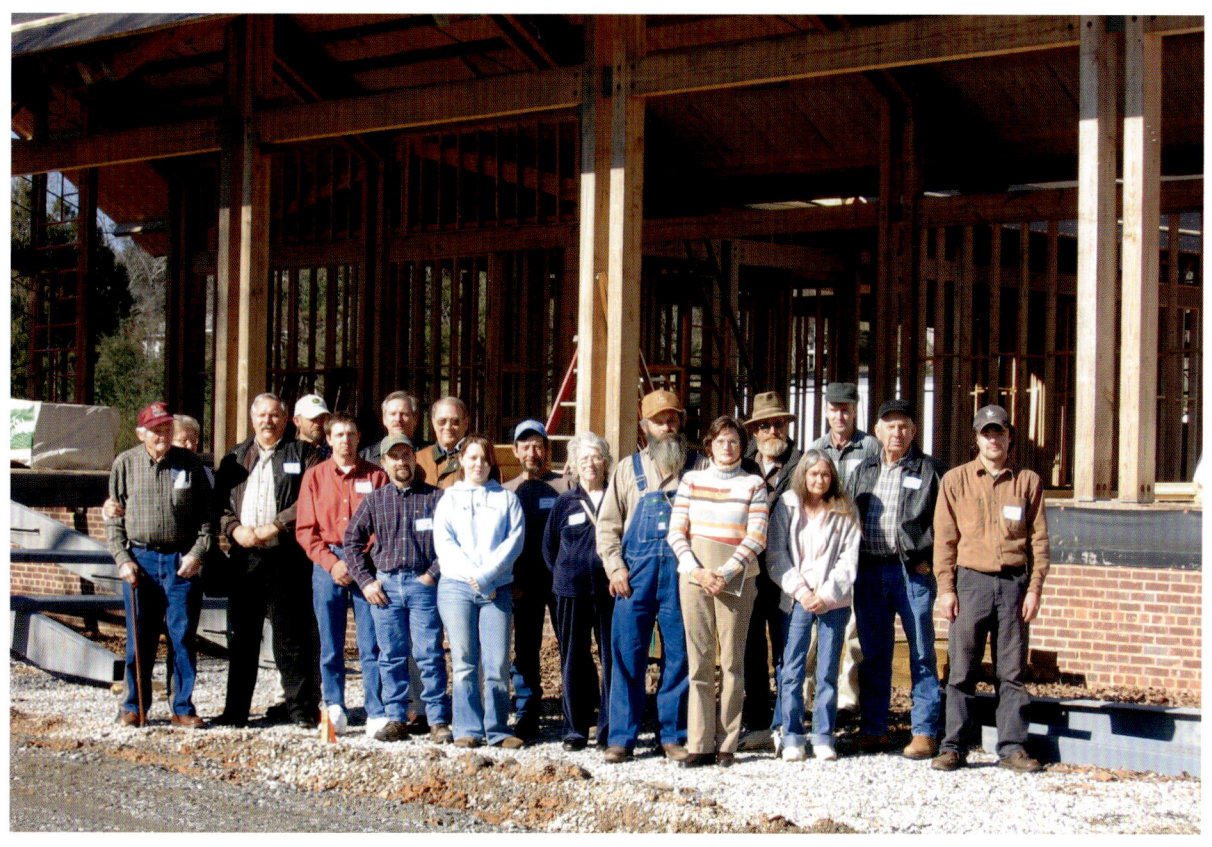

published. These interviews testify to the vitality of the tradition now, far greater than when I began my research in the 1960s. This vitality owes much to the influence of Lanier Meaders, whose death in 1998, along with that of his cousin Cleater ("C.J.") Meaders Jr. in 2003 and of Bobby Ferguson in 2005, left an enormous void in north Georgia's pottery tradition. That loss is partly compensated, however, by a new crop of potters who have taken ideas from Lanier, his mother (Arie Meaders), and others of the older generation and carry them forward creatively to delight a growing audience of collectors.

If north Georgia folk pottery is alive and well today, it is a somewhat different tradition than the one Lanier inherited from his father, Cheever, in the second quarter of the twentieth century. My account in subsequent chapters of these changes and the struggles of our grassroots potters to keep pace has implications beyond that small corner of the state, not just for ceramics but for many forms of traditional artistic expression in the modern world.

A Day with Lanier Meaders

In the Prologue to *Brothers in Clay* I describe my first meeting, in 1968, with Lanier and his admonishment to "don't be a stranger." Taking him at his word, for a good many years I made a point of visiting him at least once a month, my role as researcher soon easing into that of friend. On one of those occasions, a lazy summer day a decade after that first visit, he invited me to try my hand at his potter's wheel. I knew this was a special offer, one I'd not heard him extend to anyone before. I replied that while I'd certainly like to understand how he might teach someone, I'd tried to learn throwing several times in my life but didn't seem to have a knack for it, and that it could be a long, wasteful morning for him. He must have been feeling especially generous that day, for he wasn't deterred.

I'd often observed Lanier kicking the foot-bar of his treadle wheel as lumps of clay took form magically beneath his fingers

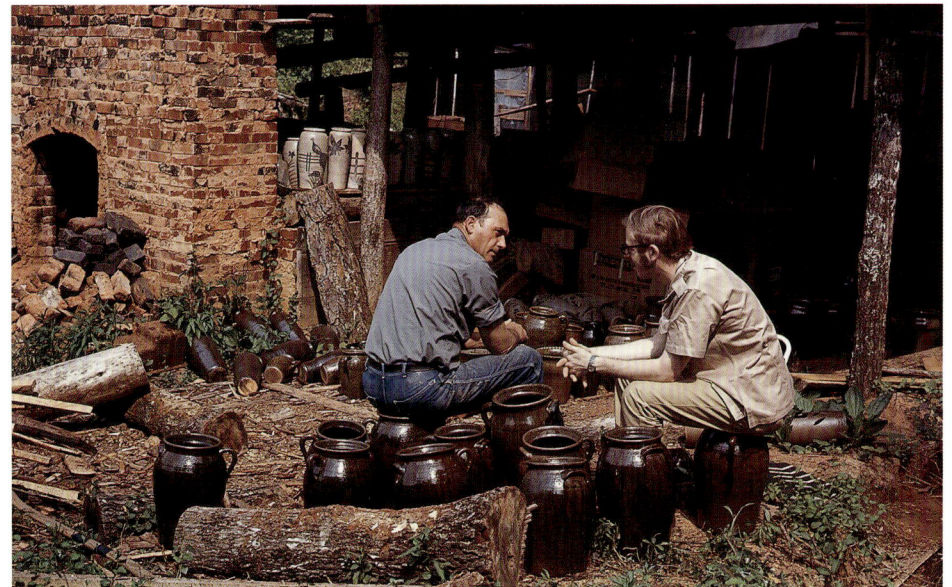

Mossy Creek potter Lanier Meaders (left) with author, 1970 (demonstrating another use for churns). Painted vases on the kiln were by Lanier's mother, Arie. *Photo: Richard Pillsbury.*

and hoped that I'd absorbed at least some of his technique by then. Without preliminaries he worked up a ball of clay, kindly centered it on the headblock for me, and stepped back to let me at it. The wheels I'd tried before were electric, so I knew I had to expend some real effort to make Lanier's human-powered wheel turn. For maybe twenty minutes I furiously pumped away at the foot treadle while Lanier stood by patiently, not saying a word but clearly suppressing a grin. Suddenly he rushed at me with a handkerchief pulled from his pocket. This attack startled me until I realized that he was wiping the blinding perspiration from my eyes. Then he spoke for the first time, declaring that I'd been turning the wheel in the wrong direction! In the Western world, at least, a potter's wheel turns counterclockwise, the clay moving toward, rather than away from, the potter's hands. No wonder I'd made little progress.

I stopped the wheel and reversed direction, beginning anew. Trying to recall how Lanier used his hands both inside and outside the pots he "pulled up," I shifted my concentration from the foot-bar to the spinning clay on the headblock. But the clay also was shifting—off center, to become a lopsided mess. Apparently I was exerting too much pressure on one side. Several times I stopped

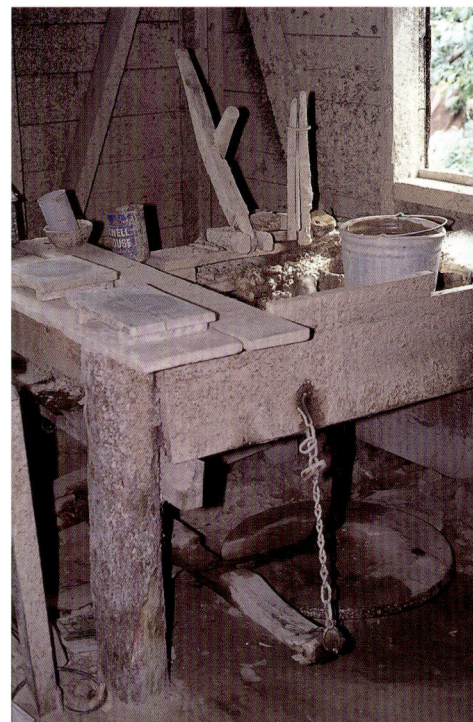

Lanier Meaders's foot-powered, treadle-and-crankshaft potter's wheel, 1977. *Photo: author.*

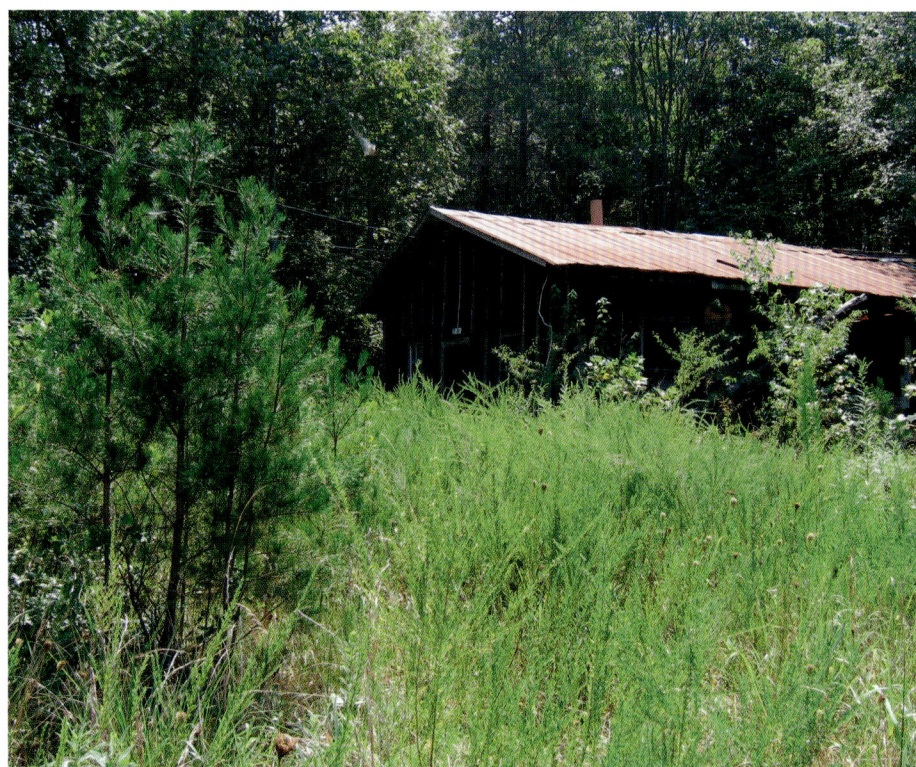

the wheel and recentered the clay. An exhausting half hour of this and I'd succeeded in creating something like a misshapen ashtray.

At this juncture a seven-year-old cousin of Lanier walked through the open door of the tar-papered shop for the first time in her life and asked if she could make something. Even after his ordeal with me he was in an obliging mood, so with just a bit of verbal instruction and his guiding her hands as she cranked the wheel, it took the little girl all of five minutes to finish a beautifully symmetrical bowl. So ended my lesson.

I tell this story when people ask if I make pottery, since I've written so much about the craft. I say that my interest springs from my appreciation of others' skill, a skill I lack but greatly admire in the subjects of this book. My craft isn't the shaping of clay but the shaping of words and pictures to create in these pages what I hope will mirror the beauty of north Georgia folk pottery.

Acknowledgments

I am especially grateful to the Hewell family of Hewell's Pottery, Clete Meaders, David Meaders, Stanley and Jamie Ferguson, Dwayne Crocker, and Lin Craven for taking time to be interviewed and for their thoughtful responses. I am also indebted to: Chris Brooks, director of the Folk Pottery Museum of Northeast Georgia, my liaison with that facility; David Greear, Emory Jones, and Chris Swanson for photographs they took for the Folk Pottery Museum, and further to Emory (grandson of Wiley Meaders) for contributing family photos; Steve Engerrand and Gail DeLoach of the Georgia Archives for permission to use historic photographs from the Vanishing Georgia Collection; Bill Selman and Dale Brubaker for graphics and design of the Meaders and Ferguson-Hewell genealogical charts; Kirk Elifson for companionship and photography on research trips; Richard Gordon, Lori Howard, and John Medlock of Georgia State University for their computer wizardry; Bob Cain and Dean and Kay Swanson for sharing photographs they commissioned of the Folk Pottery Museum; Susan Crawley and Sara Hindmarch of the High Museum of Art (Atlanta) and Tina McCalment of Berea College (Kentucky) for help with photographs in their collections and permission to use them; Henry Glassie, Terry Zug, and Betty Jean Meaders for their friendship and support; my Georgia State University folklore students Jennifer Corcoran, Laura M. Drummond, Leslie Gordon, Tyrie J. Smith, and

Anthony Souther for their potter interviews; and Divya Nair and Nicole Mullen for transcribing several potter interviews. Finally, I thank another Nicole—Nicole Mitchell, director of the University of Georgia Press—for her encouragement.

From Mud to Jug

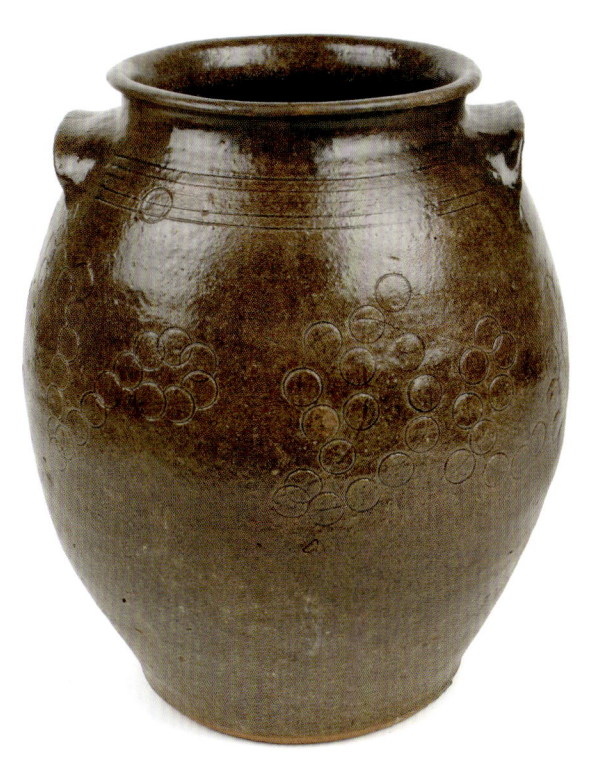

CHAPTER 1

Folk Pottery

A Handed-on Tradition

We use clay products daily, usually without thinking about where they came from. Most pottery used in the United States today is either machine-molded table- and kitchenware or the self-consciously artistic work of school-trained studio potters. These approaches to making things of clay sprang from the Industrial Revolution's mass-production technology and the resulting Arts and Crafts response. Until the mid-1800s, however, most American pottery was folk.

What sets these wares apart from those of the factory, artist's studio, and home hobby room? To folklorists, who adopted the term *folk pottery* in the 1970s, folk behavior of any kind results from informal, face-to-face learning of group-shared knowledge. Folk potters, then, are those who've learned their designs and handcrafting skills from other traditional potters and are thus human links in a chain of handed-on tradition. Drawing on this community-based resource still gives folk potters the freedom to interpret the tradition to suit their individual needs and creative impulses, accounting for the artistic developments seen today in north Georgia folk pottery.

As with all traditional arts, folk pottery is learned by observation and practice in a family or apprenticeship setting. As fourth-generation potter Clete Meaders put it, "In my family, pottery was what was going on, what was talked about. I didn't have formal training, step-by-step instruction; I just watched and learned." Members

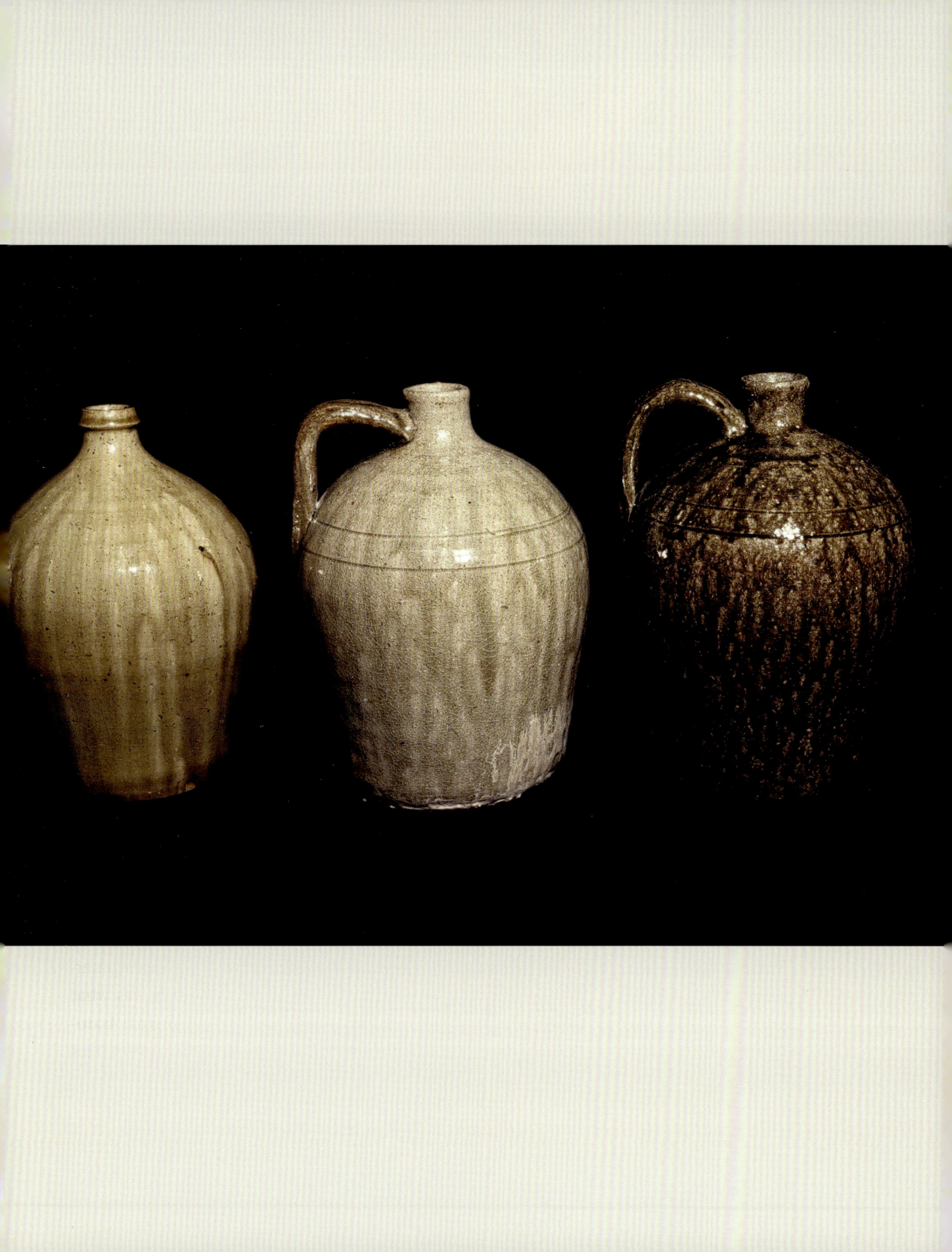

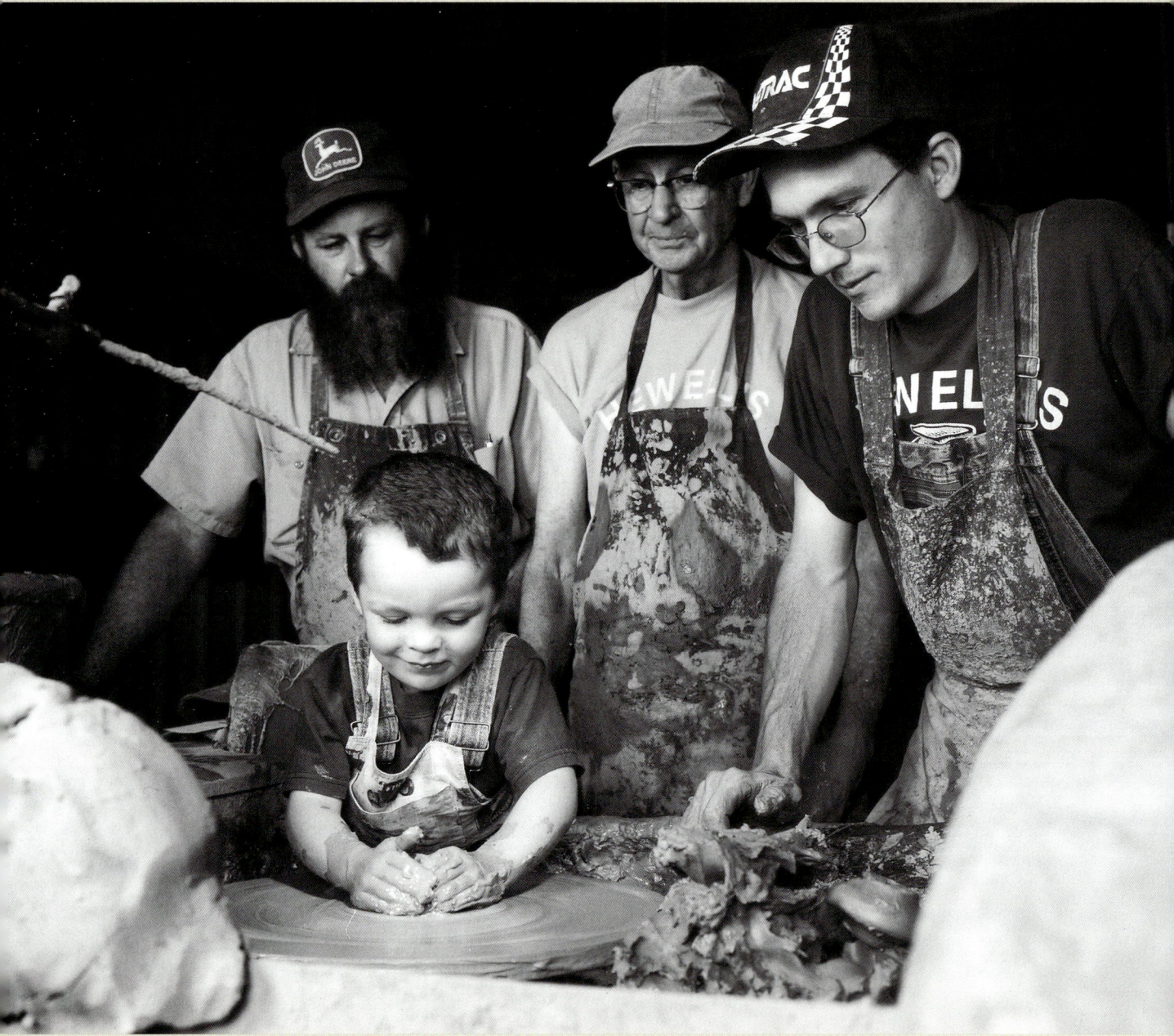

Handing on the Hewell family pottery tradition, Gillsville, 2001.
Three living generations, plus three historical ones, stand behind
the training of two-and-a-half-year-old Eli. Shown with him are
(L–R): his grandfather, Chester; great-grandfather, Harold; and
father, Matthew. *Photo: Chris Swanson.*

of families that have been making pottery for generations are immersed in the craft from childhood and identify with it as a way of life. Such early exposure offers a head start, but growing up in a "clay clan" is no guarantee of becoming a good potter. Mastering this demanding craft takes years and requires native ability, dedication, and patience.

Family learning has always been an important way of maintaining southern folk crafts, but apprenticeship—training as a teenager or adult under an experienced master—is also part of the story and has become especially important in the garden pottery tradition. Two of north Georgia's still-active "clay clans" began this way in the nineteenth century: the first Meaders potters learned from hired potters of two other White County families, and pioneer Barrow County potter Charles H. Ferguson apparently began his career back in Abner Landrum's South Carolina workshop. Much more recently, Ferguson's descendant, Bobby Ferguson of Gillsville, not only helped members of his family learn the craft but also took as apprentices others who now work on their own. So the two kinds of training can go hand-in-hand, and both have kept alive a vernacular, or locally based, ceramic tradition.

Once the norm but now a rare exception, Euro-American folk pottery (i.e., European-derived, as opposed to the Native American tradition most active in the Southwest) thrives only in northeast Georgia and North Carolina. Why and how it has survived here, in the midst of modern ways of making things, is the subject of the following chapters.

CHAPTER 2

Clay Country

Northeast Georgia

In the early 1800s, American folk potters shifted their production from relatively soft and porous earthenware to stoneware, a tough ceramic product made of fine-grained, fairly pure clay that fires gray or tan. Georgia's stoneware clay is concentrated along the Fall Line that slashes across the state's middle as well as in scattered deposits north of the Fall Line in the Piedmont Plateau.

This "clay country" also was some of Georgia's richest farmland, attracting early potters who were often farmers themselves and whose wares served the needs of their farm and plantation neighbors. The success of those pioneer potters attracted others to the craft, and by the late 1800s Georgia boasted nine pottery centers, three of them in the upper Piedmont of northeast Georgia.

Opposite: Native American bowl from Nacoochee Valley, White County, ca. 1400s, incised and paddle-stamped decoration. North Georgia's clay was used long before European settlers arrived. Earthenware pots were coil-built and pit-fired, and still are by traditional Cherokee and Catawba potters in the Carolinas. This late-Mississippian-period bowl was excavated from Nacoochee Mound in 1916 by the Museum of the American Indian (Heye Foundation) and the Smithsonian Institution's Bureau of American Ethnology. H. 8¼ inches, W. 15 inches. *Photo: David Greear; on loan to Folk Pottery Museum of Northeast Georgia (hereafter "FPM" in credits) from the National Museum of the American Indian, Smithsonian Institution, cat. no. 049431.000.*

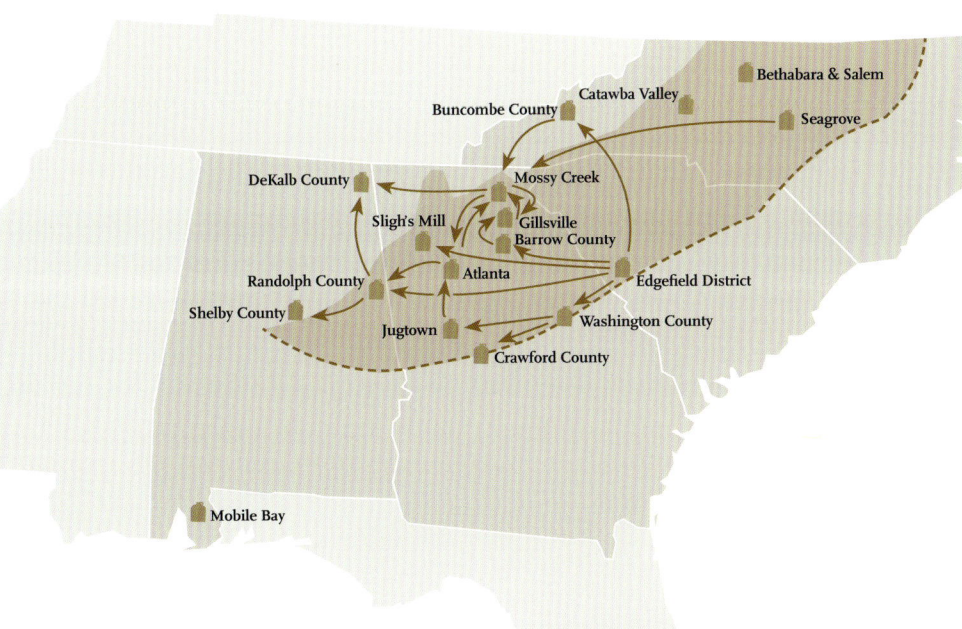

Northeast Georgia within the larger regional pattern of pottery centers, located mostly in the Piedmont (darker shaded area) where stoneware clay is concentrated. Arrows show movements of some potters, including those who spread the alkaline-glazed stoneware tradition from South Carolina's Edgefield District. *Based on a map by Staples & Charles Ltd.*

Pottery Centers
Piedmont
— — — Fall Line

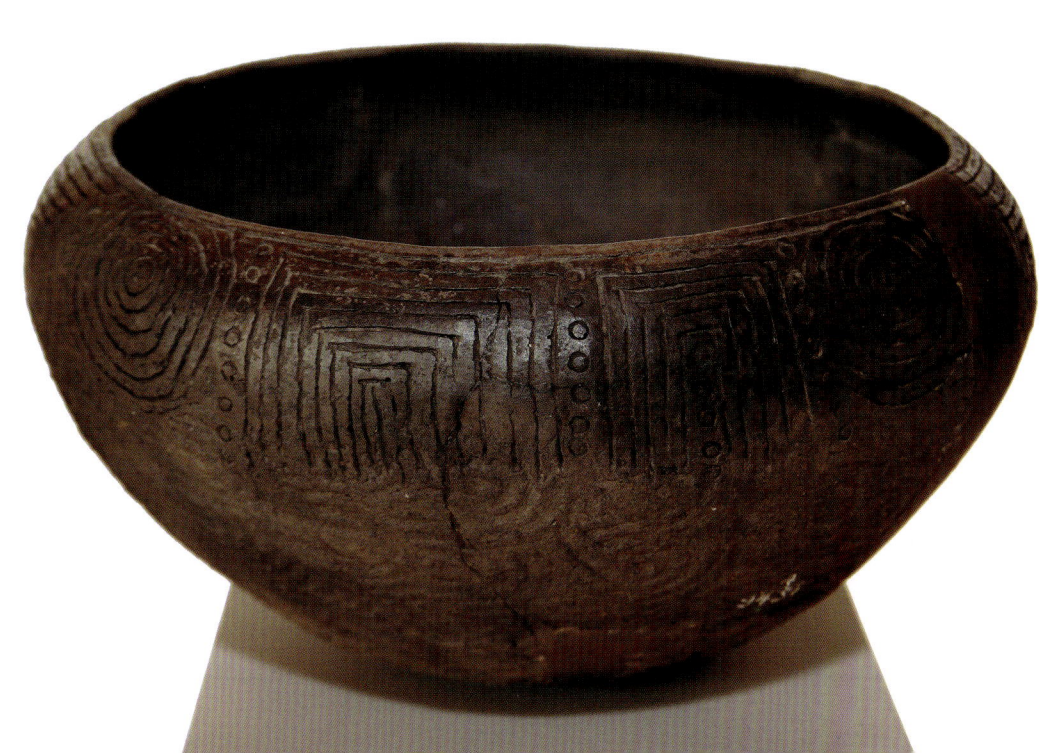

Upper Piedmont Centers

Georgia's pottery centers were farming communities where folk potters clustered. Their wares were sold directly from the pottery yard as well as wagoned by family members or middlemen peddlers. Different hauling routes eased competition in centers such as Mossy Creek, where nine shops operated "within hollering distance" in the early 1900s. General stores and whiskey distillers were their biggest customers before gift and crafts shops took over that role.

Mossy Creek, White (originally Habersham) County

This farming settlement in the foothills below Cleveland, which included the post offices of Leo and Benefit, was Georgia's largest pottery center, home to over eighty folk potters since the 1820s. The pioneer potters, including members of the Davidson, Craven, and Dorsey families, came from North Carolina.

Both ash- and lime-based alkaline glazes have been used at Mossy Creek. Specialized forms include multinecked "flower jugs" (jugs intended as vases to display cut flowers), squatty-pitcher-type "cream risers," and later face jugs (jugs featuring applied human faces). The Meaders family entered the craft late but carries it on today.

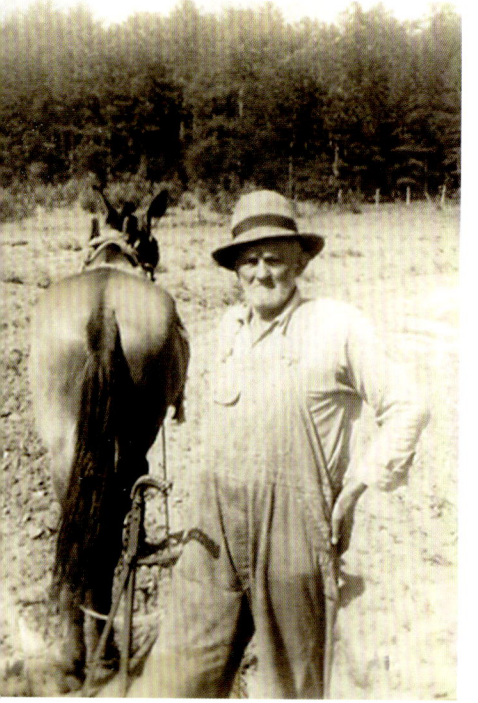

Wiley Meaders plowing with a mule, Mossy Creek, early 1940s. Many north Georgia folk potters were also farmers, and some still are (Gillsville's Chester Hewell raises cattle; his cousin, Wayne Hewell of Lula, raises poultry). Wiley was the eldest of six potter sons of Meaders Pottery founder John Milton Meaders. *Courtesy of Emory Jones.*

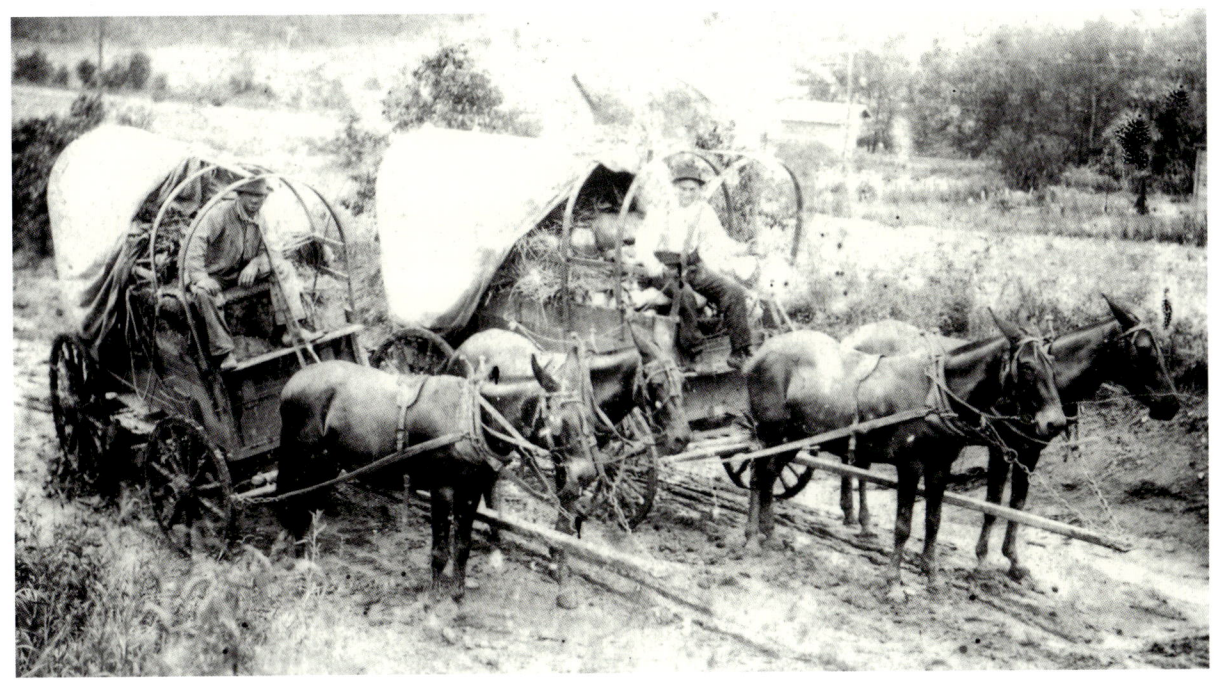

Mule-drawn covered wagons loaded with straw-cushioned pottery from Daddy Bill Dorsey's Mossy Creek shop on a selling trip, ca. 1910. One of the drivers is a Dorsey, the other a Meaders. *Courtesy of Leone Palmer and Emory Jones.*

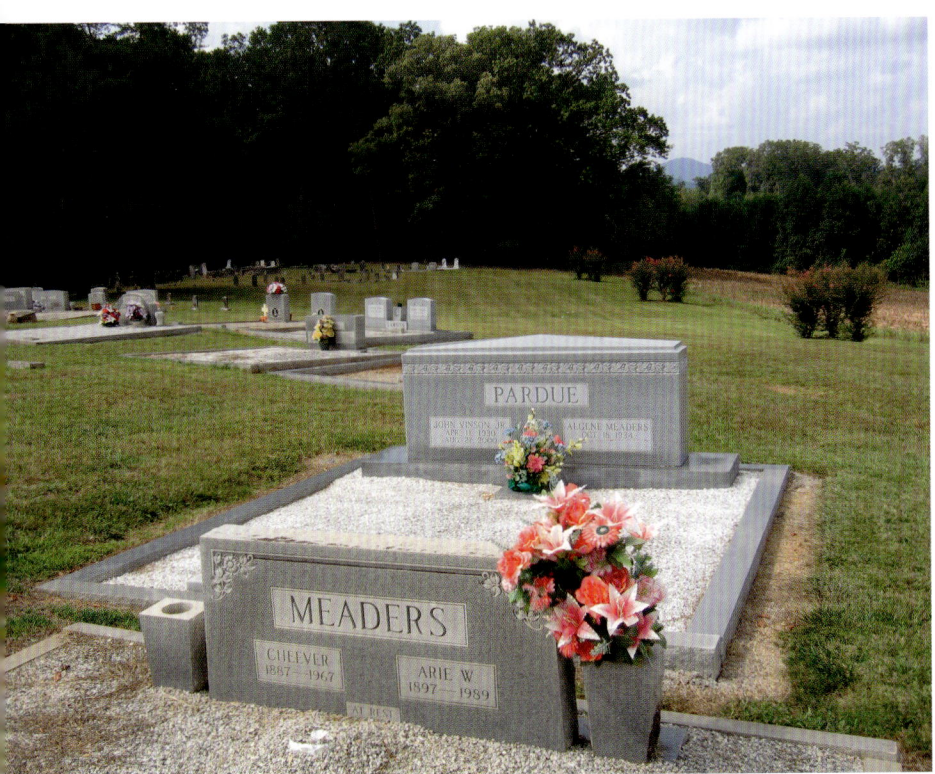

Mossy Creek Methodist Church cemetery, 2008, in rolling upper-Piedmont terrain. Buried in the older section in distance is Frederick Davidson, a church founder and likely pioneer potter; in the foreground are the graves of Cheever Meaders, who ran Meaders Pottery 1920–67, and his wife, Arie, who created designs that are now part of the north Georgia tradition. *Photo: author.*

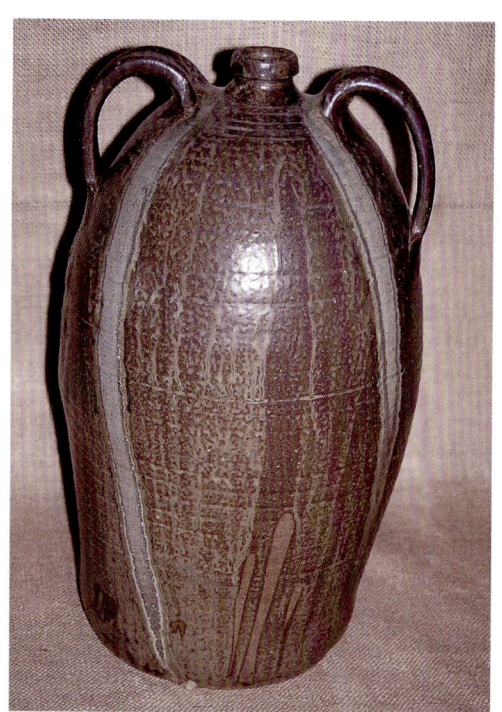

Five-gallon syrup jug attributed to the Davidson family, ca. 1850, alkaline (ash) glaze. The decorative technique of glass placed on handles or rims and melted in the kiln was concentrated in North Carolina; its rare use on Mossy Creek wares points to the origin of that north Georgia center's pioneer potters. H. 19½ inches. *Photo: author; author's collection.*

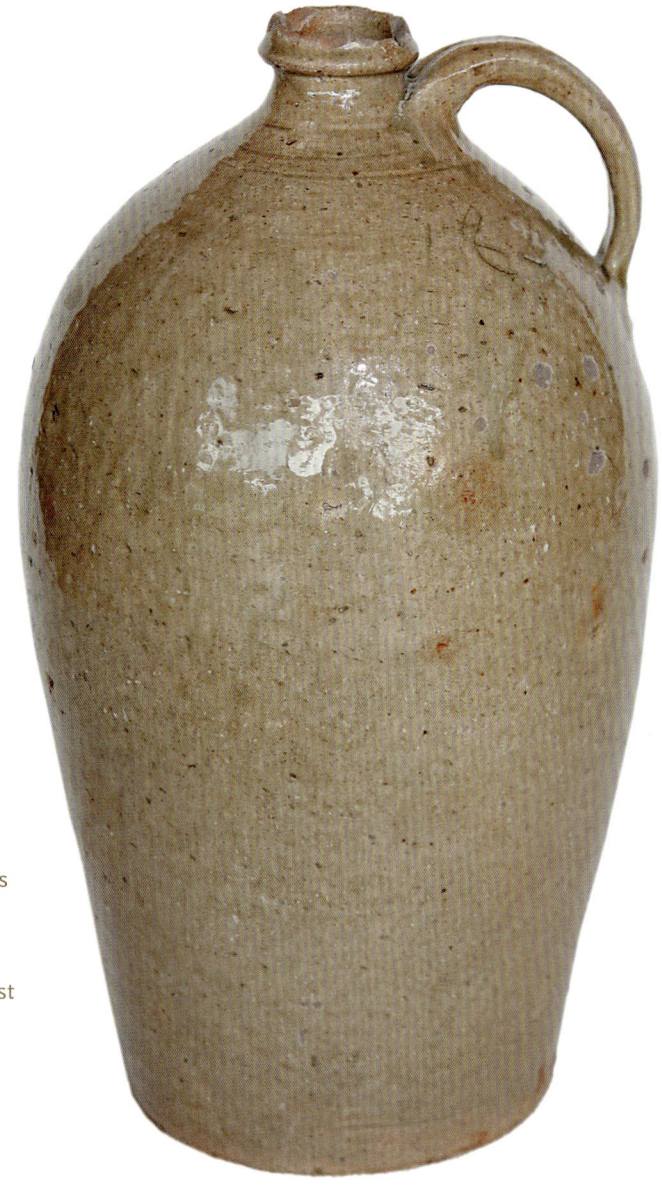

Three-gallon syrup jug, maker unknown, 1846 (incised date), alkaline (lime) glaze. Found in a White County smokehouse, it has the pronounced lip of antebellum jugs and the elongated shape of syrup jugs from this center. The light clay and glaze are in contrast to the more typically dark north Georgia wares. H. 16¼ inches. *Photo: David Greear; on loan to FPM by Atlanta History Center.*

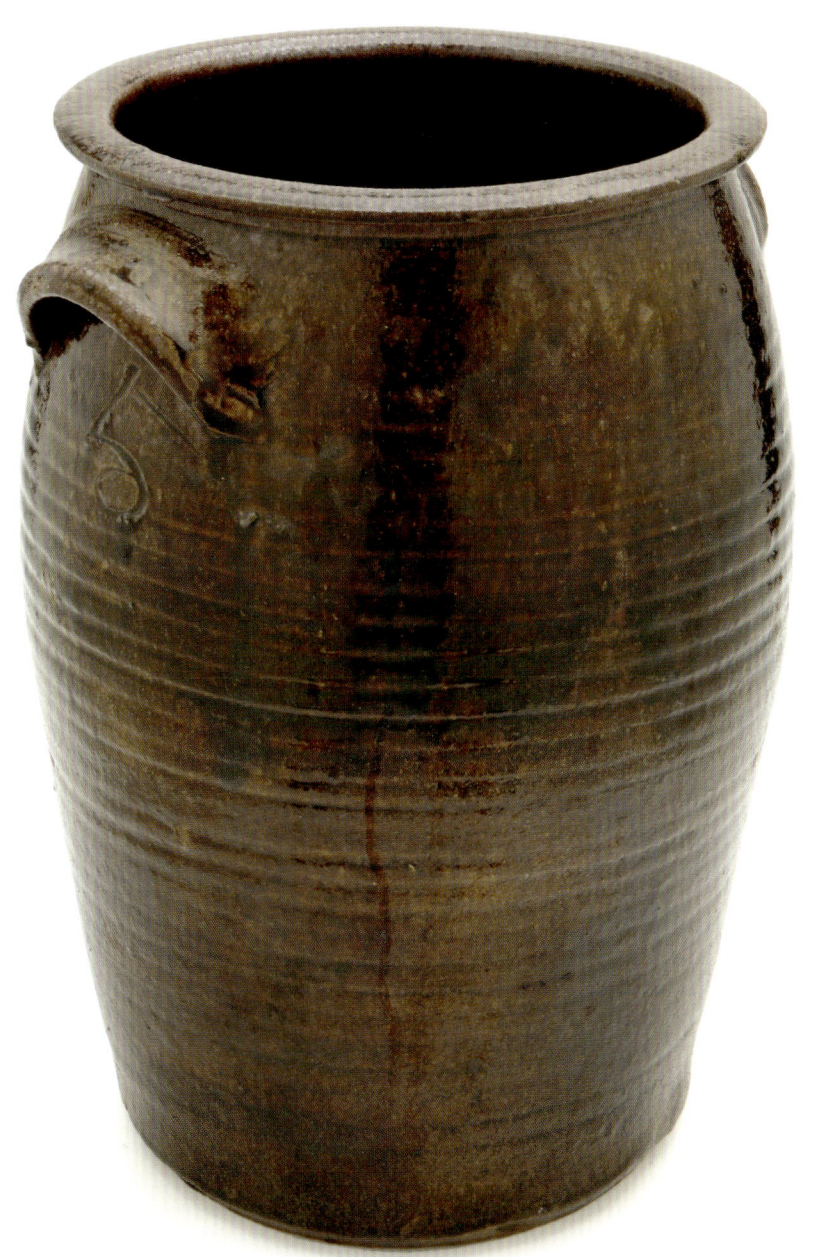

Five-gallon storage jar, Isaac H. Craven, 1870s–1880s, alkaline (ash) glaze. On larger jars he used the flattened rim (typical of his father's home state, North Carolina) to scratch the gallon capacity in Roman numerals, in this case "V" (with the Arabic numeral incised below each lug handle for good measure). H. 15½ inches. *Photo: David Greear; FPM collection.*

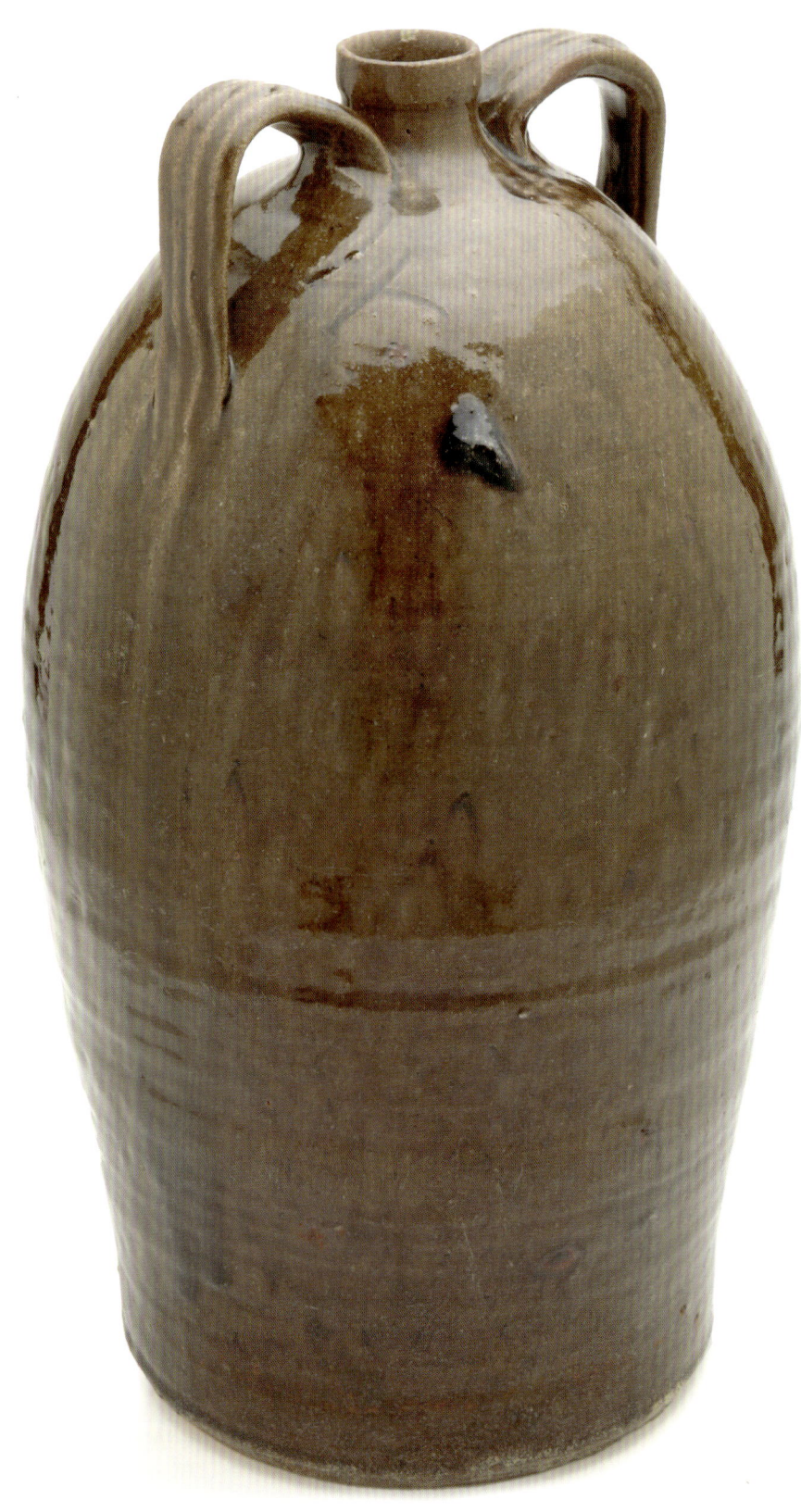

Four-gallon syrup jug attributed to Joseph Tarplin ("Tarp") Dorsey, 1880s, alkaline (lime) glaze. It has the elongated shape of earlier Mossy Creek syrup jugs and Tarp's usual ring-collar at the mouth. He was a son of pioneer White County potter Davey Dorsey. The Dorseys used both ash and lime glazes. H. 19½ inches. *Photo: David Greear; FPM collection.*

Jug Factory, Barrow (originally Jackson) County

Charles H. Ferguson was trained in the early alkaline-glazed stoneware tradition of Edgefield District, South Carolina. He moved to Georgia and by 1847 had set up a "Jug Factory" (as shown on early maps) just east of present-day Statham. He began a sixty-potter dynasty that, through marriage, came to include the DeLay, Archer, Dial, Robertson, and Hewell families.

During the Civil War, potters added ash-glazed plates and cups to their usual food-storage wares to substitute for factory-made tableware kept out by the Union blockade. Later pottery was salt glazed over Albany slip (see description of Albany slip in chapter 3). By 1900 most Barrow County shops had closed, leaving only Henry H. Hewell of Winder and the Bell Pottery of Bethlehem to operate into the early twentieth century.

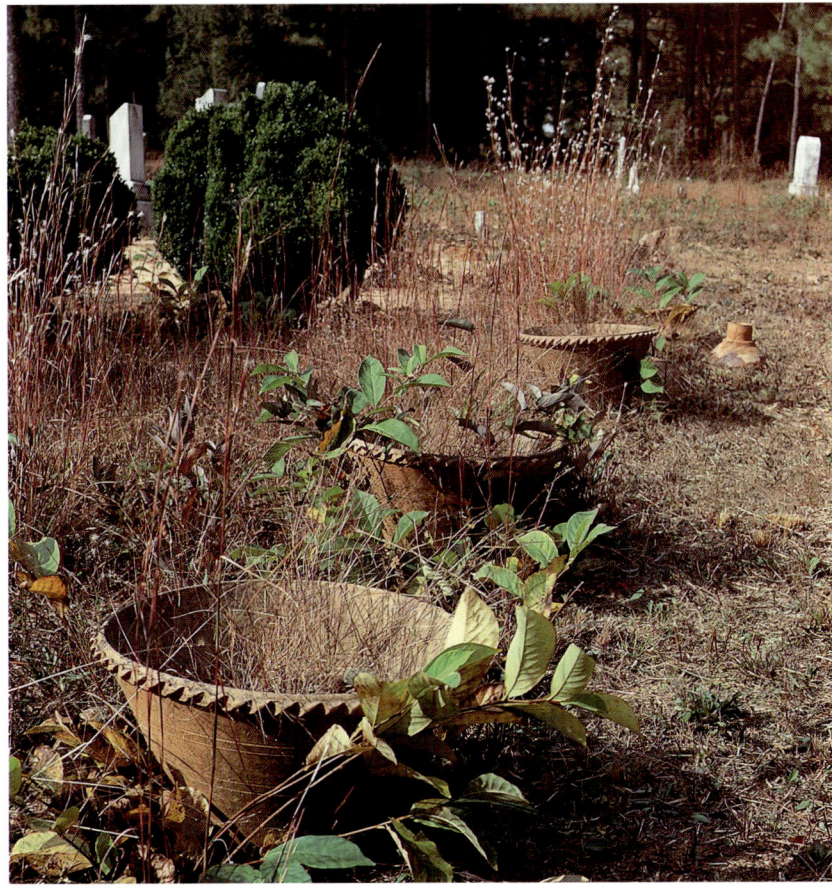

DeLay Cemetery near Statham, 1978, where some Barrow County potters are buried. This is the only north Georgia pottery center known to have made ceramic grave markers; the unglazed, fluted-rim tub planters have since sunk to ground level. *Photo: author.*

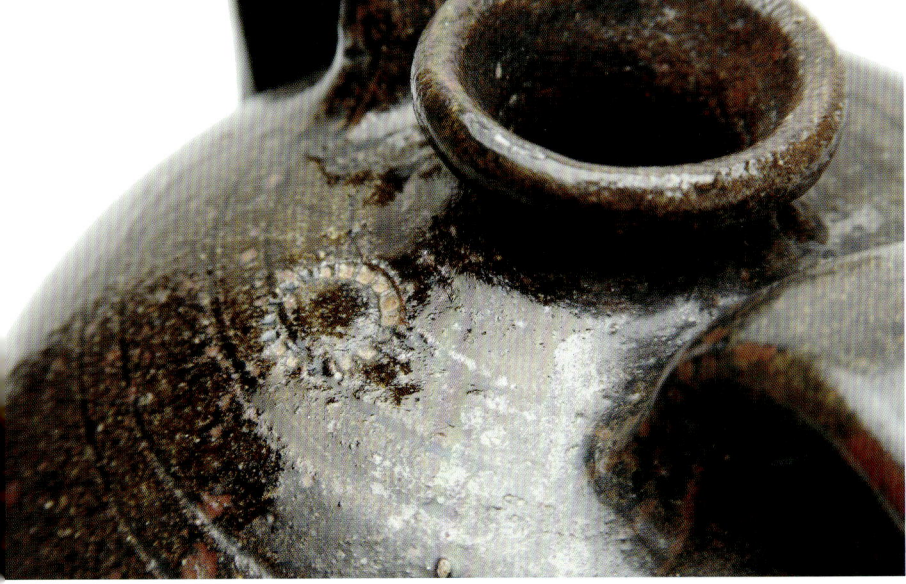

Detail of circular mark on shoulder of George Ferguson syrup jug; similar maker's marks are found on wares of other Barrow County potters. *Photo: David Greear.*

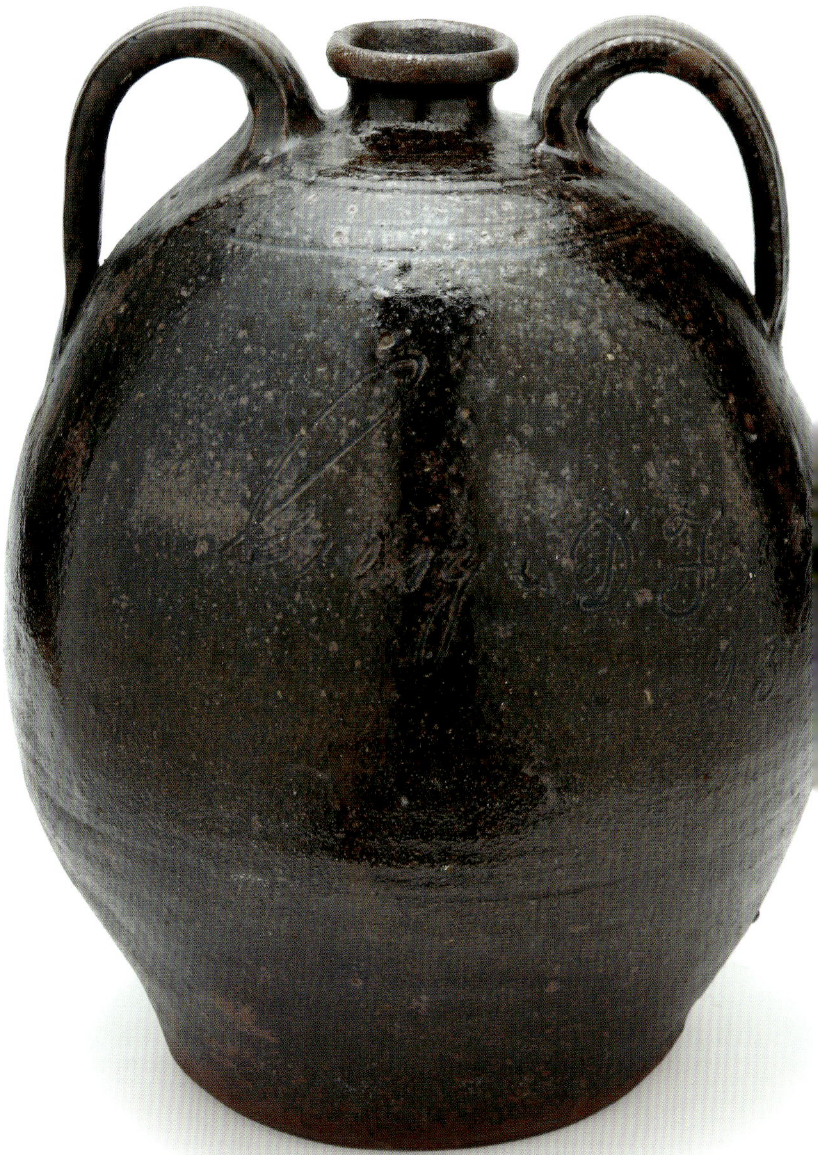

Four-gallon syrup jug, George D. Ferguson, 1868 (incised signature and date), alkaline (ash) glaze. His grandfather, Charles H. Ferguson, was associated with stoneware pioneer Abner Landrum back in Edgefield District, South Carolina, and by 1847 had opened the Jug Factory in what is now Barrow County. H. 16½ inches. *Photo: David Greear; FPM collection.*

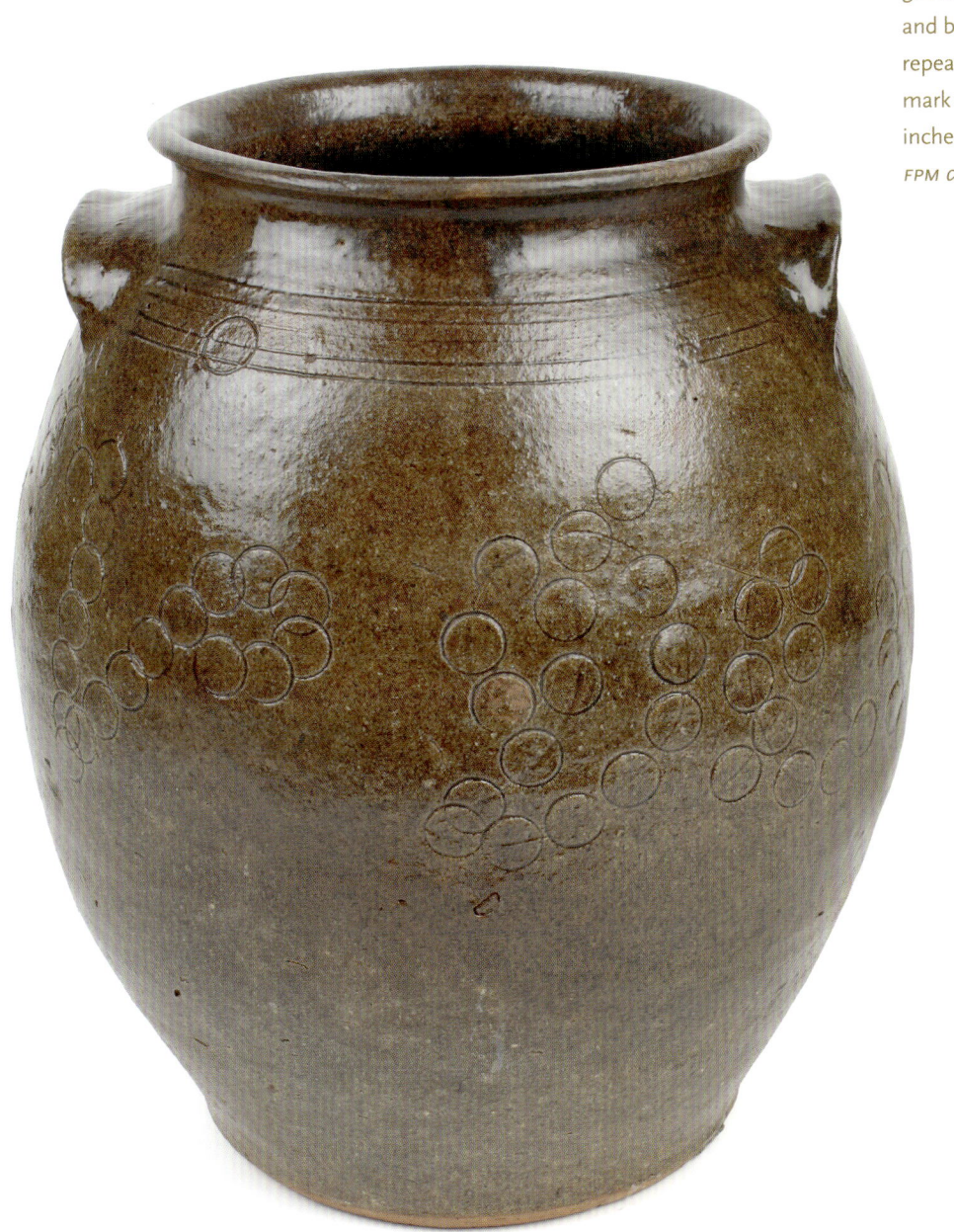

Four-gallon storage jar, Russell Van DeLay, ca. late 1860s, alkaline (ash) glaze. He likely became a potter through marriage to pioneer potter Charles H. Ferguson's granddaughter, Martha Ann, and boldly signed this piece by repeating the local ring-stamp mark to spell his name. H. 14½ inches. *Photo: David Greear; FPM collection.*

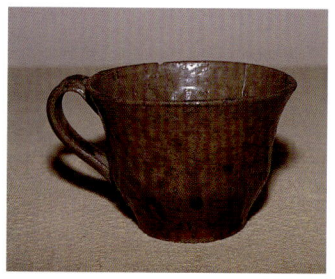

Teacup thought to have been made at Ferguson and Dial Pottery ca. 1863 in lieu of imported, factory-made tableware blockaded by the Union, alkaline (ash) glaze. H. 3½ inches. *Photo: author; ex-collection of Mr. and Mrs. William W. Griffin.*

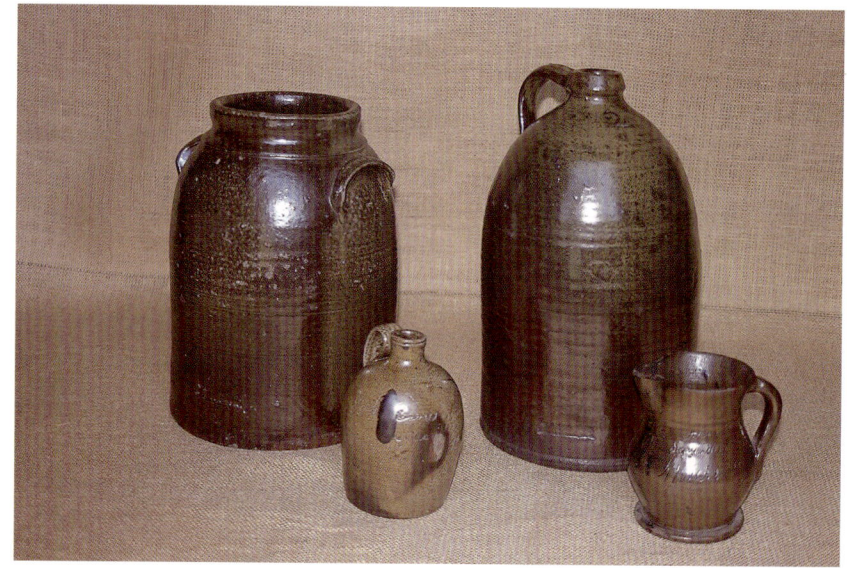

Postbellum wares by Barrow County–trained potters, Albany-slip glaze, all but the pitcher showing salt glaze as well. Larger jug and crock stamped "W. C. Robertson / Barbers Creek P.O."; small jug possibly by W. R. Addington, inscribed "John Crow / Gillsville, Ga."; pitcher attributed to Marcus Archer, inscribed "Mrs. Arrie B. Archer / Aug. 4 1879 / Mallorysville, Ga." *Photo: author; ex-collection of Mr. and Mrs. Levon Register.*

Gillsville, Hall County

This small town east of Gainesville, at the juncture of the Banks County and Jackson County lines, blossomed as a pottery center in the late 1800s, fed by migrants from Mossy Creek to the north and Jug Factory to the south. The first known potter in the area, in 1860, was Clemonds Chandler of White County; the next, in 1880, was William Addington of Barrow County. A few years later another White County potter, John Robert Holcomb, arrived and built a shop, which his grandson, Samuel Rayburn ("Ray") Holcomb, maintained until 1945.

In the 1940s, Gillsville potters reacted to falling demand for their Albany slip–glazed farm wares by shifting to unglazed garden pottery. The Hewells, Cravens, Sims, and Wilsons (the first two still in production) made such pottery on a large scale and trucked it all over the country.

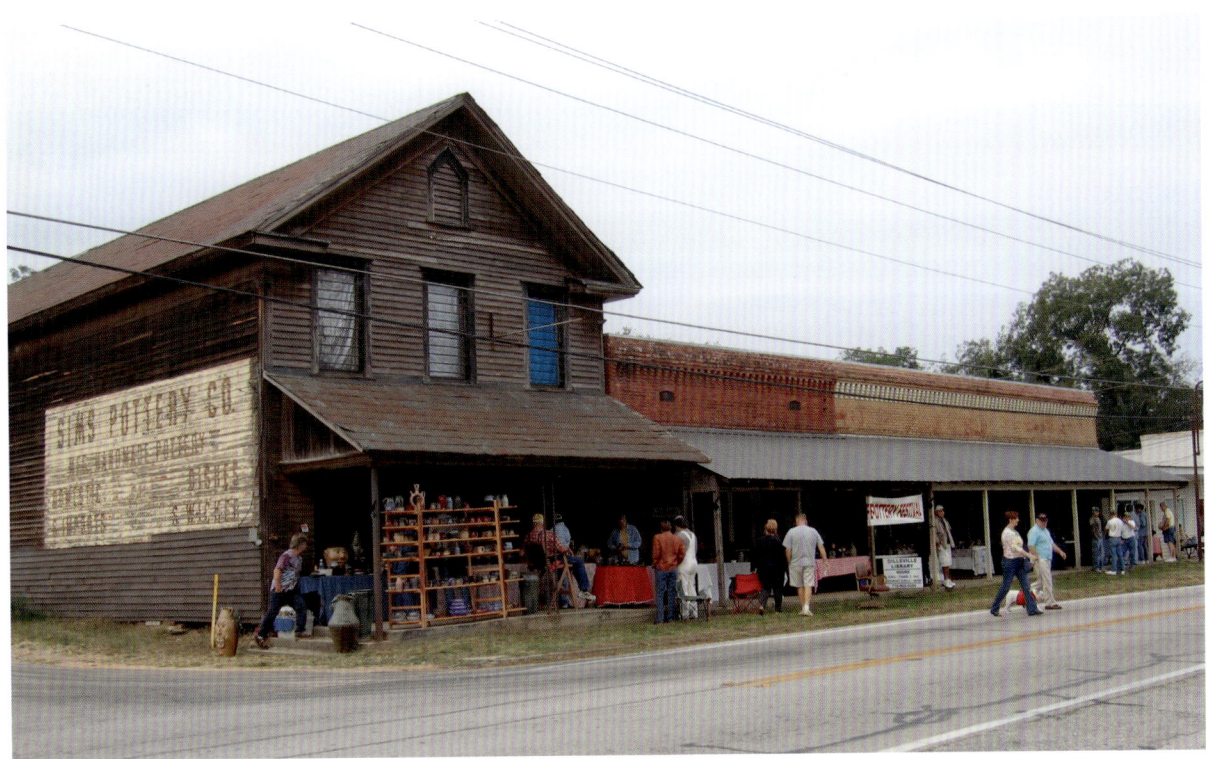

Gillsville town center, with local potters and dealers selling wares, 2005. *Photo: author.*

Holcomb Pottery, ca. 1928. In front of weatherboarded-log shop are potter William Cicero ("Bunk") Holcomb and wife Savannah; the boy, Eugene Dodd, was related by marriage and also a potter. Bunk's father, Mossy Creek potter J. R. Holcomb, moved to Gillsville ca. 1885; Bunk's son, Ray, closed the shop ca. 1945. Among the Albany slip–glazed churns and jugs are stacks of flowerpots (foreground center), a portent of change to come. *Courtesy of B. R. Holcomb.*

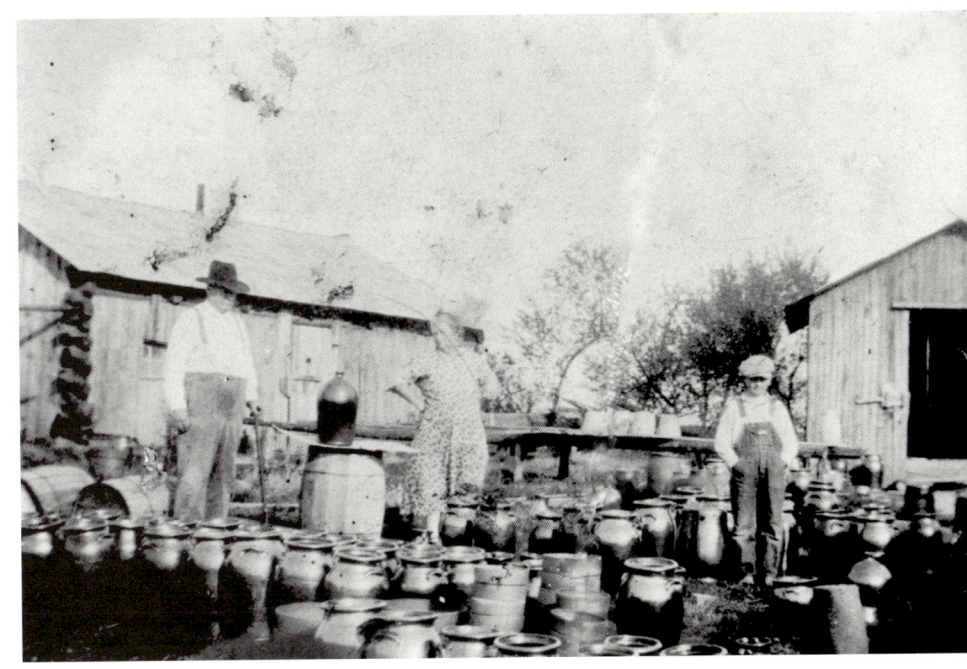

Mountain Potteries

The sparse mountain population depended mainly on wagoners from the upper Piedmont centers for their farm wares, but there were a few scattered shops in northeast Georgia's rugged uplands. These included the Jones Pottery of Young Cane, near Blairsville, and the Rabun Gap shop of George Dillard. Sanford Tilman and Peter Howard were listed as potters in the 1850 census for Lumpkin County, perhaps attracted by gold-mining operations there.

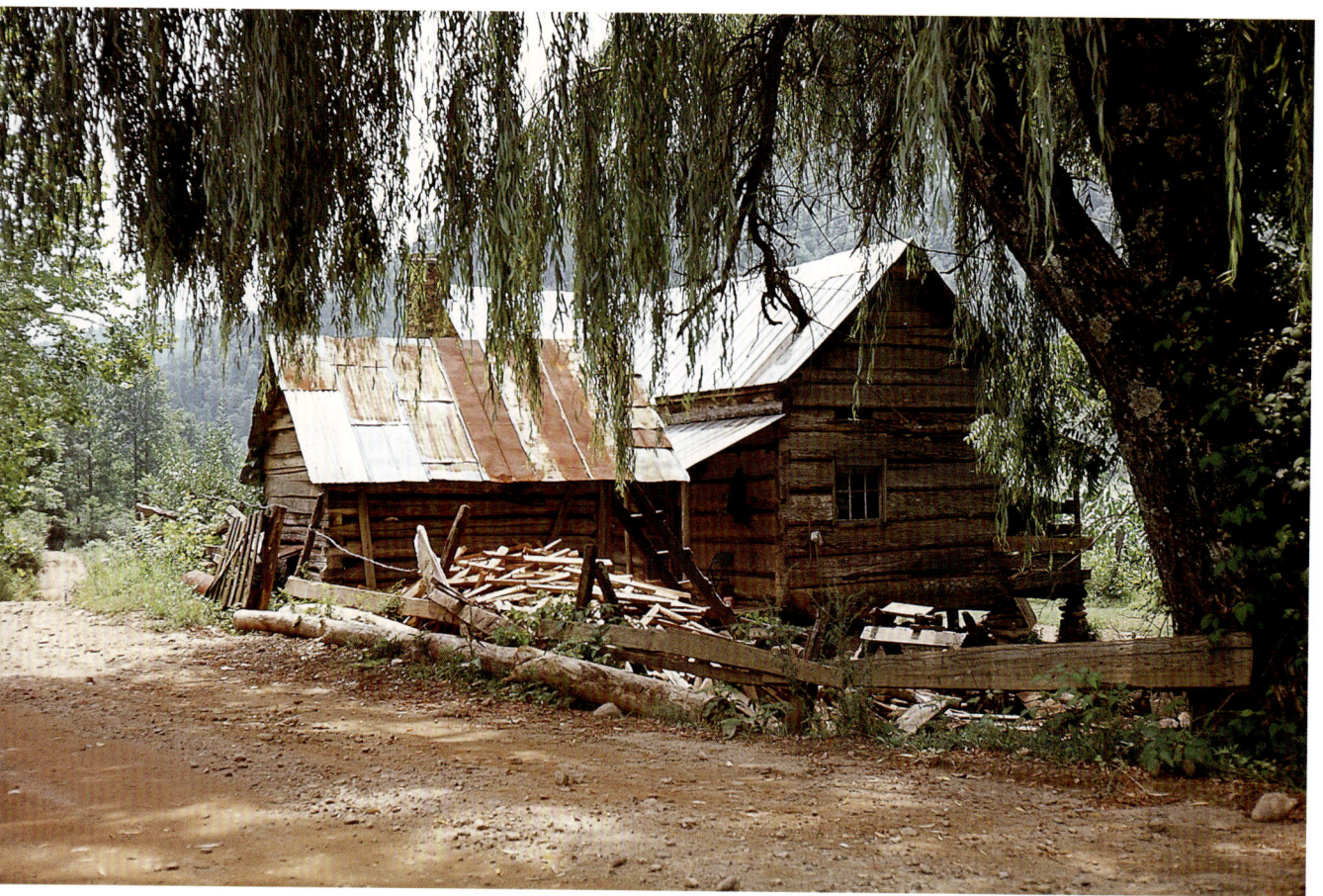

Georgia mountain home of farmer, fiddler, and herb doctor Arthur Young, 1969 (electricity hadn't yet reached this remote location). In the 1800s such farms would have used wares by the few mountain potters as well as those wagoned from the upper Piedmont. *Photo: author.*

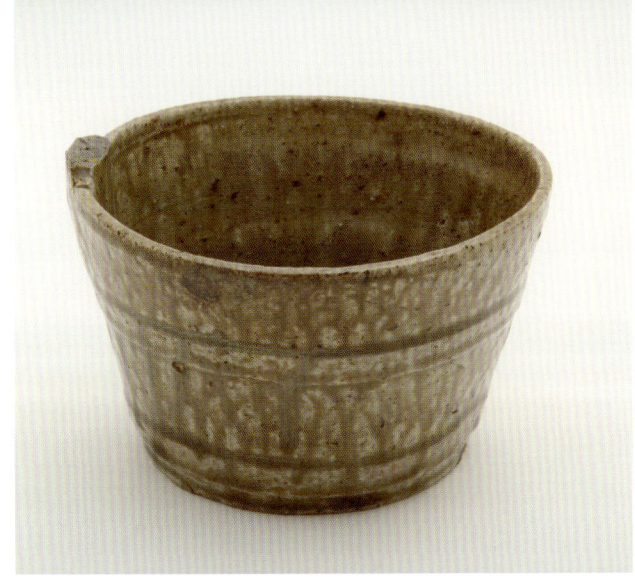

Noggin, probably Lumpkin County, 1850s, alkaline (ash) glaze. Found in the Dahlonega area being used to serve butter, it may have been made by Sanford Tilman or Peter Howard, listed as potters in the 1850 census. With its extended-stave handle (now broken) and simulated horizontal bands, it's a small stoneware version of coopered wooden noggins for eating porridge in the British Isles; similar earthenware "luggies" were made in Scotland. H. 3½ inches. *Photo: David Greear; FPM collection.*

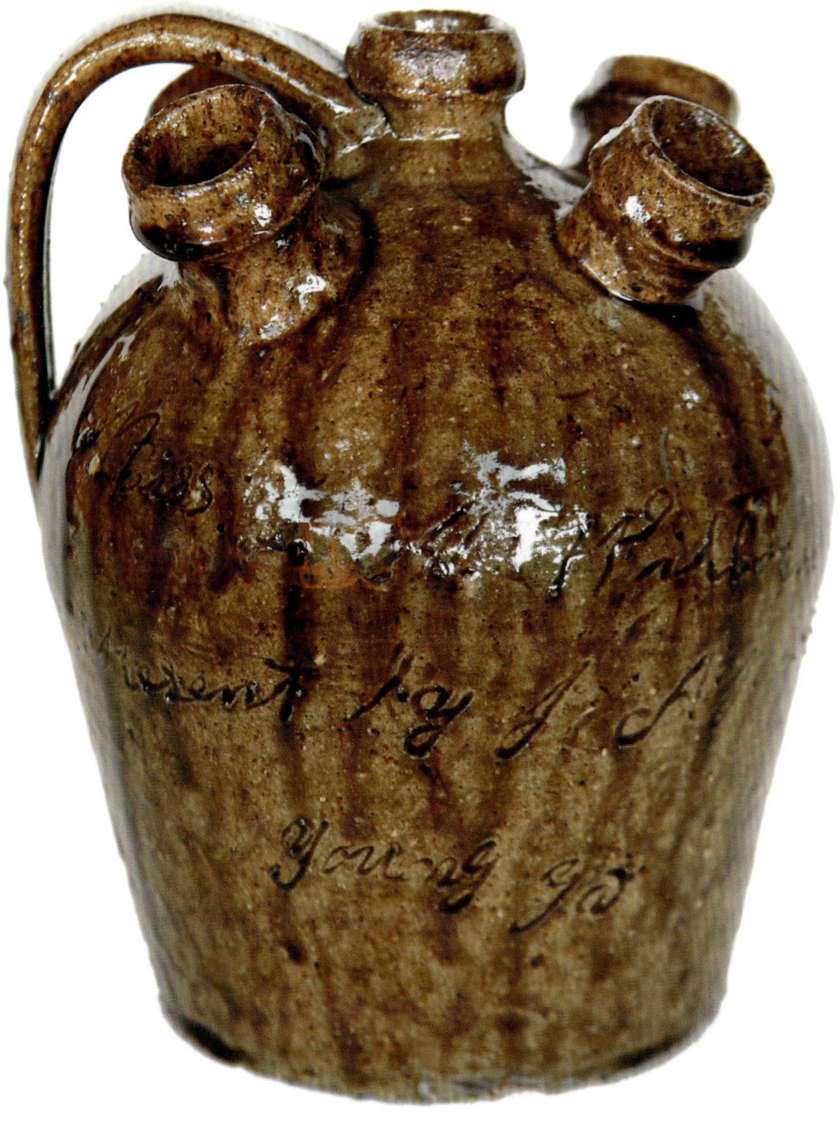

"Wedding jug," James Jones, Young Cane, Union County, ca. 1870s, alkaline (ash) glaze. According to the oral history of this mountain piece, inscribed "Miss L. A. Wilborn / a present by J. A. Jones," it was used to celebrate a wedding; such multinecked flower jugs were also made at Mossy Creek as early as the 1850s. H. 9 inches. *Photo: David Greear; author's collection, on loan to FPM.*

CHAPTER 3

From Near and Far

Roots of the Tradition

Where did north Georgia's pottery tradition come from? After more than thirty years exploring this question, I can offer a number of conclusions with some certainty, whereas others amount to educated guesswork. The picture that emerges is a complex one, with the Carolinas as the most immediate source and Britain, Germany, and possibly China (indirectly via print media) and Africa (via the slave trade) as more distant sources of pottery making in Georgia.

First, this was a stoneware tradition, producing a durable ceramic product made of fine-grained clay. Other than pre-Removal Native American pottery and Gillsville's post-1930s garden pottery (planters and yard ornaments), there is no evidence that earthenware—which is made from coarse-grained clay containing a good deal of iron, thus typically reddish brown when fired and sometimes called "redware"—was made in north Georgia. During the early 1800s, when much of north Georgia was being settled, stoneware was becoming the dominant type of American folk pottery, supplanting earthenware, whose lead glaze was coming to be recognized as hazardous. (Georgia's neighbors to the north, North Carolina and Tennessee, did make such lead-glazed redware and continued to do so after stoneware was adopted there.)

The glaze first used on north Georgia stoneware was alkaline glaze, a distinctly southern type apparently developed in Edgefield District, South Carolina, where the earliest dated example was made in 1820 by pioneering stoneware manufacturer Abner Landrum.[1]

He may have come across a published description of Chinese high-firing, woodash- and lime-based glazes and began experimenting with them as an alternative to the salt used to glaze stoneware farther north and in Europe. The green or brown alkaline glazes were spread westward into Georgia by his workmen, among whom was Charles H. Ferguson, who began one of north Georgia's three pottery centers with his Jug Factory in what is now Barrow County. There, only the ash-based version of alkaline glaze is known to have been used.[2]

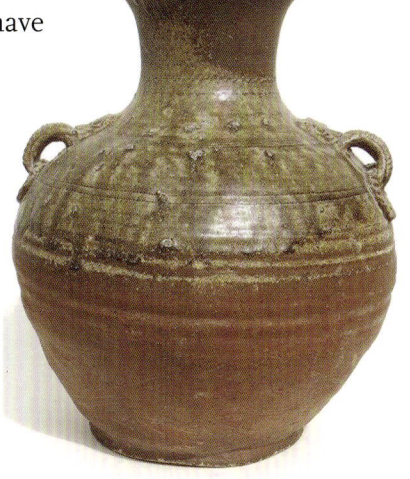

Jar, China, Han dynasty (206 BC–AD 220), ash glaze on upper half similar to that later used in the American South. Such glazes were described in *Du Halde's History of China* (1736). H. 12½ inches. *Private collection.*

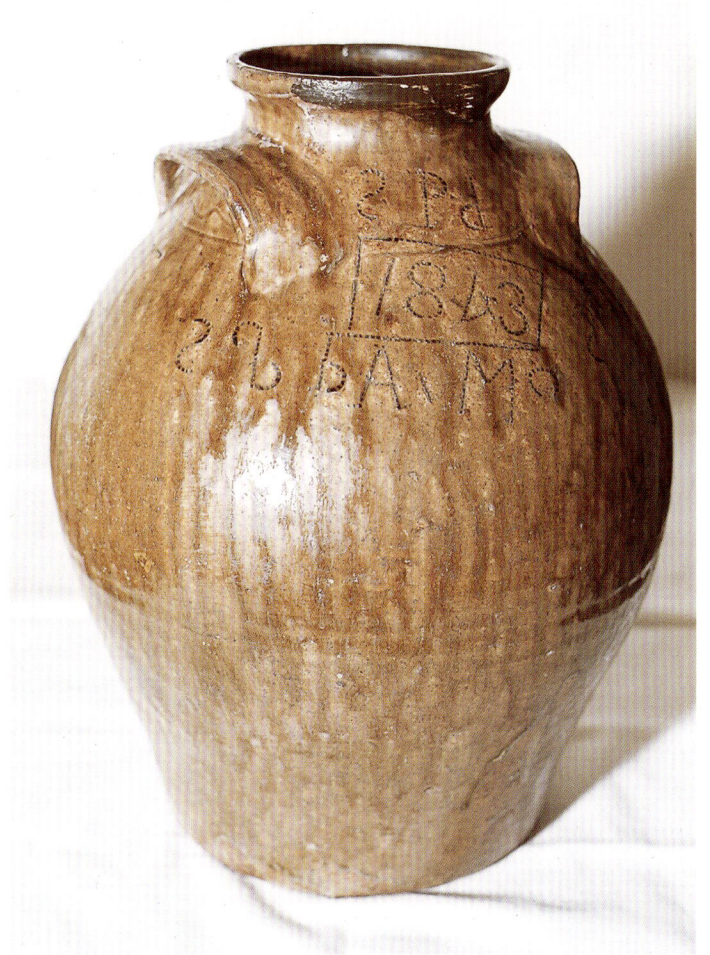

Pickle jar attributed to Clemonds Chandler, Mossy Creek, dated 1843 (initials said to be those of his brother-in-law, Samuel P. Densmore). This ash version of alkaline glaze was known to later Meaders potters as "Shanghai" glaze, suggesting a memory of Asian inspiration. H. 12 inches. *Photo: author; private collection.*

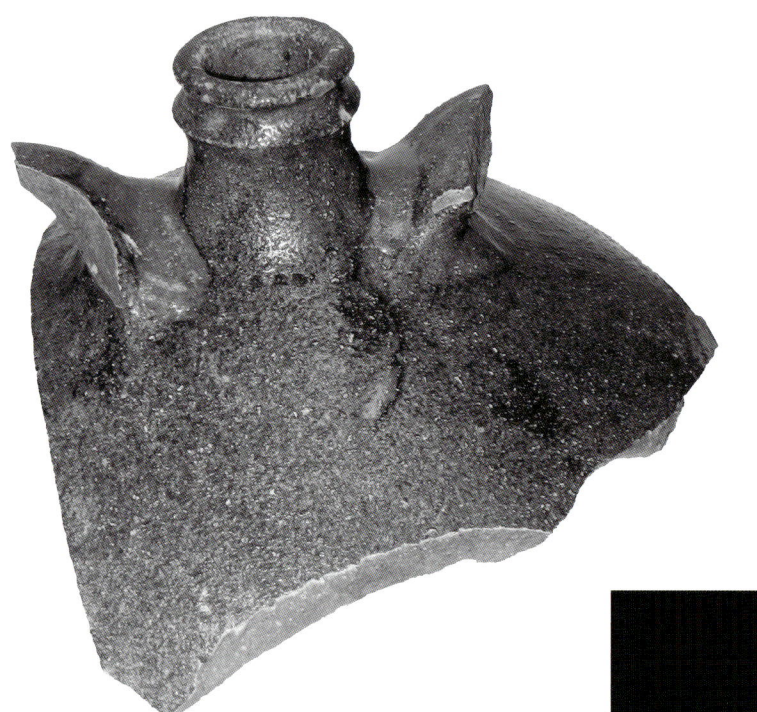

Four-gallon syrup jug shard found by Chester Hewell on his Gillsville property. Double-collared neck, alkaline (underfired ash) glaze, and punctated dots indicating gallon capacity are typical of antebellum Edgefield District, South Carolina, but it probably was made in Barrow County in the 1840s, perhaps by Edgefield-trained Charles H. Ferguson. Partially melted glass at the juncture of handles and neck, a decorative technique in North Carolina, likely was added in this case to strengthen the bond. *Photo: author; author's collection, gift of Chester Hewell.*

Four-gallon syrup jug, Pottersville Stoneware Manufactory, Edgefield District, South Carolina, 1830s, alkaline (lime) glaze. The double-collared neck typical of antebellum Edgefield jugs was initially reproduced by Edgefield-trained Georgia potters. H. 16½ inches. *Photo: author; author's collection.*

In the 1870s, Barrow County's ash glaze was replaced by the easier-to-prepare Albany slip, a natural clay glaze imported from New York. Barrow County potters often threw salt into the kiln to relieve the smooth, brown slip with patches of mustard tan or green where the sodium vapor concentrated. This double-glazing technique may have taken its inspiration from the brown salt-glazed stoneware of Britain and Germany, where pots were dipped into an iron wash before firing. It is not known how salt glazing was introduced to Barrow County, since it was virtually nonexistent elsewhere in northeast Georgia. It was, however, used in Atlanta in the 1870s, and contact with potters there such as the Browns may have given Barrow County potters the idea.

Eight known or suspected pioneer Mossy Creek potters all migrated from North Carolina, moving south through upper South Carolina into northeast Georgia. Both Hezekiah Chandler and Frederick Davidson (born in Virginia and Buncombe County, North Carolina, respectively) were at Mossy Creek by 1820, a year after the Cherokee land cession that created Habersham County. There is no confirmation that either was a potter, but an ash-glazed jar dated 1843 is attributed to Chandler's son, Clemonds, and five of Davidson's sons were known potters. Another likely suspect, Nathaniel Pitchford, was next to arrive, acquiring land in 1822; five of his sons also were potters. Then, in 1825, came the three Craven brothers, John V., Isaac N., and Thomas W., descendants of reputed pioneer potter Peter Craven, who settled in Randolph County, North Carolina, in the 1760s. Finally, there were Basil and David L. Dorsey, probably cousins. Basil was born in Lincoln County, North Carolina, and was at Mossy Creek by 1828 when he married Nathaniel Pitchford's daughter, Nancy; by 1850 the couple had moved to Alabama, where Basil was listed as a potter in that year's census. "Davey" Dorsey came from Macon County, North Carolina, settling by 1840 at Mossy Creek, where he is listed as a potter in the 1860 census.

The kind of wares made by the first Mossy Creek potters once they built their shops remains a mystery; we don't know who introduced alkaline glazes (both the ash and lime types used there),

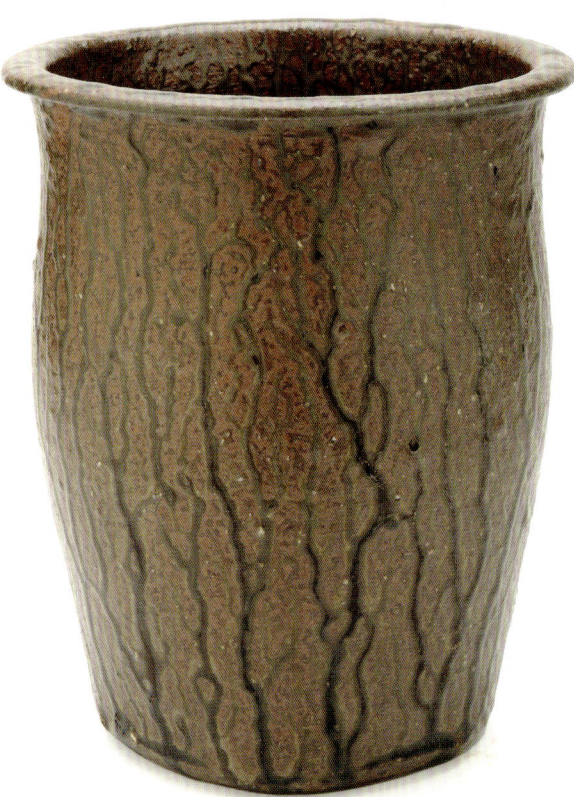

Cream pot attributed to Isaac H. Craven, Mossy Creek, 1870s–1880s, alkaline (ash) glaze. His jar shapes, with their flattened rim, echo those of his father's home state, North Carolina. H. 9 inches. *Photo: David Greear; FPM collection.*

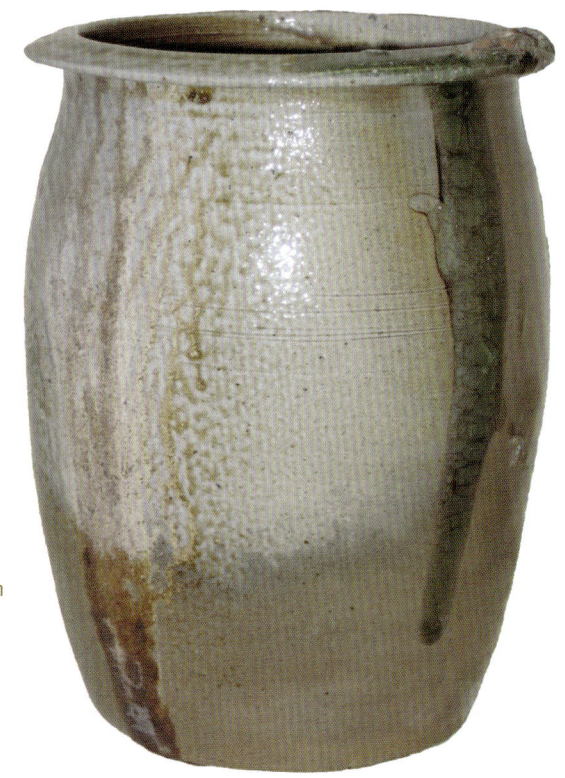

Cream pot attributed to Solomon Loy, Alamance County, North Carolina, ca. 1850s, salt glaze. This type of cream pot from North Carolina's eastern Piedmont is a forerunner of those by Isaac H. Craven. H. 9½ inches. *Photo: author; author's collection.*

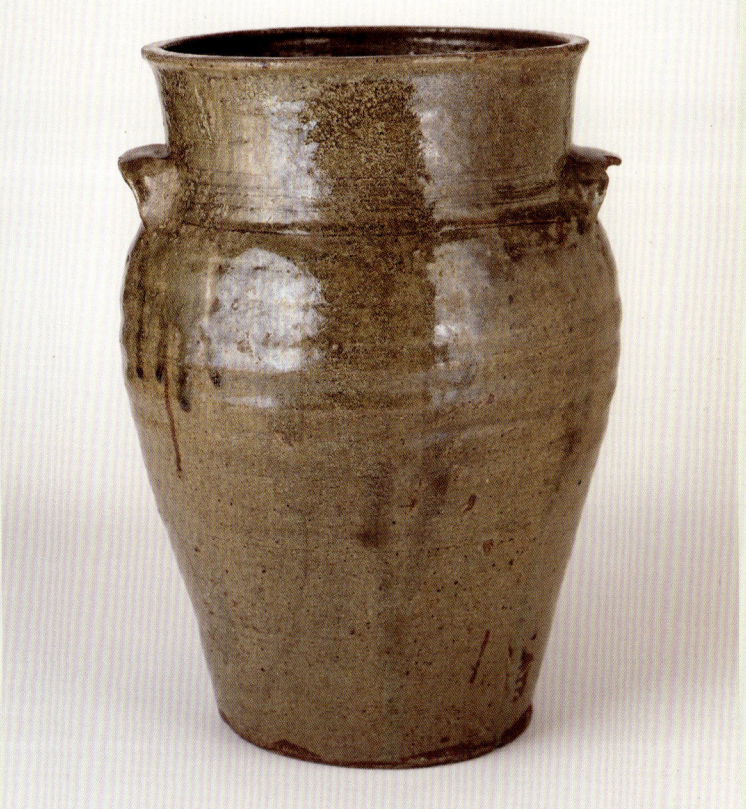

Four-gallon jar, maker unknown, probably Mossy Creek, alkaline glaze. Found in White County, this is the earliest dated pot from north Georgia known (assuming the date is the year it was made). Incised on the base is "Josiah / Vandufer his year / the 25 of September / 1832." Josiah possibly was a son of Adam Poole Vandiver, who came to Habersham County from upper South Carolina in 1822. The 1850 census lists "J.V." as an eighteen-year-old farmer in Adam's household, so the jar may have been made by a pioneer potter to mark Josiah's birth. H. 16½ inches. *Courtesy of High Museum of Art, Atlanta; purchased with funds from the Decorative Arts Acquisition Trust and the Decorative Arts Endowment, 1990.72.*

or from where. The earliest date—1832—on what is thought to be Mossy Creek stoneware appears on an alkaline-glazed jar. In North Carolina's eastern Piedmont, where the Cravens came from, lead-glazed earthenware was joined by salt-glazed stoneware beginning in the 1820s, but neither ceramic type can be documented at Mossy Creek. By the 1870s John V. Craven's son, Isaac H., had embraced ash glaze and even developed his own subtype, called "iron sand." None of the pioneers, on their way to Georgia, is known to have passed as far south in South Carolina as Edgefield District, where these glazes are thought to have originated. And alkaline glaze— only the ash-based type, at that—does not seem to have been used in North Carolina (in the western Piedmont and mountains) until the 1830s or 1840s.

So much for the origin of early north Georgia stoneware glazes. The next consideration is the pottery forms, or function-based shapes. Some, such as lug-handled storage jars—that is, jars with horizontal slab handles—and double-handled syrup jugs, have parallels in eighteenth- and early-nineteenth-century Britain, especially northern England, where they can be found both in earthenware and stoneware.[3] This is no great surprise, since some of the oldest southern pottery families, such as the Cravens, came from Britain, where family history claims their beginnings in the craft. Such transatlantic similarities, however, may be coincidental rather than proving descent.

The origin of the face jug form, which features faces applied in clay to the surface, is especially problematic. The first known north Georgia face jugs were made at Gillsville around 1900 by Charles H. Ferguson's grandson, Charles P. ("Charlie") Ferguson. Charlie likely was carrying on a tradition that his grandfather acquired from his home area, Edgefield District, where a white potter, Thomas Chandler, made a signed example in about 1850 and where enslaved African American potters made face jugs at Thomas Davies' Palmetto Fire Brick Works in 1863–65. In his sojourns up north Chandler may have seen Remmey family face vessels that I believe were descended from the German *Bartmannskrug*, a type of stoneware jug with a bearded face molded on the neck. The

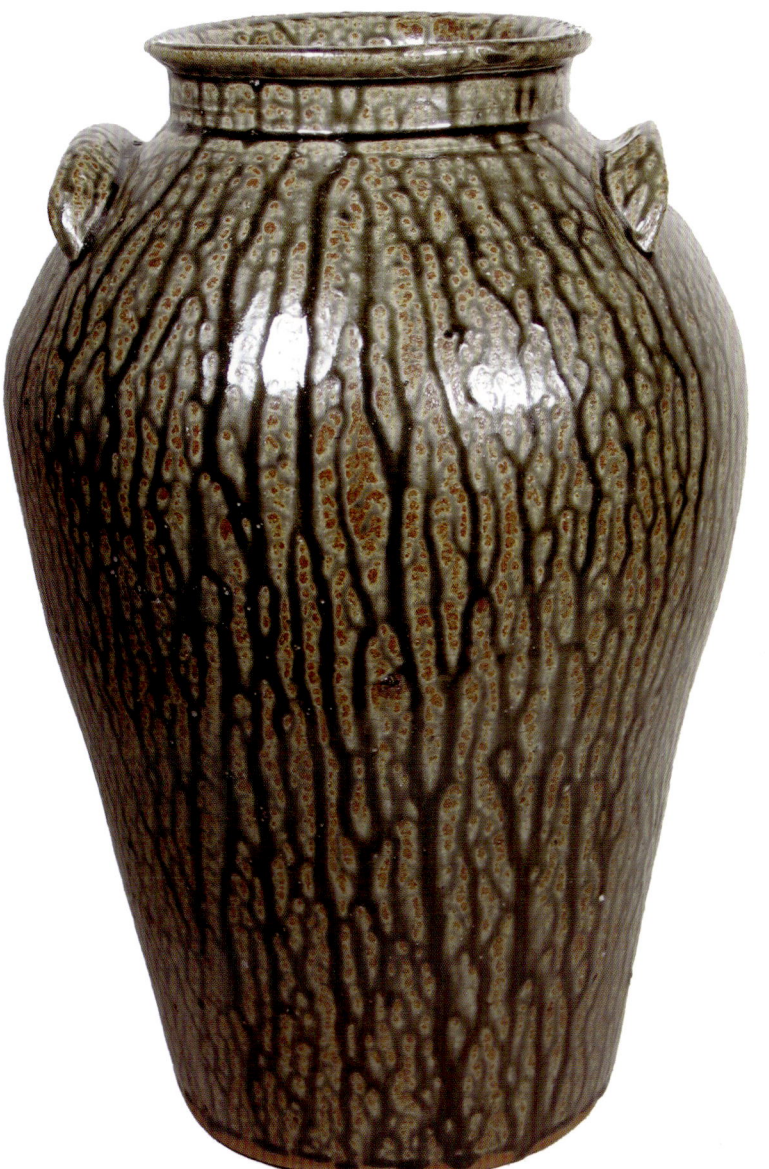

Five-gallon jar, Cleater ("C.J.") Meaders Jr., Cleveland, Georgia, 1991, alkaline (ash) glaze. In what C.J. called "real folk art," he re-created—apparently without being aware of it—an early White County, and British, jar form. H. 18¼ inches. *Photo: author; author's collection, gift of the maker.*

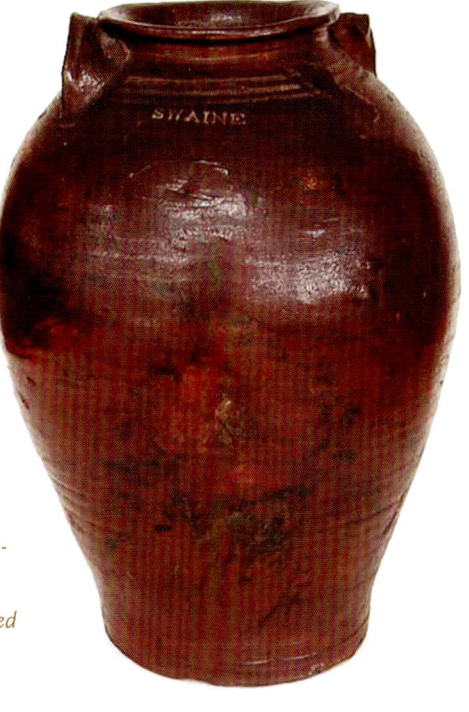

Four-gallon jar, Thomas or Robert Swaine, Prescot, Merseyside, England, 1820s–40s, brown salt-glazed stoneware. The form of this lug-handled jar from the little-known Liverpool-area stoneware tradition is similar to those of north Georgia. H. 16 inches. *Courtesy of Recycled Collectibles, Virginia Beach, Va.*

slave-made examples, on the other hand, may have carried on an African tradition of anthropomorphic "spirit" pots to honor ancestors. Charles H. Ferguson left South Carolina in 1827, before face jugs are known to have been made there, but he could have kept in touch with later developments in Edgefield. It can't be determined whether Charlie's examples, then, were ultimately inspired by a similar idea from Germany or Africa, or whether his tradition was independently invented in South Carolina or Georgia. We do know, however, that there was a lineage of face jugs by Anglo-southern potters prior to those by the Meaders family.[4]

Finally, we turn to the origins of key features of the production technology. The treadle-and-crankshaft potter's wheel used to shape American (not just southern) folk stoneware seems to have been developed in England in the late 1700s; I saw such wheels still being used for earthenware at the Harris Pottery near Farnham, Surrey, in the 1980s. I thought that southern potters were the only ones to use the "ball-opener" lever mounted on the wheel crib to make the initial plunge in the clay to create a vessel until I came across a photograph of one being used in 1979 by a German stoneware potter.[5] Southern wood-fueled, rectangular kilns are similar to those used for stoneware since the 1600s in Germany and France, although English delftware (white-glazed earthenware) kilns of the 1600s also are similar. Whatever its origin, this type of kiln, very different from the round kilns of the North, seems to have first come to the South via eighteenth-century Virginia.

The continuity of ceramic traditions brought from the Carolinas and, more remotely, from the Old World, offers only a partial explanation of how northeast Georgia's pottery tradition came to be. Much of the current tradition arose through the creative efforts of individual potters in that corner of the state in response to the needs of their customers and to the twentieth-century changes described in later chapters. These local developments, then, occurred both as practical solutions to problems and as the artistic visions of influential potters, notable among whom were members of two key families.

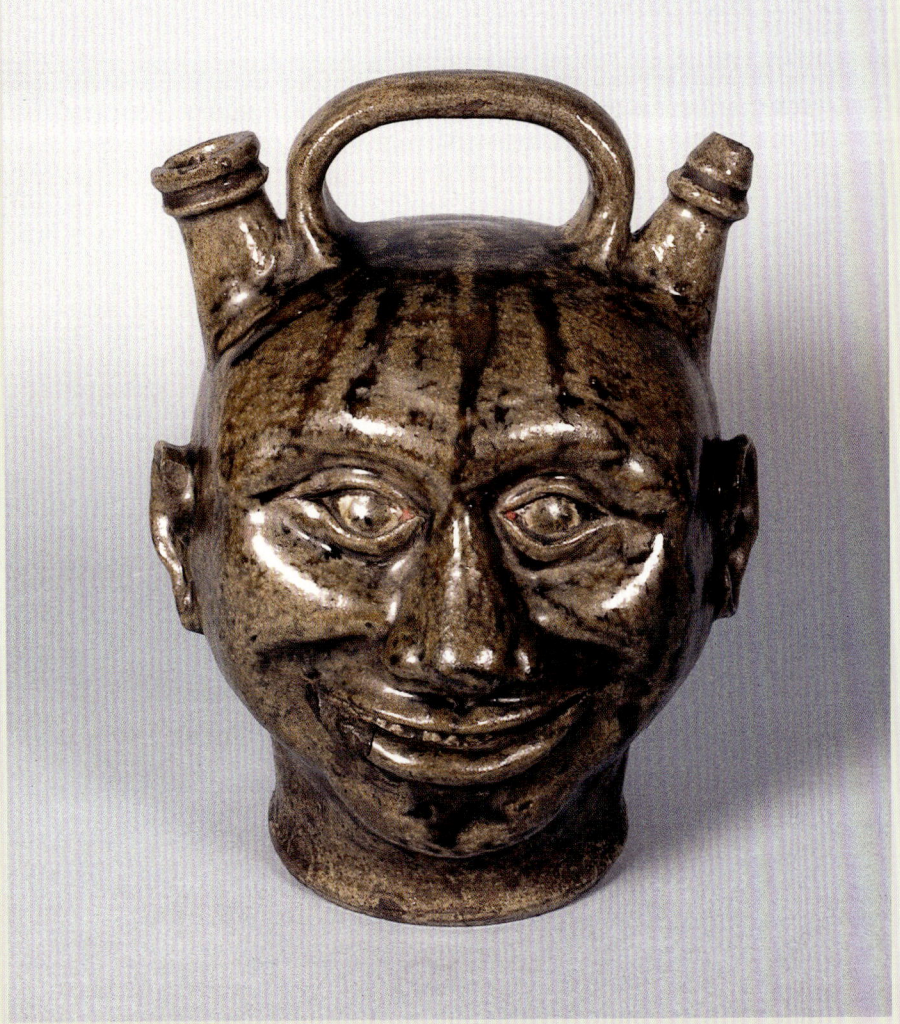

Face jug in monkey form (a water vessel type common in Africa and Mediterranean Europe), Thomas Chandler (stamped "CHANDLER / MAKER"), Edgefield District, South Carolina, ca. 1850, alkaline (ash) glaze. Edgefield face jugs may have led to those by north Georgia's Fergusons and were perhaps descendants of a German or African tradition. H. 11½ inches. *Private collection; courtesy of McKissick Museum, University of South Carolina.*

CHAPTER 4

Clay Clans

Two Pottery Dynasties

In the past, Georgia's traditional crafts, including pottery, were maintained more through kinship than formal apprenticeship. A young man often became a folk potter by being born or marrying into a potting family. Some families have been involved in the craft for many generations and have played a major role in shaping their communities' ceramic traditions. Intermarriage between members of two existing pottery families created several large pottery dynasties or clay clans.

The Meaders Family

The Meaders (pronounced *Medders*) Pottery of Mossy Creek was launched in 1892–93 by John Milton Meaders, who saw the success of potter neighbors (his sister, Fannie, had married shop owner "Daddy Bill" Dorsey in 1872) and thought this would be a good trade for his six sons. He hired members of older local pottery families—D. Marion Davidson and Williams Dorsey—to work in his new log shop and train his boys. The older brothers then established their own shops in the area, while the youngest, Cheever, took over the original Meaders Pottery in 1920, with crafts enthusiasts eventually becoming his main customers. In the 1950s Cheever's wife, Arie, began making decorative wares for those seeking a more artistic product. Her creative vision, and Cheever's insistence on operating the old-fashioned way, set the stage for their son, Quillian Lanier.

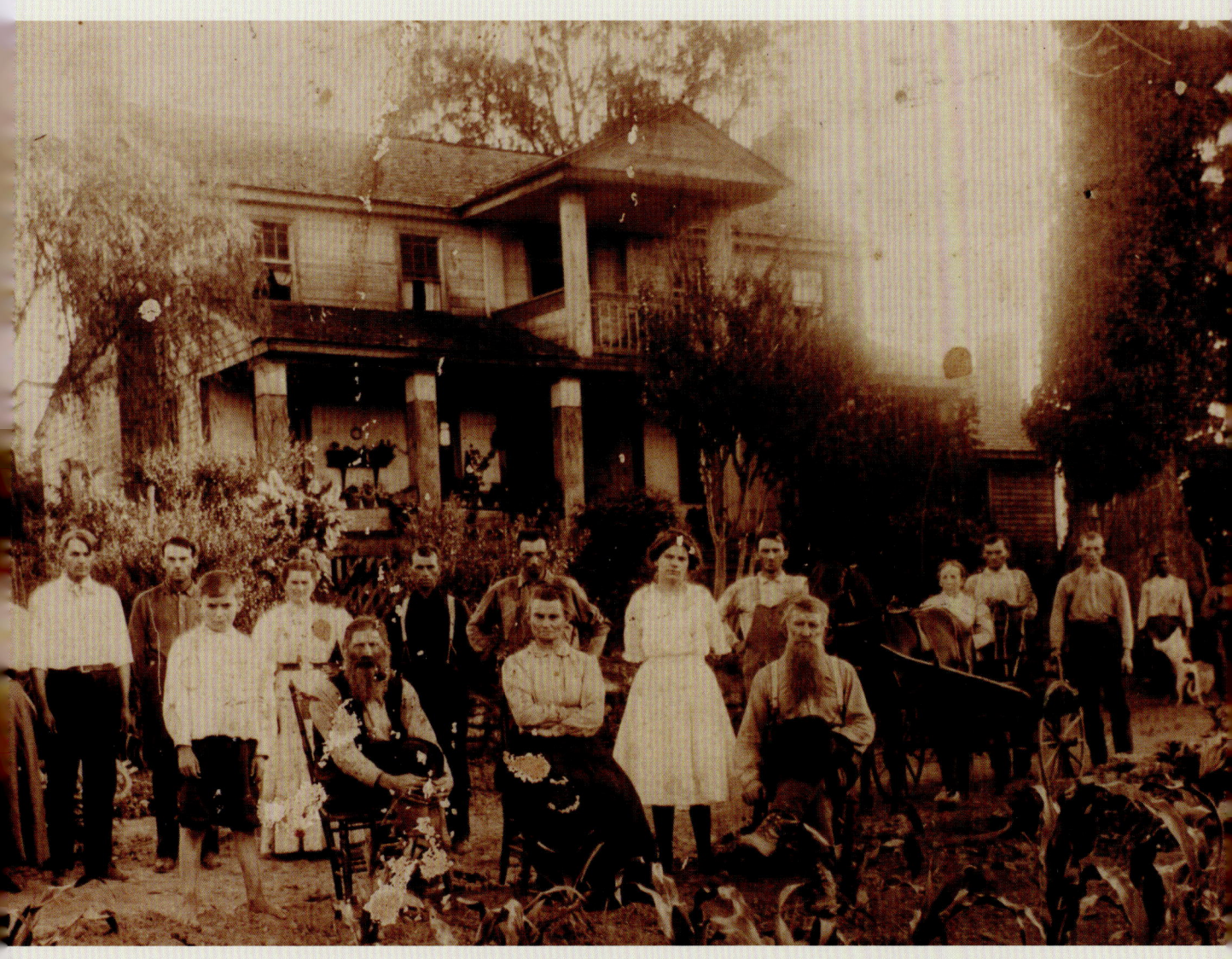

Home of William F. ("Daddy Bill") Dorsey, Mossy Creek, ca. 1900. It was built
ca. 1860 by merchant and planter Christopher Meaders, whose son, John Milton
Meaders, founded Meaders Pottery in 1892. Pottery owner Daddy Bill married
Christopher's daughter, Frances ("Fannie"), sealing a union between the two
families. Seated in front are (L–R) Daddy Bill, wife Fannie, John M. Meaders; behind
them are (L–R) Meaders potters L.Q. (dark shirt), Cheever, Caulder, and Casey
(behind buggy). *Courtesy of White County Historical Society.*

Meaders Selective Genealogy

Emphasizing White County Potters

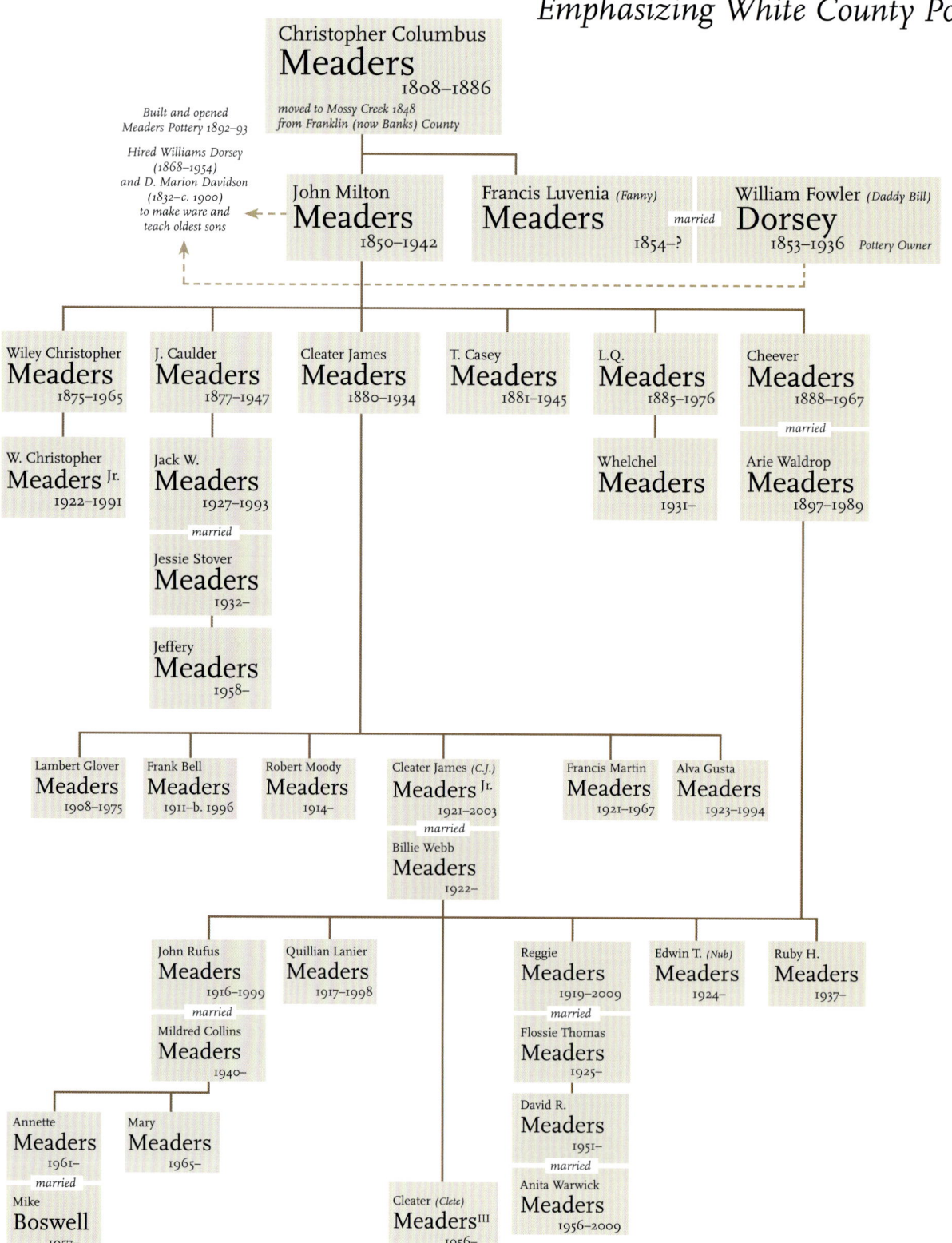

Christopher Columbus **Meaders** 1808–1886
moved to Mossy Creek 1848 from Franklin (now Banks) County

Built and opened Meaders Pottery 1892–93

Hired Williams Dorsey (1868–1954) and D. Marion Davidson (1832–c. 1900) to make ware and teach oldest sons

John Milton **Meaders** 1850–1942

Francis Luvenia *(Fanny)* **Meaders** 1854–?   *married*   William Fowler *(Daddy Bill)* **Dorsey** 1853–1936 *Pottery Owner*

Wiley Christopher **Meaders** 1875–1965

J. Caulder **Meaders** 1877–1947

Cleater James **Meaders** 1880–1934

T. Casey **Meaders** 1881–1945

L.Q. **Meaders** 1885–1976

Cheever **Meaders** 1888–1967
married

W. Christopher **Meaders** Jr. 1922–1991

Jack W. **Meaders** 1927–1993
married
Jessie Stover **Meaders** 1932–
Jeffery **Meaders** 1958–

Whelchel **Meaders** 1931–

Arie Waldrop **Meaders** 1897–1989

Lambert Glover **Meaders** 1908–1975

Frank Bell **Meaders** 1911–b. 1996

Robert Moody **Meaders** 1914–

Cleater James *(C.J.)* **Meaders** Jr. 1921–2003
married
Billie Webb **Meaders** 1922–

Francis Martin **Meaders** 1921–1967

Alva Gusta **Meaders** 1923–1994

John Rufus **Meaders** 1916–1999
married
Mildred Collins **Meaders** 1940–

Quillian Lanier **Meaders** 1917–1998

Reggie **Meaders** 1919–2009
married
Flossie Thomas **Meaders** 1925–
David R. **Meaders** 1951–
married
Anita Warwick **Meaders** 1956–2009

Edwin T. *(Nub)* **Meaders** 1924–

Ruby H. **Meaders** 1937–

Annette **Meaders** 1961–
married
Mike **Boswell** 1957–

Mary **Meaders** 1965–

Cleater *(Clete)* **Meaders** III 1956–

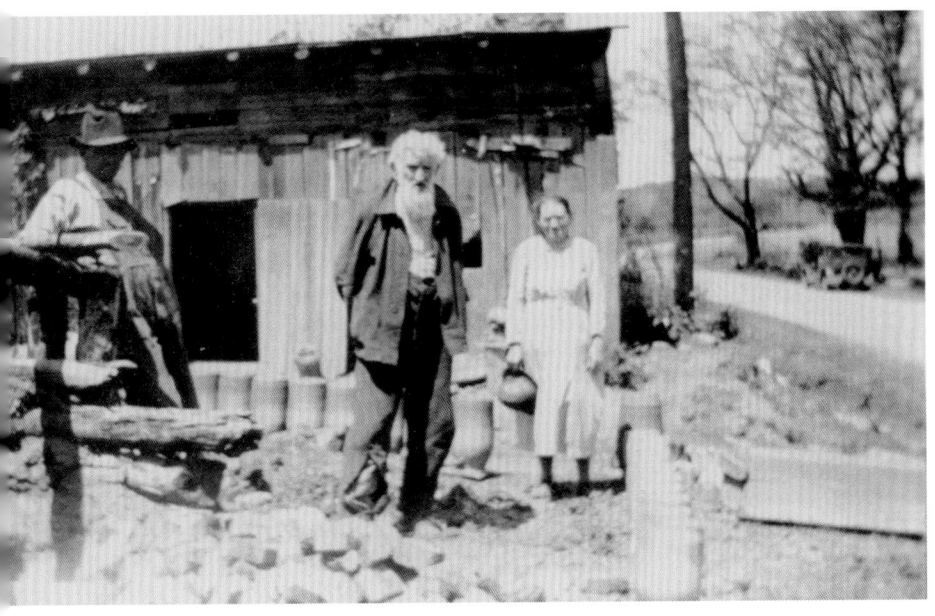

Meaders Pottery ca. 1930, with founder John Milton Meaders, daughter Camilla, and (at left) youngest son, Cheever, who by then was running the weatherboarded log shop. *Courtesy of Emory Jones.*

Pitcher, Cheever Meaders, ca. 1930s, alkaline (ash) glaze. Cheever continued to use alkaline glazes until his death in 1967; his favorite was "Shanghai," an ash glaze containing creek "settlin's" (silt) and crushed glass. His wares typically have an accenting line or two incised around the body and a signature loop handle attached at a slight angle with thumb print at top where he pushed it into wall. H. 9½ inches. *Photo: David Greear;* FPM *collection.*

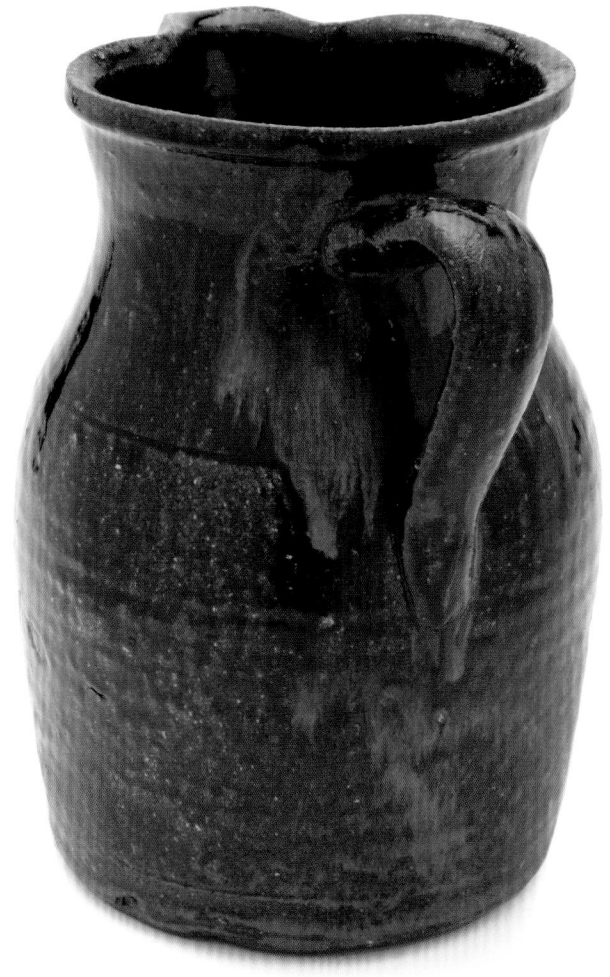

With Cheever's death in 1967, Lanier, at age fifty, took over the shop, encouraged by the Smithsonian Institution's documentary filming and its sale of his wares at the first Festival of American Folklife earlier that year. Lanier was awarded a National Heritage Fellowship by the National Endowment for the Arts in 1983, and was recognized by the state with a Governor's Award in the Arts (1987) and Georgia Council for the Arts dinner at the Governor's Mansion (1993). In continuing and refining the tradition of alkaline-glazed stoneware, Quillian Lanier Meaders (1917–1998) was a crucial link between the past and the future of southern folk pottery.

In 1921 one of Cheever's brothers, Cleater Meaders, opened a shop at Cleveland, the seat of White County. It closed in 1938, but in 1983 his son, Cleater Jr. ("C.J."), built a wood-burning kiln north of Cleveland where he made runny-textured ash-glazed wares with his wife, Billie, until his death in 2003. Their son, Clete, runs an old-fashioned shop at Hoschton, Jackson County, and other members of the family also have taken up the craft.

Pottery and home of Cleater Meaders Sr. at Cleveland, the White County seat, ca. 1930. In 1921 Cleater moved from Mossy Creek to town, where he could take advantage of tourist traffic. At left is mule-turned clay mill, shop and kiln behind, and miniature kiln in foreground where his children fired their wares (displayed on table right of center). *Courtesy of White County Historical Society.*

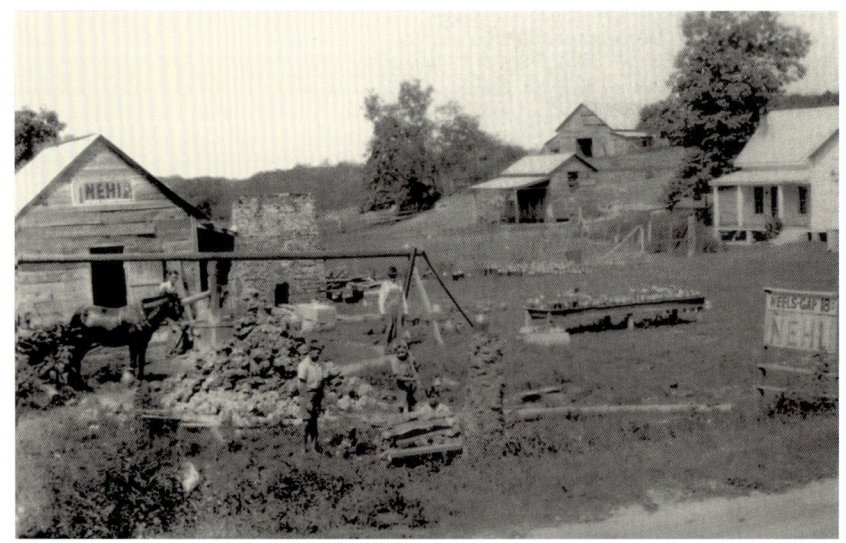

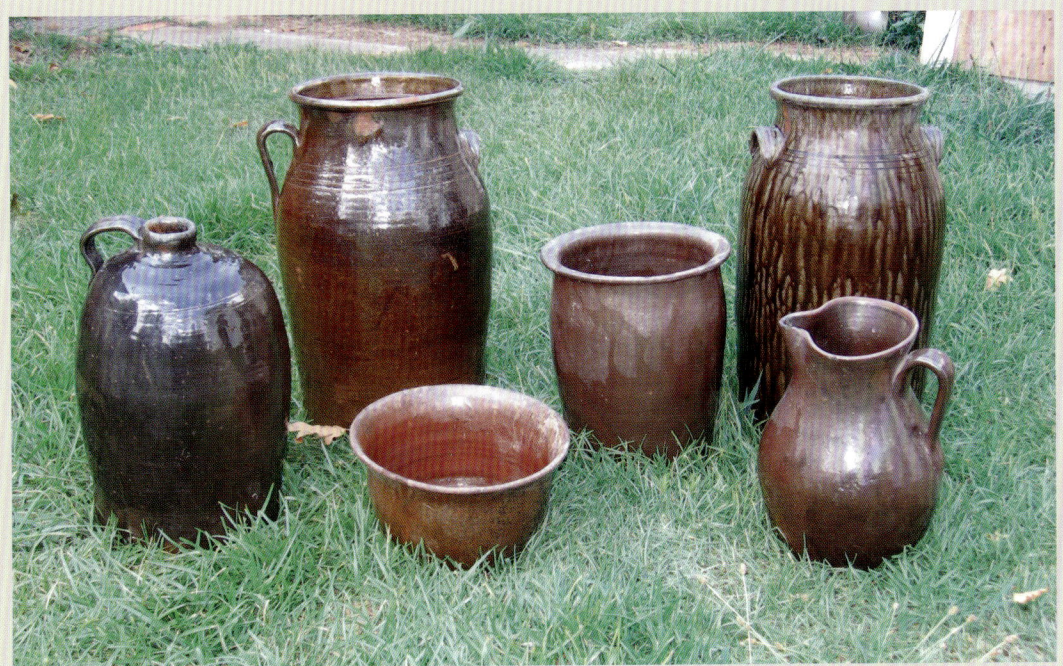

Utilitarian wares, Cleater Meaders Sr., ca. 1920s. Churn or jar at right is ash-glazed; the others are glazed with Albany slip, which Cleater sometimes mixed with feldspar, flint, and whiting. He incised lines around the shoulder of larger wares to indicate gallon capacity; the bowl is unusual for White County. *Photo: author; FPM collection, gift of Marviene Brand.*

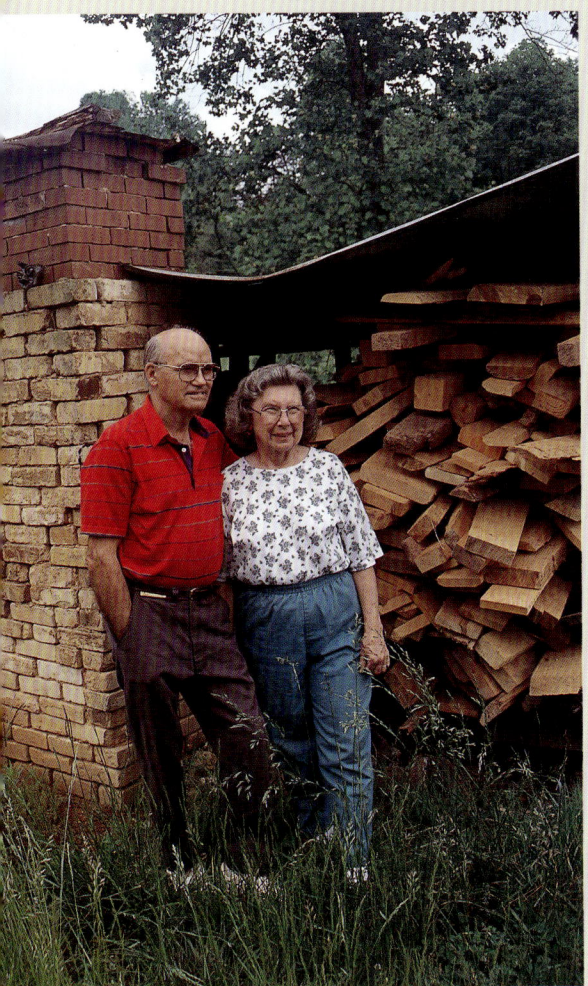

Cleater ("C.J.") Meaders Jr. and wife Billie at wood-fueled tunnel kiln on their summer place near Cleveland, Georgia, 1992. They worked as a team, C.J. turning and Billie sometimes burning the kiln and decorating; she signed their pots with both names. *Photo: author.*

The Hewell Family

The first known potter of this family was Nathaniel Hewell, who made alkaline-glazed stoneware during the Civil War in the Jug Factory center. His son, Eli, migrated to Gillsville in the 1890s. Eli's second marriage, to Frances Ferguson—granddaughter of Edgefield-trained, pioneer Barrow County potter Charles H. Ferguson—and the marriage of Eli's daughter from his first marriage, Catherine, to Frances's brother, Charles P. Ferguson, consolidated an enormous pottery dynasty.

Chester Hewell, the current manager of Hewell's Pottery, declares, "We're inventors, not imitators." That philosophy has allowed the Hewells to adapt successfully as the pottery market has changed. Unglazed, hand-thrown horticultural wares became their main product in the 1940s as demand for food-related wares fell. Then, responding to a growing collectors' market in 1983, the Hewells built a wood-burning tunnel kiln and revived their early family tradition of producing alkaline-glazed stoneware as a sideline to their garden pots. They again make face jugs, as William Hewell had in the early 1900s. They work in a modern plant but demonstrate the old methods at their annual fall Turning and Burning festival in Gillsville. Speaking in 1973 of the endurance of this family business, Chester's father, Harold Hewell, declared, "We must have been born with clay in our veins." Harold's great-grandson, Eli, began throwing at age two and, with his younger sister Susannah, is taking the craft into its seventh generation.

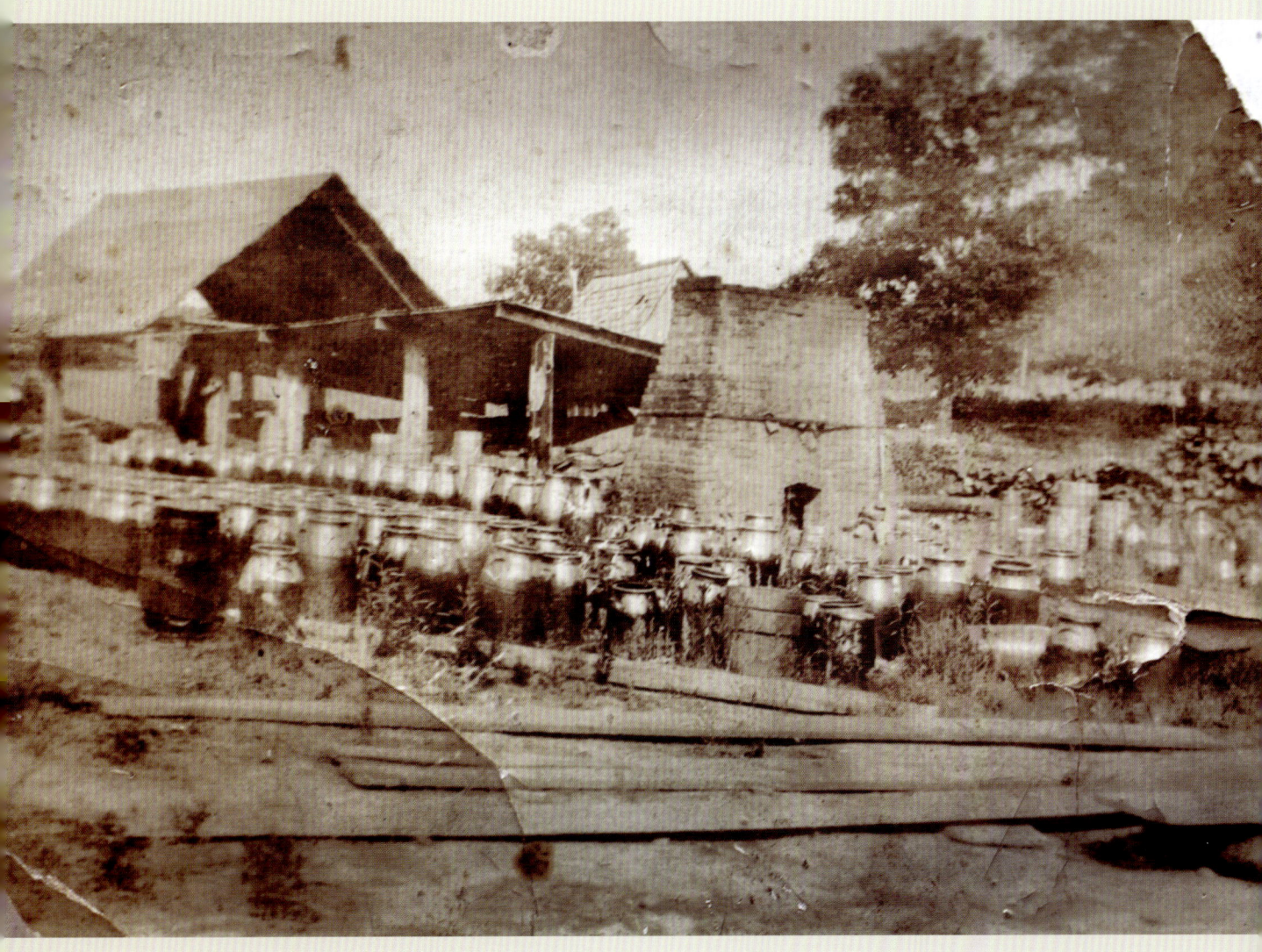

Hewell's Pottery, 1920s, with Albany slip–glazed food-storage wares far outnumbering the stacked flowerpots, a ratio that would later change. *Courtesy of Hewell family and David Greear.*

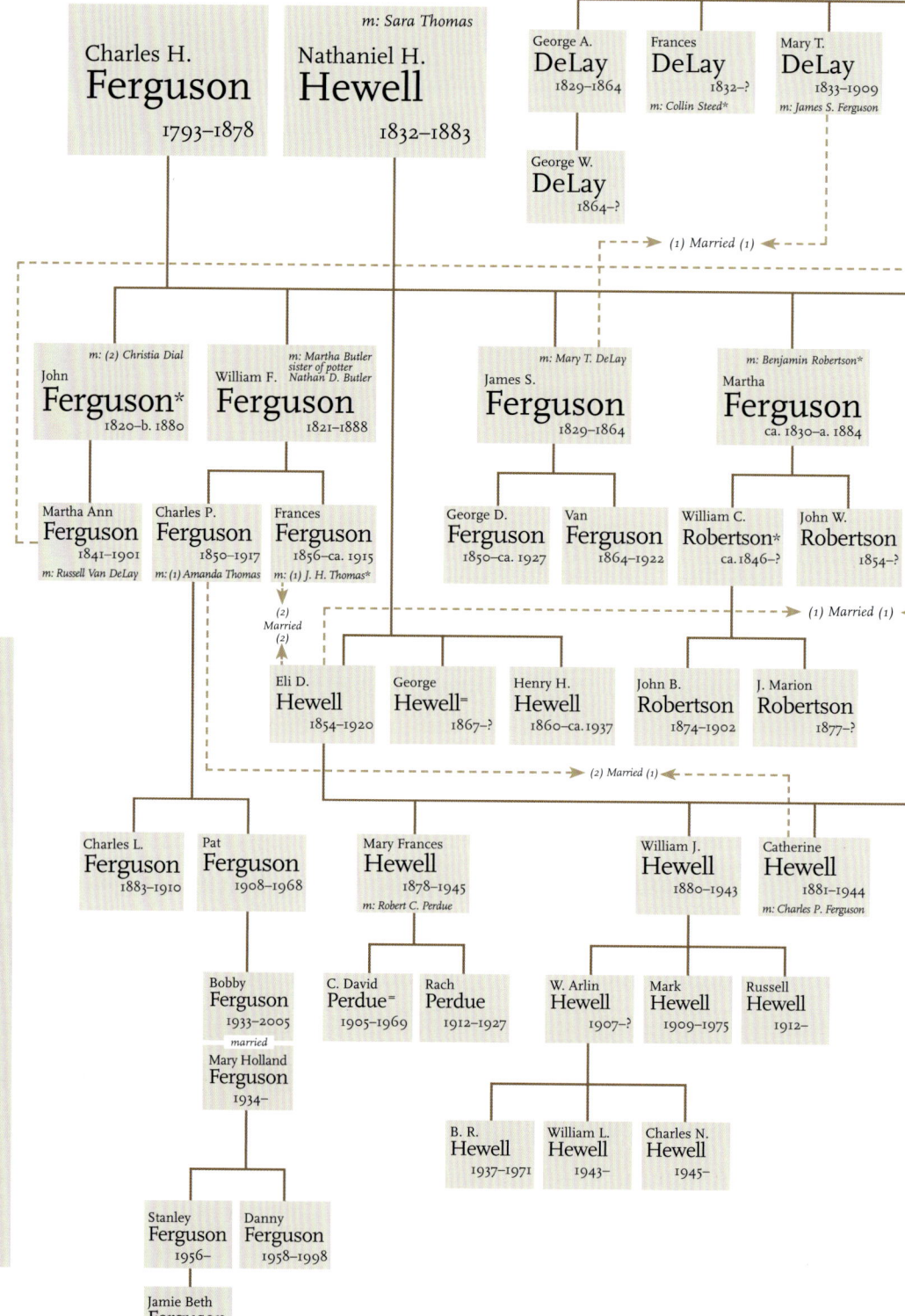

Key to Symbols

* suspected of, but not established as, being a potter

= limited involvement (eg., as owner but not potter)

m marriage (women shown contributed to family consolidation; Catherine & Grace Hewell were potters)

ca. circa (about)

b. before

a. after

--- potter families combined by marriage

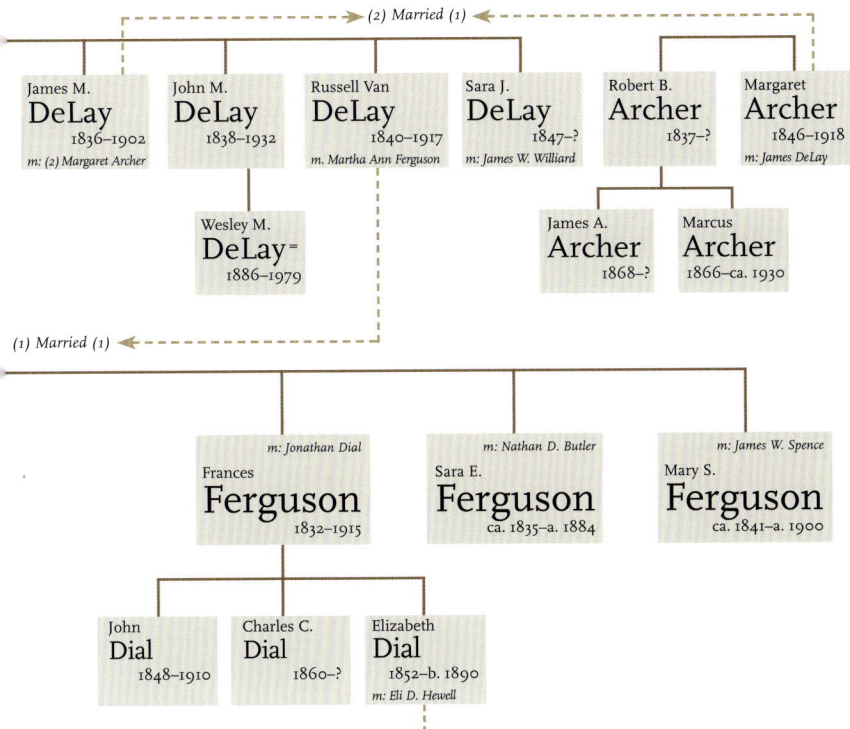

(2) Married (1)

| James M. **DeLay** 1836–1902 m: (2) Margaret Archer | John M. **DeLay** 1838–1932 | Russell Van **DeLay** 1840–1917 m. Martha Ann Ferguson | Sara J. **DeLay** 1847–? m: James W. Williard | Robert B. **Archer** 1837–? | Margaret **Archer** 1846–1918 m: James DeLay |

Wesley M. **DeLay**= 1886–1979

James A. **Archer** 1868–?   Marcus **Archer** 1866–ca. 1930

(1) Married (1)

m: Jonathan Dial
Frances **Ferguson** 1832–1915

m: Nathan D. Butler
Sara E. **Ferguson** ca. 1835–a. 1884

m: James W. Spence
Mary S. **Ferguson** ca. 1841–a. 1900

John **Dial** 1848–1910   Charles C. **Dial** 1860–?   Elizabeth **Dial** 1852–b. 1890 m: Eli D. Hewell

Ferguson and Hewell Genealogy

with Allied Potters

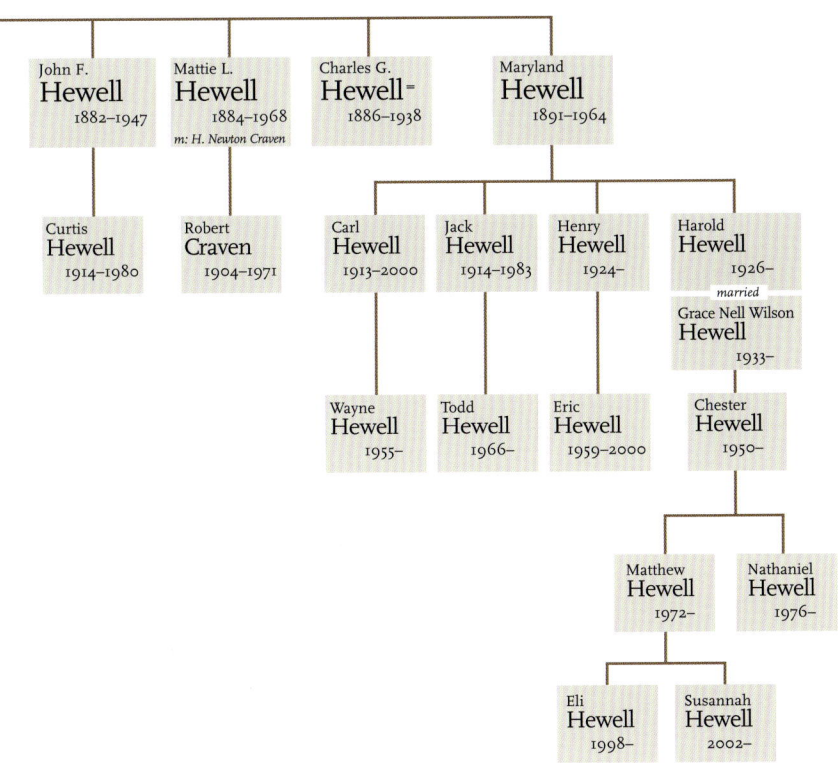

| John F. **Hewell** 1882–1947 | Mattie L. **Hewell** 1884–1968 m: H. Newton Craven | Charles G. **Hewell**= 1886–1938 | Maryland **Hewell** 1891–1964 |

Curtis **Hewell** 1914–1980   Robert **Craven** 1904–1971

Carl **Hewell** 1913–2000   Jack **Hewell** 1914–1983   Henry **Hewell** 1924–   Harold **Hewell** 1926–
married
Grace Nell Wilson **Hewell** 1933–

Wayne **Hewell** 1955–   Todd **Hewell** 1966–   Eric **Hewell** 1959–2000   Chester **Hewell** 1950–

Matthew **Hewell** 1972–   Nathaniel **Hewell** 1976–

Eli **Hewell** 1998–   Susannah **Hewell** 2002–

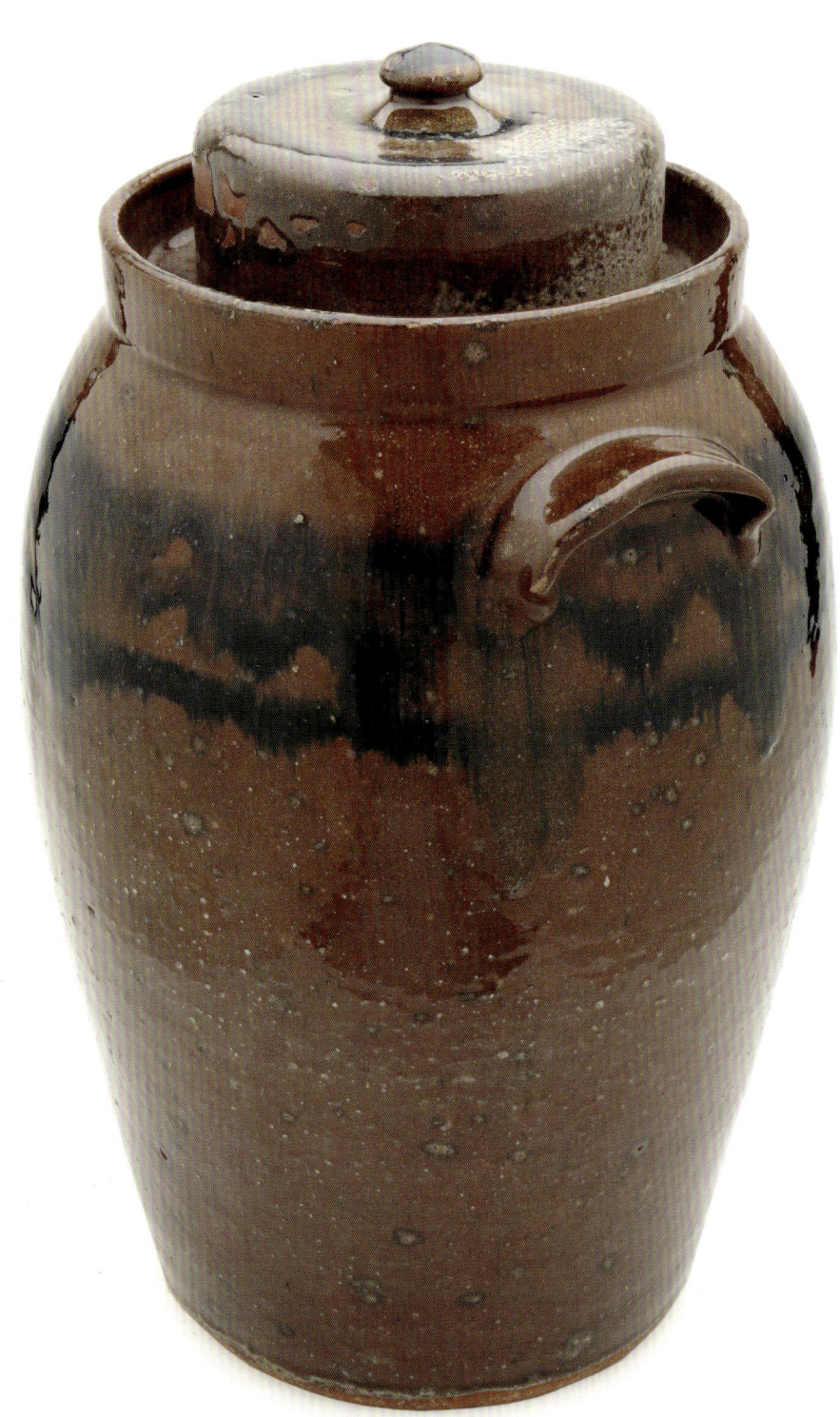

Five-gallon homebrew crock attributed to Maryland ("Bud") Hewell, ca. 1930, alkaline ("glass") glaze with cobalt blue decoration. This specialized form for fermenting malt liquor was popular during Prohibition; the lid sat in water-filled well around mouth, allowing gases to escape but excluding airborne bacteria that would sour contents. Bud adopted this version of ash glaze, with its high proportion of crushed glass, while working for J. D. ("Jug") Johnson at Lanford Station, South Carolina. H. 20½ inches. *Photo: David Greear; FPM collection.*

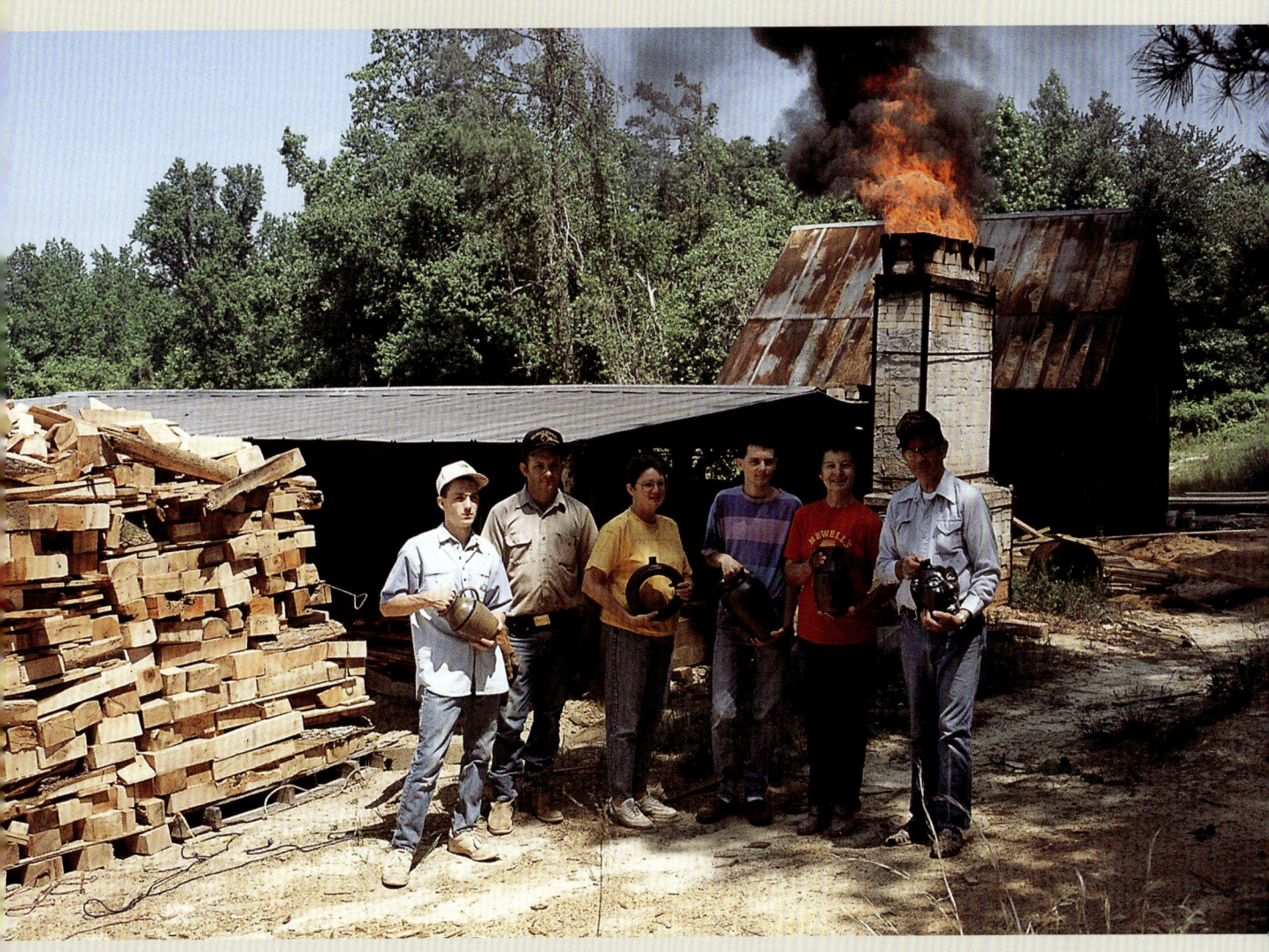

Three generations of Hewells at their wood-burning tunnel kiln and new old-timey shop, 1993. L–R: Matthew, Chester, Sandra, Nathaniel, Grace, and Harold. *Photo: author.*

CHAPTER 5

From Mud to Jug

The Production Process

Most north Georgia folk potters combined pottery with farming on a seasonal basis, but they were nonetheless professionals in the sense that they made their wares to sell. Folk pottery was—and still is—a business. As Lanier Meaders put it: "People now think of pottery as an art form, but for us it was our livelihood. It put food on our table." Acquired through years of training and practice, the skills of these potters were supported by specialized equipment, some of it outdoors, the rest housed in a log or frame workshop. Many of today's folk potters still use elements of the regional hand-crafting technology carried over from the nineteenth century.

Clay

Early Georgia potters didn't have the luxury of buying ready-to-use clay; they had to find their basic raw material locally and process it themselves. Stoneware clay normally is found in stream bottomland under several feet of topsoil. Cleater Meaders Sr. and Jr. used a long iron "clay auger" to locate good clay on their White County land, drilling into the ground to extract a test sample before shoveling up the clay. On a grander scale, the Hewells now dig clay with back-hoes, and keep a hill of clay outside their Gillsville plant. Chester Hewell recalls his grandfather, "Daddy Bud" (Maryland Hewell), saying, "Everything you need to make pottery is in the clay."

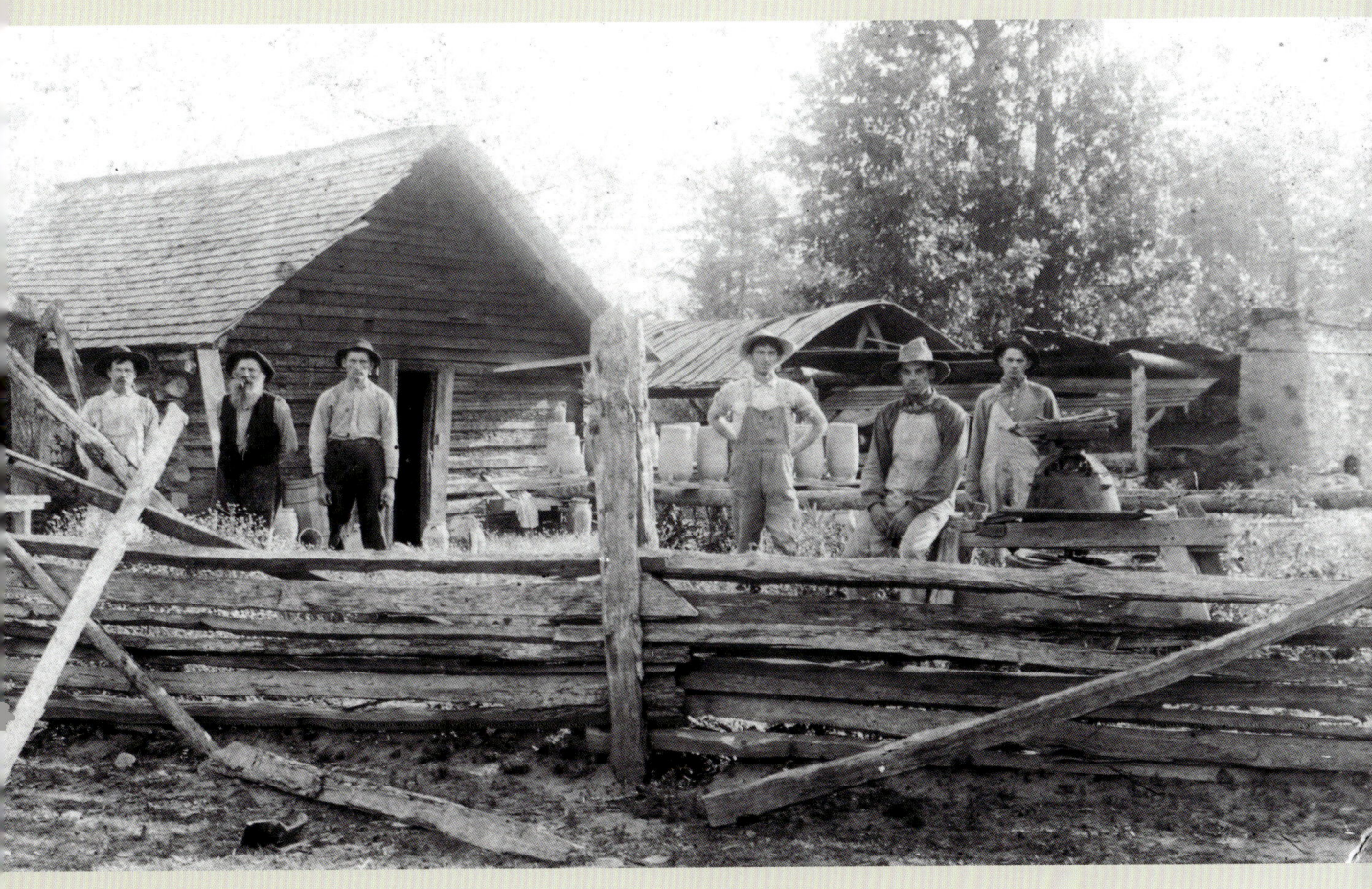

Pottery of William F. ("Daddy Bill") Dorsey, Mossy Creek,
ca. 1910. Daddy Bill (second from left, smoking pipe) is
flanked by hired potters of Hewell or Brown families, with
his sons Albert, Herbert, and Charlie at right. *Courtesy of
Leone Palmer and Emory Jones.*

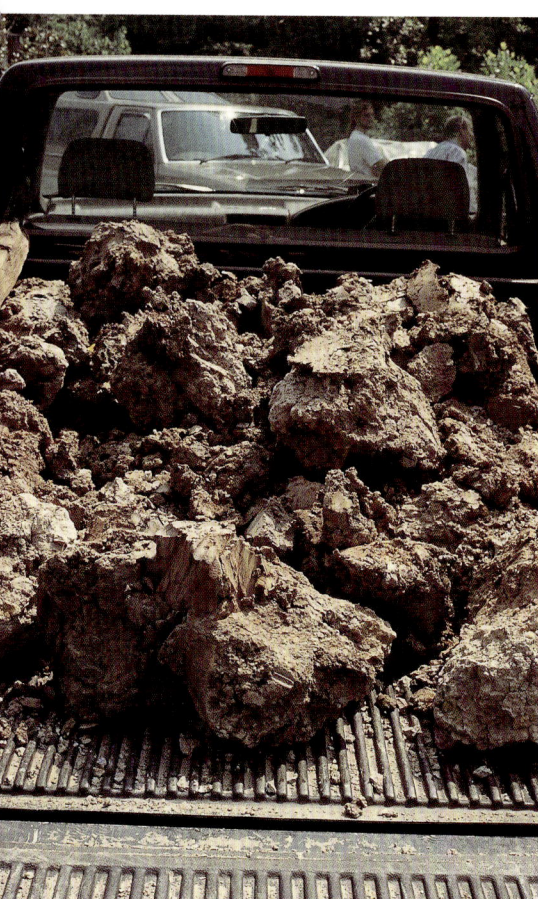

Pickup truckload of stoneware clay hand-dug by Cleater ("Clete") Meaders III from his family's Tesnatee River bottomland north of Cleveland, Georgia, 1995. *Photo: author.*

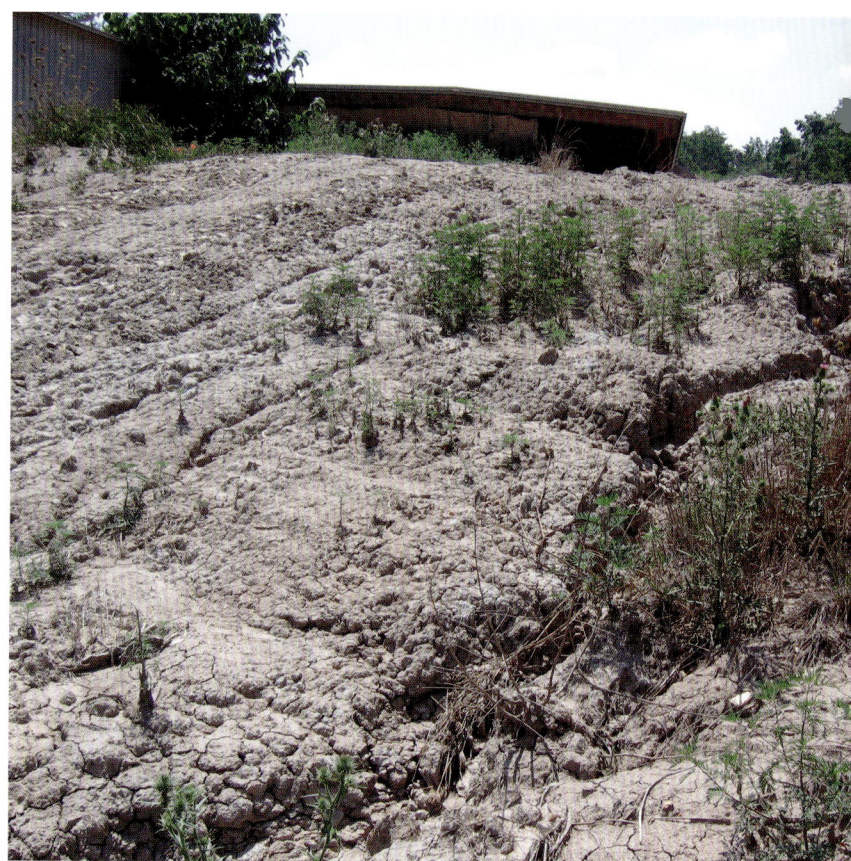

Clay supply at Hewell's Pottery, Gillsville, 2008. It was dug mechanically and is expected to last decades. Clay is fed to an electric-powered processor from the shed in the distance. *Photo: author.*

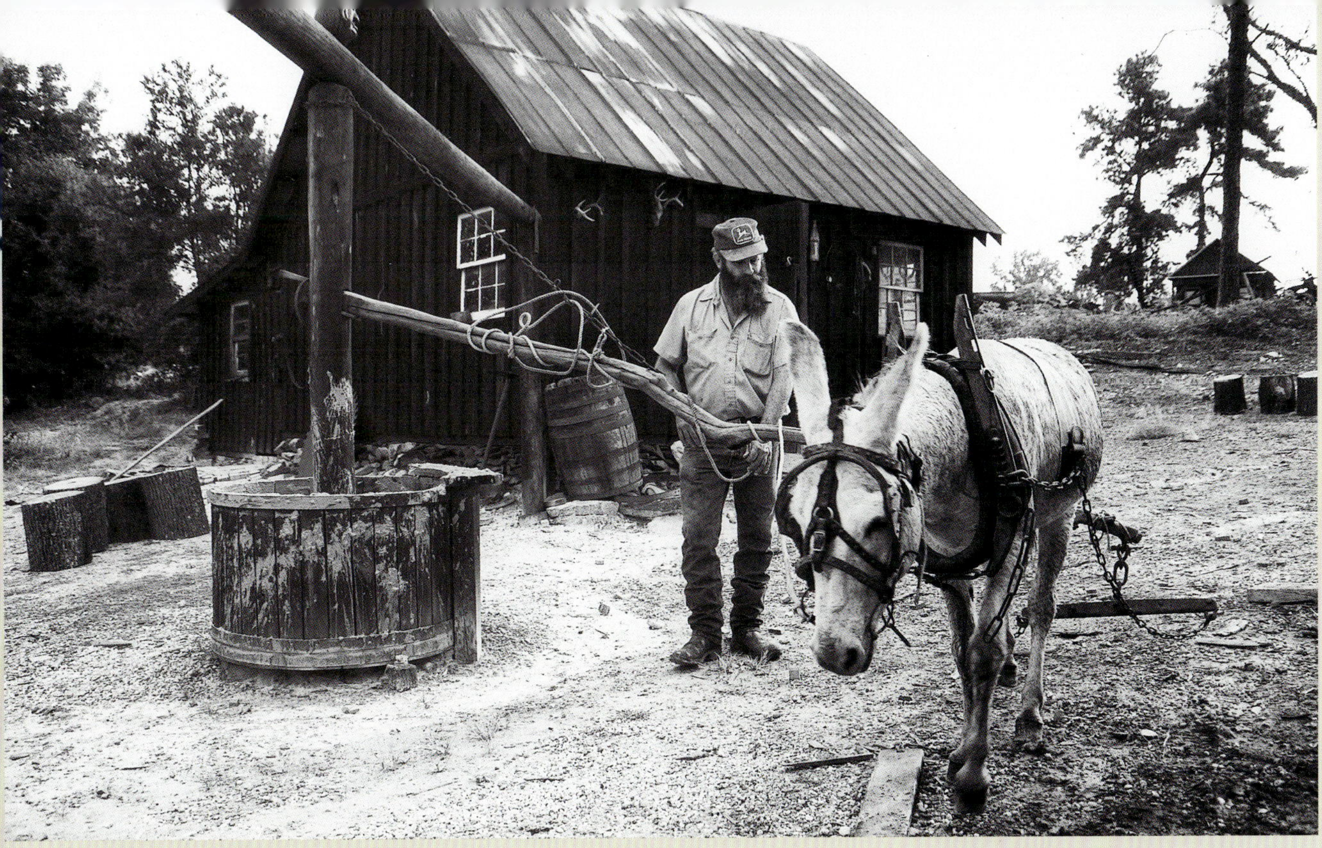

Chester Hewell mixing clay the traditional way with a mule-powered mill, 2001. Horizontal pins inside the tub churn clay and water until heavy impurities drop to the bottom. Both mill and frame shop were built to demonstrate old methods at the Hewells' Turning and Burning festival in Gillsville. *Photo: Chris Swanson.*

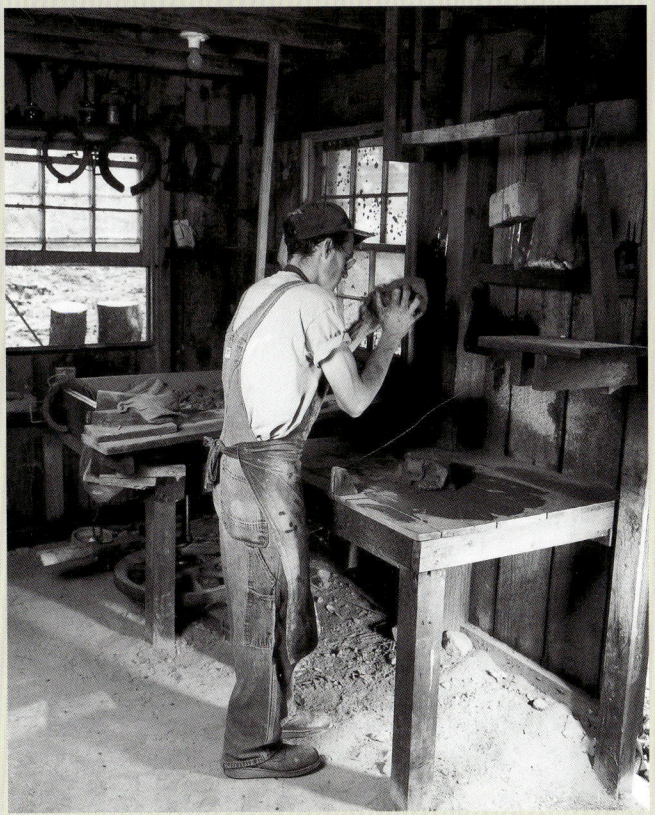

Matthew Hewell wedging clay at the "ball board" in Hewell's Pottery old-timey shop, 2001. The lump is split by the wire as it's slammed down, homogenizing the clay while expelling air and exposing bits of twigs and rocks that could cause blowout holes. *Photo: Chris Swanson.*

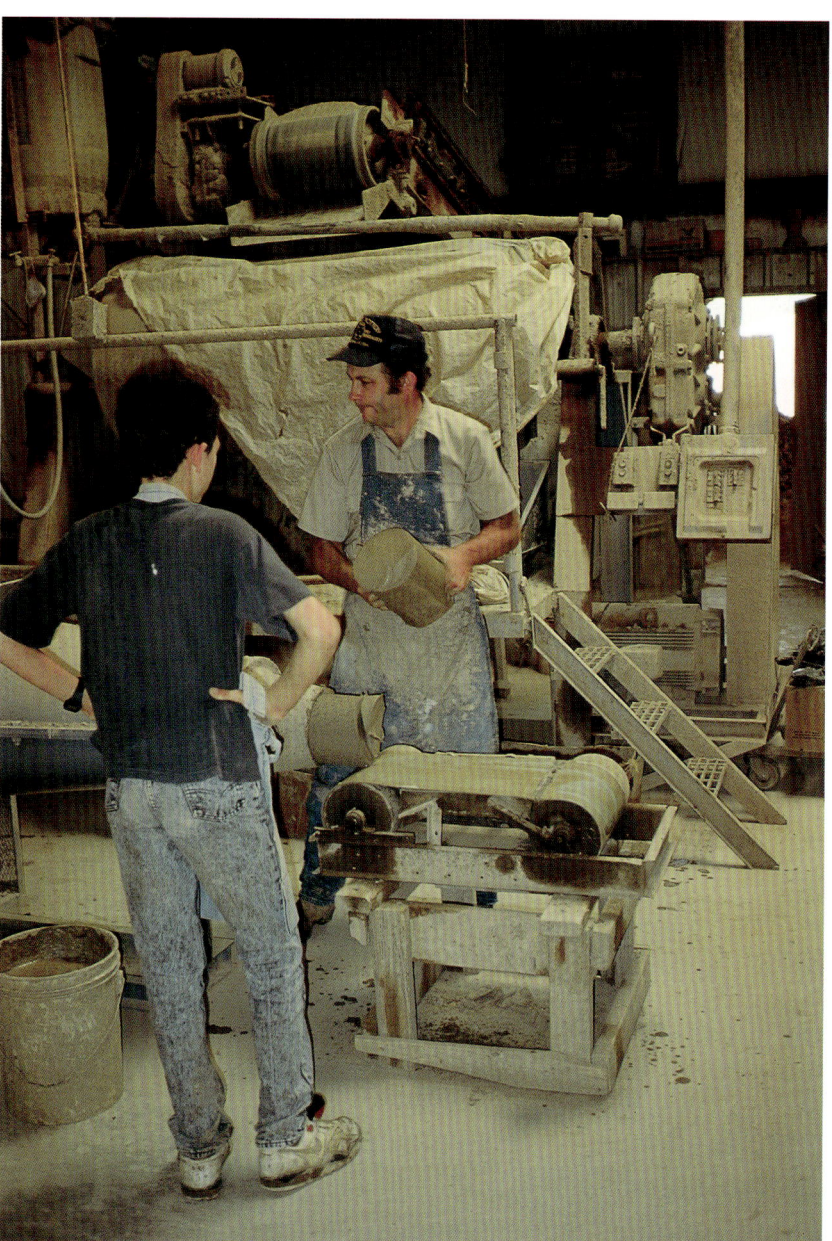

Chester Hewell and son
Nathaniel cutting clay slugs
extruded from a mechanical
mixer, Gillsville, ca. 1990.
Photo: author.

North Georgia folk potters once mixed their clay in mule-turned
mills; now they use motor-driven mills. It's then manually wedged,
or kneaded, to homogenize it and remove air, roots, and stones that
could cause blowout holes when fired. The resulting clay "balls,"
weighed so that pieces of the same shape and size are uniform, are
now ready to be thrown.

Turning

The skill that most defines southern folk potters as craftsmen is turning or throwing: the process of shaping the clay on a potter's wheel. In the old days this was men's work, although women sometimes helped. "It takes longer to learn to make a good piece of ware than it does to get a college education," declared Ada Hewell (who worked up the clay and added "ear," or lug, handles to butter churns for her husband Maryland at Gillsville). Several years of practice under the watchful eye of an older potter were needed to develop this throwing skill.

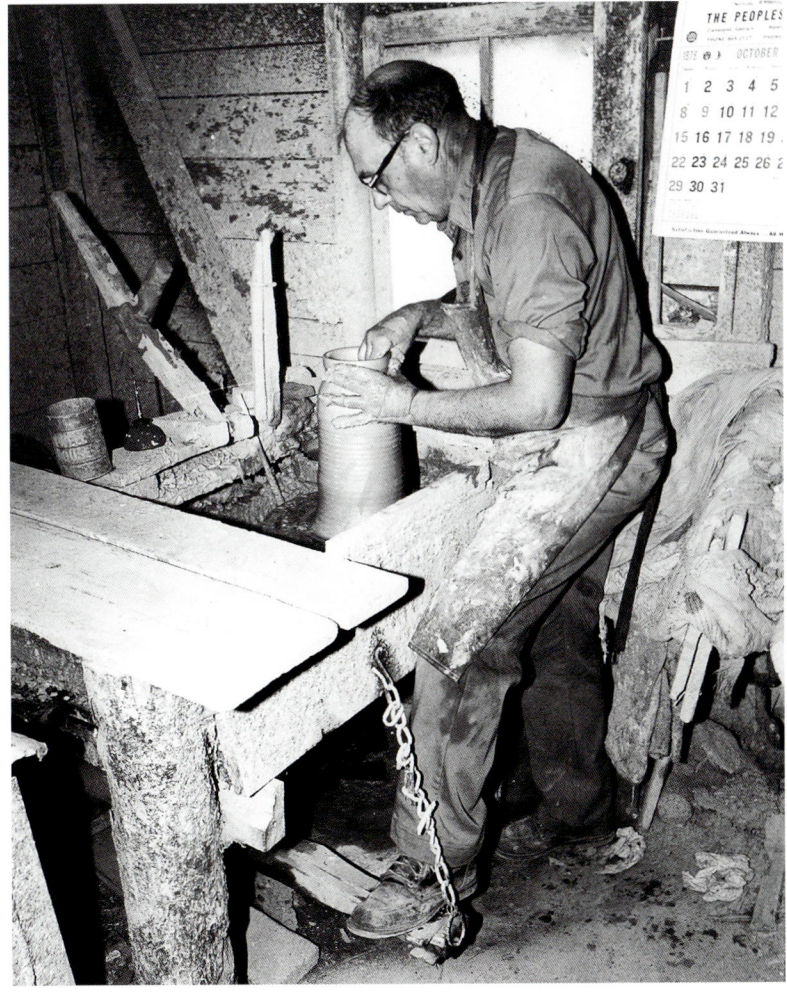

Lanier Meaders at his potter's wheel, Mossy Creek, 1978. Developed in 1700s England, the treadle wheel, with its foot-bar linked to a crankshaft, became the norm for American stoneware potters. Southern potters operate it in a standing position, as does Meaders here. Note the ball-opener lever in its resting position at left. *Photo: author.*

The type of potter's wheel used by American stoneware potters is the treadle wheel, developed in eighteenth-century England; with one leg the potter pushes back and forth a horizontal bar linked to a crankshaft to turn the wheel. In England and in the North such wheels had a seat, but southern potters operate them in a standing position, leaning against a padded rail, so they can pull up, or shape, big pieces more easily. The hinged ball-opener lever for creating the initial opening in the clay for a vessel form is another regional feature. Some Georgia folk potters now use electric motor-powered wheels.

Glazes

Glaze is the glassy sealing finish on pottery (thought of in Asia as the "flesh" covering the clay "bones"). Well-fired stoneware clay normally won't leak, but it's still glazed both as a precaution and as an enhancement to the appearance of the finished product. Traditionally, northeast Georgia folk potters coated their "raw," or unfired, wares with a solution of either homemade alkaline glaze or "bought" Albany slip.

Alkaline glazes are named for the wood ashes or lime they contain that, when mixed with water, become a caustic-base flux that helps to melt the other ingredients: clay (which binds the glaze to the pot and contributes silica) and an extra silica source such as sand. These glazes turn green or brown as the iron in the clay reacts to the kiln atmosphere. An alkaline glaze becomes green in a smoky (reduction) atmosphere and brown in a free-burning (oxidation) atmosphere; the exact shade is influenced by the clay beneath, since when properly fired the glaze is semitransparent. The ash-based type often has a drippy "tobacco spit" texture, while the lime version tends to be smoother. Some Mossy Creek potters replaced the regular sand in their alkaline glazes with dark "iron sand," "flint" (quartzite), and later, powdered glass. The glaze solution was refined in a hand-turned stone mill, a back-breaking chore later eliminated with the addition of preprocessed ingredients to glaze recipes.

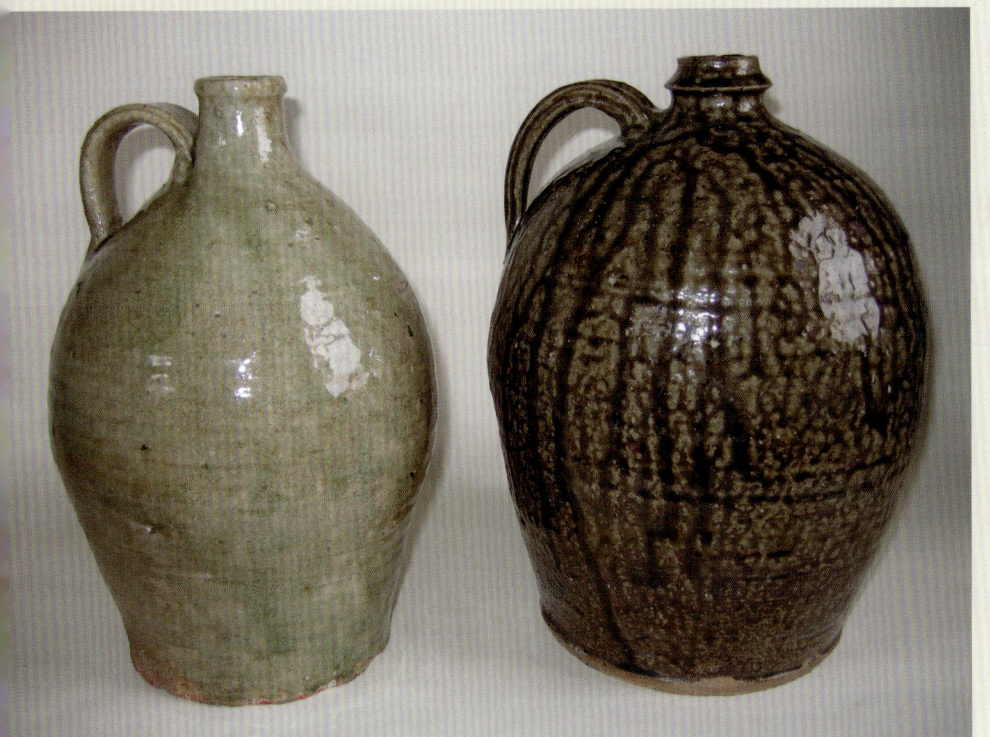

Alkaline-glazed whiskey jugs attributed to antebellum north Georgia. At left, a typically smooth lime-based version over light-colored clay; at right, a typically drippy-textured ash version over darker clay. Wood ashes contain minerals that also deepen color. H. each 11 inches. *Photo: author; author's collection.*

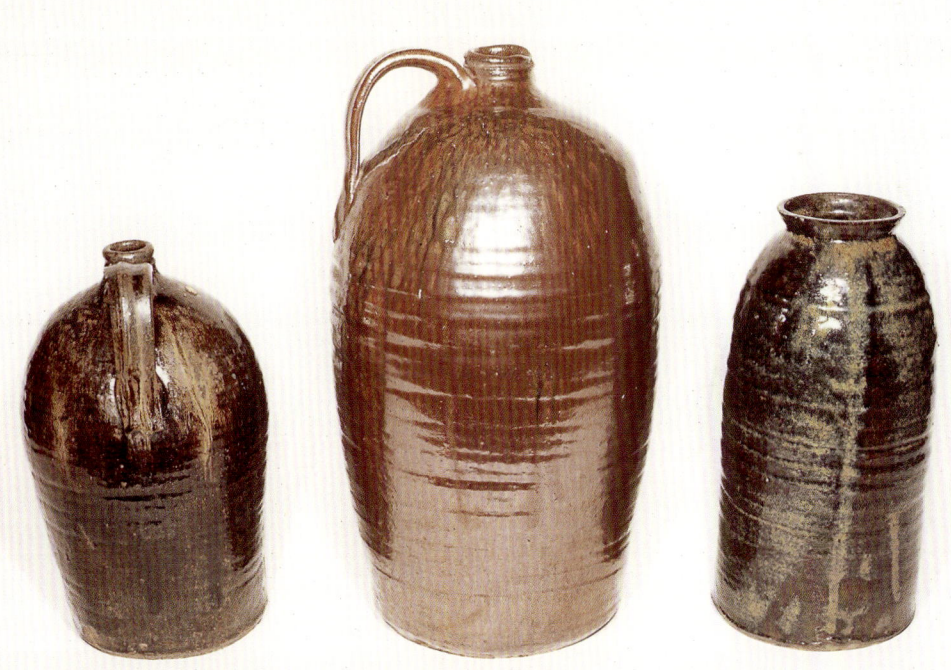

Whiskey jug, syrup jug, and canning jar, Isaac H. Craven, Mossy Creek, 1870s–80s, showing color variations in his "iron sand" version of ash glaze. He collected the dark sand from a local roadbed, where it washed down from adjacent banks. H., L–R: 11¼ inches; 16½ inches; 12¼ inches. *Photo: author; author's collection.*

These alkaline glazes are remarkably similar to those of the Far East dating to the time of Christ. A description of Chinese high-firing, ash- and lime-based glazes was published in 1735 in French and the following year in English; Abner Landrum of Edgefield District, South Carolina, may have read about them and was in any case using them by 1820. Their readily available ingredients made alkaline glazes a practical alternative to the European and northern practice of glazing stoneware with salt, a precious commodity in the southern backcountry. Migrating Edgefield-trained potters spread alkaline glazes into Georgia and by the 1850s as far west as Texas.

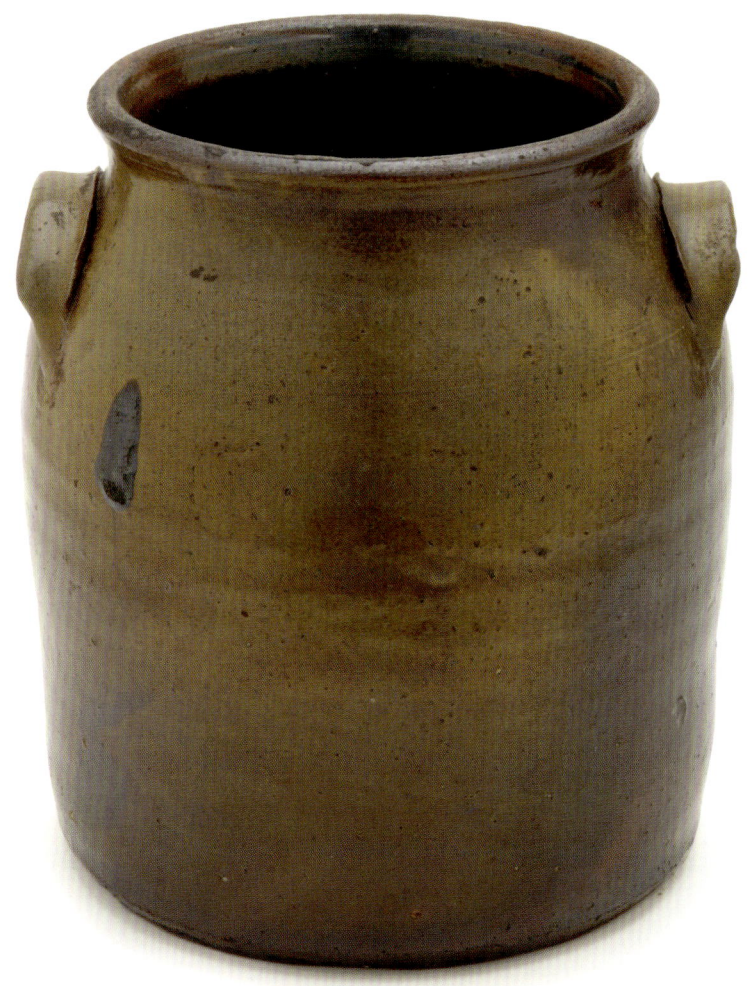

Two-gallon crock attributed to Henry H. Hewell at W. R. Addington shop, Gillsville, late 1880s, salt glaze over Albany slip (a double glaze brought from Barrow County). The lighter-colored area is where the sodium vapor concentrated; the dark drip is an unintentional by-product of salt glazing (hydrochloric acid in the smoke corrodes the bricks in the kiln ceiling, causing them to drip onto the ware). H. 10¼ inches. *Photo: David Greear;* FPM *collection.*

Albany slip is a natural clay glaze mined in the Hudson River Valley near Albany, New York. First used on northern stoneware, the smooth, brown glaze became available to southern potters once trade with the North resumed after the Civil War. Its simple preparation—just mixing with water into a slip, or liquid clay—and its ease of cleaning for customers (compared with the sometimes rough alkaline glazes) were worth the expense for some Georgia potters.

Barrow County potters adopted Albany slip in the 1870s. By throwing salt in the kiln at the height of firing they created a more visually interesting double glaze: tan or green where the sodium vapor concentrated. Gillsville potters referred to Albany slip as "the black glazin'," since it turns black when fired very hot. Mossy Creek potters began using this "patent" glaze about 1895, but not many there abandoned the alkaline glazes altogether.

Burning

Made of earth and water, pots become usable only when hardened by air and fire. Southern folk potters accomplished this transformation with wood-fueled, rectangular kilns (pronounced in the South with a silent *n* as *kills*, and very different from the North's round kilns). In north Georgia they were built above ground and called tunnel kilns, in contrast to the middle Georgia "groundhog" version enclosed by earth. Folk pottery typically is fired only once, as opposed to more delicate ceramics, which are bisque-fired and then fired a second time with glaze.

A typical north Georgia tunnel kiln might measure eighteen by eight feet, hold four hundred gallons of ware (traditionally, size was reckoned in terms of gallon capacity), and take twelve to fifteen hours to "burn" or fire. The full stoneware temperature of 2300°F is held in the last hours by "blasting off," or constantly feeding wood into the firebox, with smoke and flames billowing from the chimney. Trial pieces are drawn from an opening in the chimney end to see if the glaze has properly melted; then the firing can stop and the kiln is allowed to cool for a couple of days before unloading.

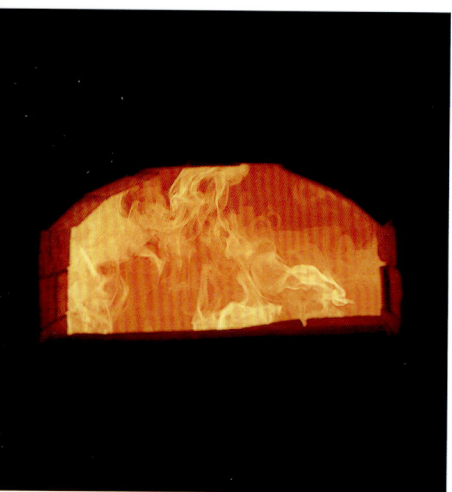

Looking through the firebox to the ware chamber of Hewell's Pottery tunnel kiln at the height of burning. *Photo: author.*

Burning one of these wood-fueled kilns is a hot, sweaty job with unpredictable results, but a connection with the past and the organic quality of the finished products, with their variegated surfaces, are the rewards. Hewell's Pottery, Wayne Hewell, Clete Meaders, David and Anita Meaders, Clint Alderman, and Pat and Janice Shields still burn their stoneware this old-fashioned way, but other north Georgia folk potters now use gas or electric kilns.

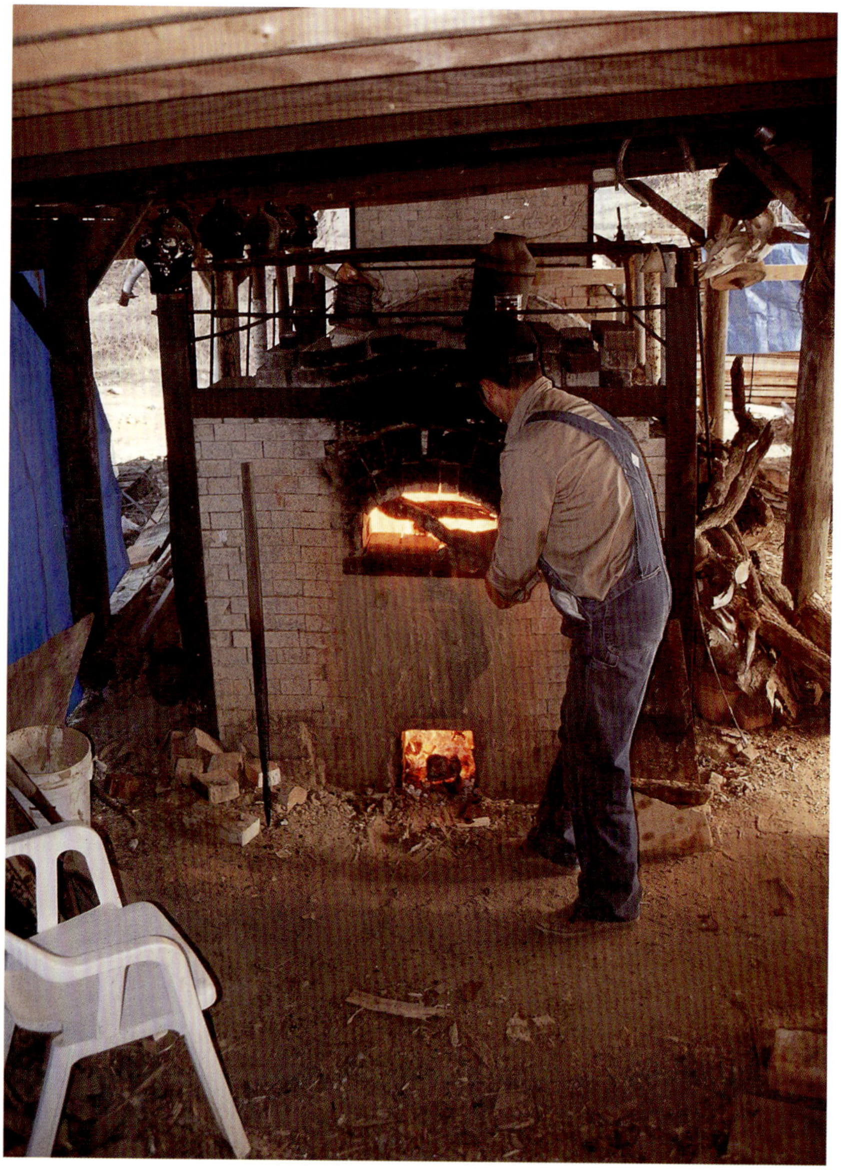

Chester Hewell feeding wood into the firebox of his tunnel kiln, Gillsville, 1992. *Photo: author.*

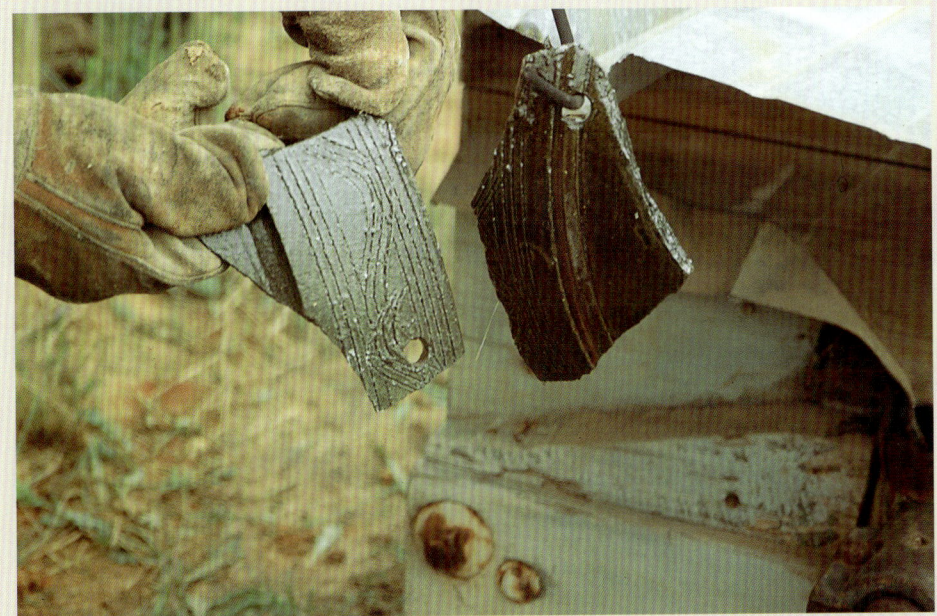

Chester comparing draw-trials (flowerpot fragments drilled and glazed), the one at right just removed with a hooked iron rod; a loose brick in the kiln's chimney allows access to the ware chamber. The ash glaze has properly melted, an indication that burning can stop. *Photo: author.*

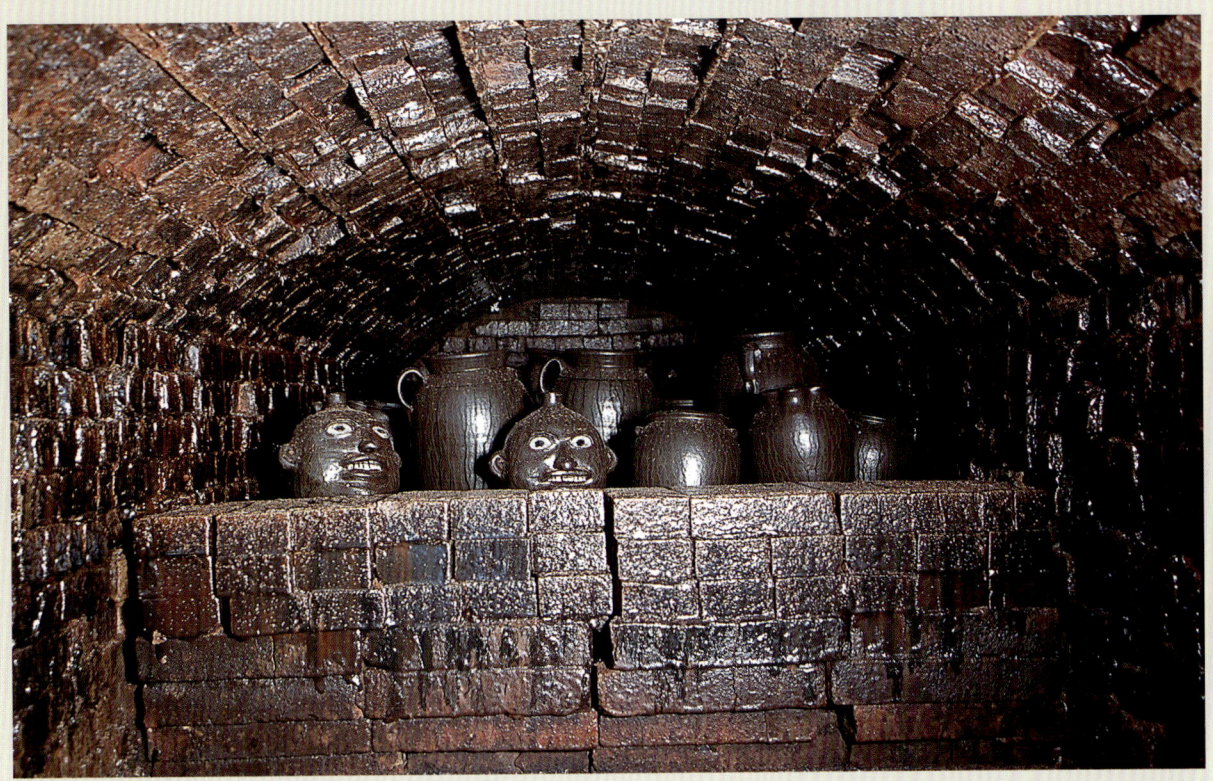

Cooled Hewell's Pottery kiln interior with ash-glazed wares ready to be unloaded, 2001. *Photo: Chris Swanson.*

CHAPTER 6

Staying Alive

Original Uses of Folk Pottery

Before modern canning and refrigeration, clay vessels for keeping food and drink were essential to survival. According to Lanier Meaders, potters were essential in north Georgia's farming society: "Just about everything else at one time in this part of the country depended upon it." To list the products of these craftsmen—jugs for whiskey, cane syrup, and water; jars for preserving vegetables, fruit, and meat; milk crocks, pitchers, and churns—is to describe a "homemade" life hard-won from nature. If you could travel back to 1900, the places you'd most likely see folk pottery on a north Georgia farm would be the springhouse, kitchen, smokehouse, and whiskey still.

The Springhouse

Using basic engineering skills acquired from "making do" on the farm, north Georgians turned a freshwater spring into a natural refrigerator by enclosing it and lining the catchment floor with stone. Stoneware milk crocks, cream risers for skimming cream, butter jars, and buttermilk pitchers were set in the cold, running water to keep dairy products from spoiling in the warm climate.

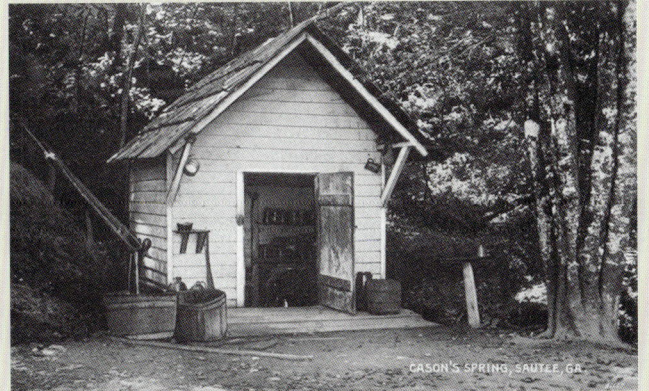

Cason's springhouse (retouched postcard photo), Sautee, White County, early 1900s. A trough fed water from the spring above to the tub for drinking, with overflow spilling into a below-ground chamber through a hole in the plank flooring. Canning jars can be seen on shelves inside; syrup jugs and a churn stand outside.

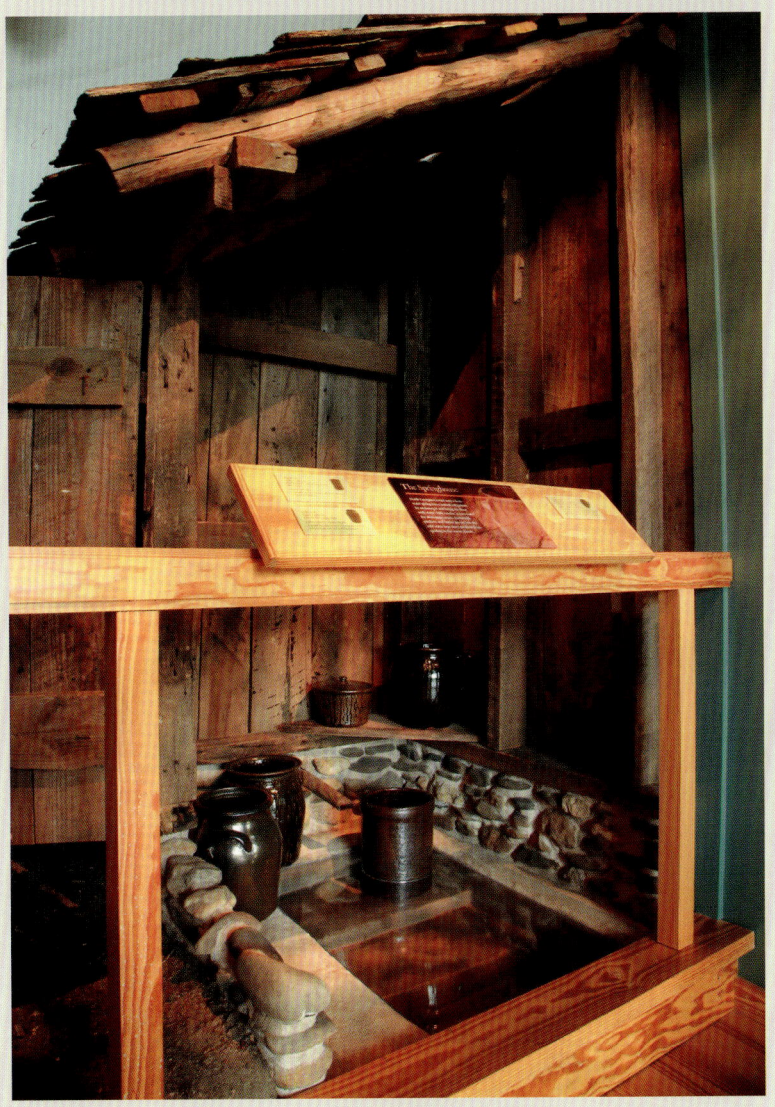

Springhouse interior with dairy wares (milk crocks, butter pots, and cream riser), re-created at the Folk Pottery Museum. *Photo: David Greear, Silver Image Studio, Helen, Ga.*

The Kitchen

In frontier days, cooking was done on the open hearth of the fireplace; a dedicated kitchen room did not become common on smaller farms until cast-iron stoves became available. In either case, food stored in pottery jars could be kept handy in a cupboard. Clay churns outnumbered wooden ones; churning was done at the fireside in winter, the heat speeding up bacterial "clabbering" of the cream so that it could be broken down into butter and buttermilk by pumping the dash-stick.

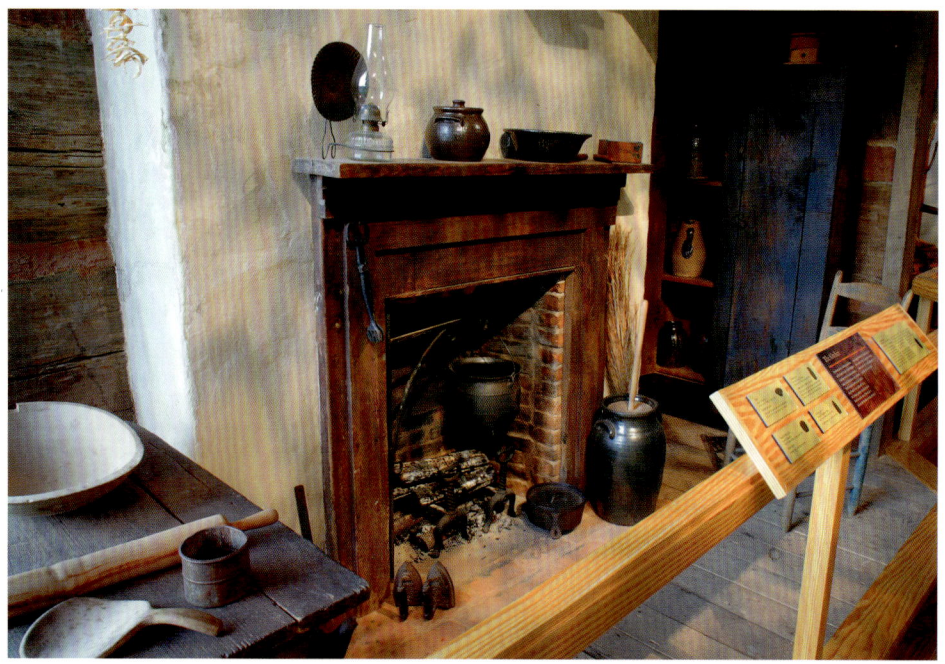

Kitchen with Albany slip–glazed churn on hearth and ash-glazed canning jars in cupboard, re-created at the Folk Pottery Museum. North Georgia farmers used clay churns (more than wooden ones) to make butter from the milk of their cows. Cream skimmed from whole milk would first "clabber," or sour, aided in cold weather by placing the churn near the fire. A wooden dash stick, with a crosspiece at the lower end, was then pumped up and down by hand until the butterfat separated from the liquid and "gathered" at top. Butter was removed, washed to remove buttermilk, and cooled in the springhouse, then served. The tangy liquid left in the churn was buttermilk, a favorite drink of rural southerners. *Photo: David Greear, Silver Image Studio, Helen, Ga.*

The Smokehouse

In this important outbuilding of north Georgia farms, hams, bacon, and sausages were preserved with salt and wood-smoke after the fall hog butchering. Located near the kitchen, the smokehouse doubled as a convenient storehouse for homemade cane syrup and canned produce, which were kept in pottery vessels.

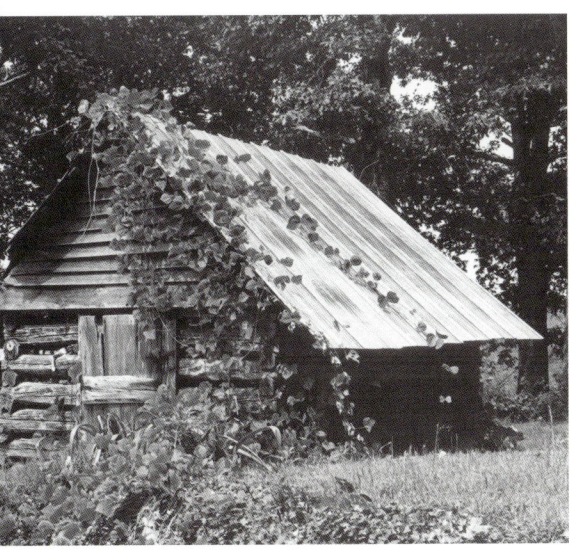

Log smokehouse built in late 1800s at the John Meaders home, Mossy Creek, across road from Meaders Pottery (kudzu was overgrowing it when photo was taken in 1975). Inside, nails in joists marked where hams and bacon hung for smoking with a hardwood-chip fire.
Photo: author.

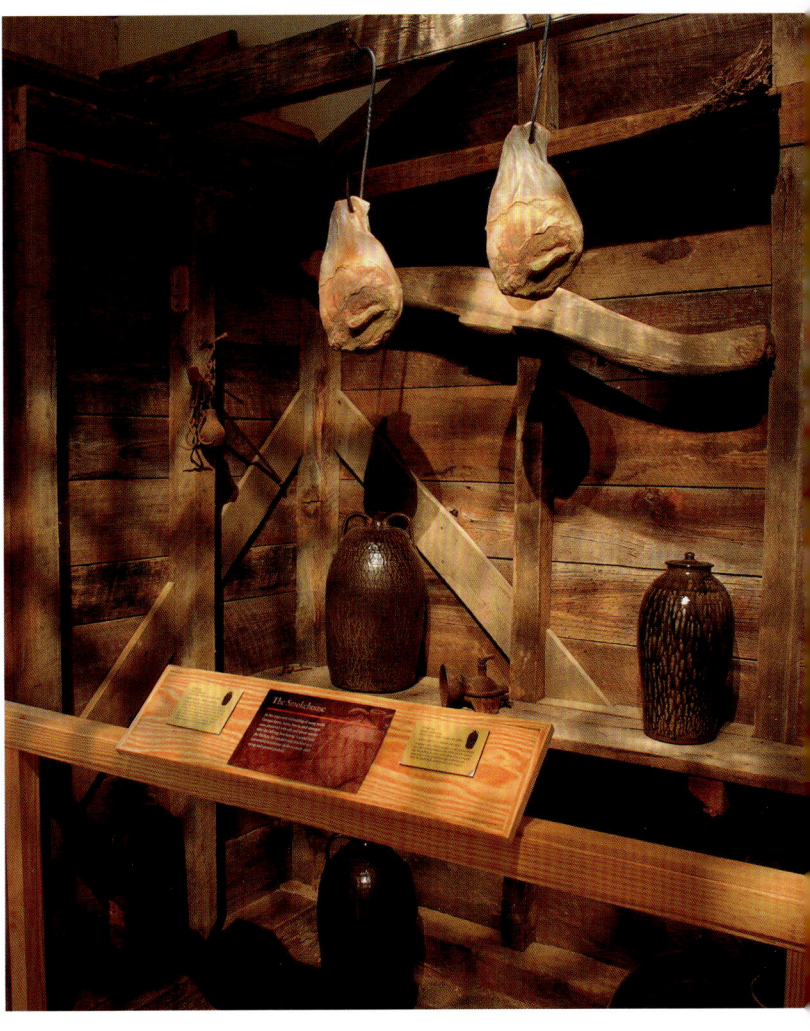

Smokehouse interior with food-storage wares (syrup jugs and lard jar), re-created at the Folk Pottery Museum.
Photo: David Greear, Silver Image Studio, Helen, Ga.

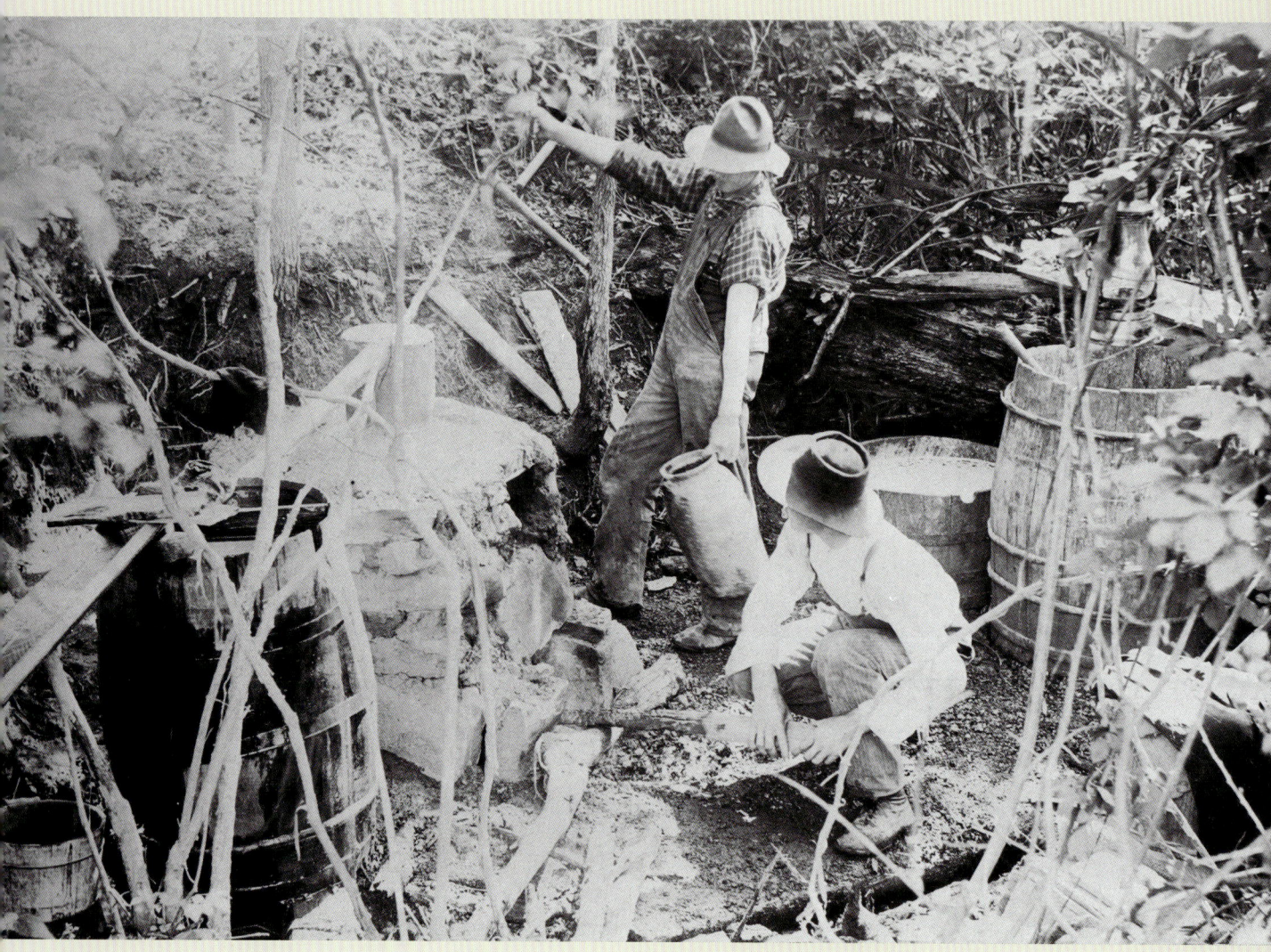

Moonshiners distilling illicit whiskey in the mountains of Rabun
County, Georgia, early 1900s, with a stoneware churn used to carry
"beer" (fermented cornmeal mash and malt) from the tub. *Courtesy of
Georgia Archives, Vanishing Georgia Collection, rab137.*

The Moonshine Still

Moonshining (illegal whiskey making) became a source of income for some north Georgians. A tradition brought by Scots-Irish settlers and adapted to American corn, "blockading," as it also was called, created potent "white lightning." Copper stills, encased in rock furnaces, were hidden in the woods to escape detection by the law.

Dawson County was north Georgia's "moonshine capital," but there were smaller pockets closer to the pottery centers, such as Long Mountain near Mossy Creek and Peckerwood near Gillsville, giving moonshiners there immediate access to the jugs they once needed to package their product. Ranging in size from a quart to two gallons, whiskey jugs were the chief stock-in-trade of some north Georgia folk potters.

CHAPTER 7

Changing Times
Threats to Functional Folk Pottery

In the industrialized North, the making of folk pottery was in decline by the mid-1800s and was nearly extinct by that century's end. But in the South, the agrarian lifestyle that supported the use of folk pottery continued into the early twentieth century. However late in coming, big changes were to affect the lives of north Georgians at that time.

In the twentieth century rural self-sufficiency slowly gave way to dependence on a cash economy, and many of the old skills, including home food production, were abandoned. At the same time, potters were lured away from their shops by factory wages. North Georgia's stoneware tradition was nearly dealt a death blow by the Great Depression of the 1930s, when cash was so scarce that potters could no longer count on fellow farmers to buy their products. This followed a series of events that caused the range of wares needed on the farm to shrink dramatically.

Prohibition

In 1907 the Georgia State Legislature passed an act making it illegal to make and sell alcoholic beverages. That did little to curb moonshining, but it caused Georgia potters to lose the business of legal distillers, who ceased operations. With national Prohibition

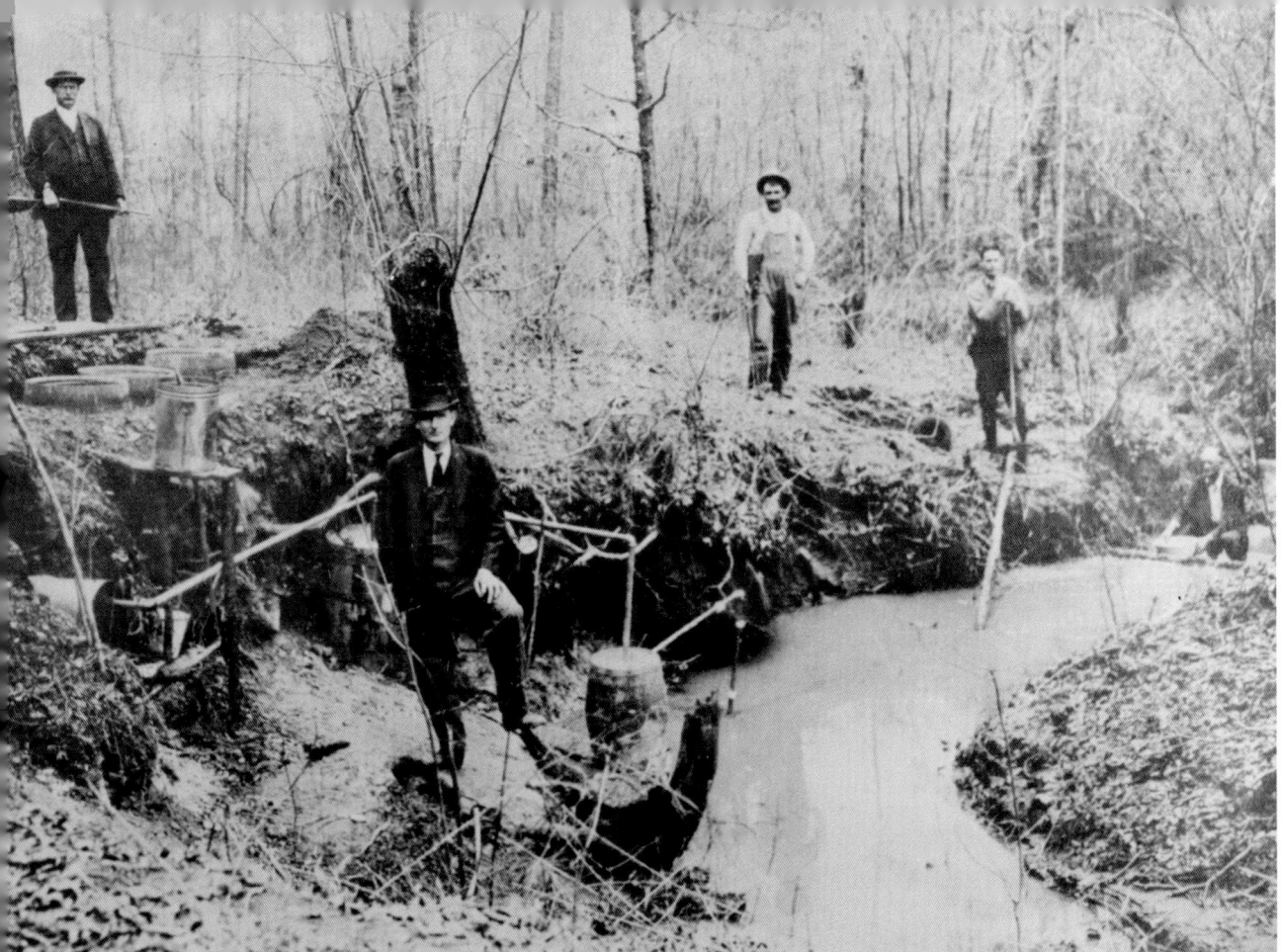

(1920–33) came a concerted federal crackdown on illicit stills. This government pressure forced potters who specialized in whiskey jugs to diversify—or quit.

Glass and Metal Containers

Factory-made glass and metal containers had a big impact on pottery used for food preservation. Glass canning jars, including Mason's patented screw-top, became available after the Civil War but were not always affordable. Steve Lewis of White County (Lanier Meaders's father-in-law) recalled "when there wasn't a dozen glass fruit cans in the district. Used to, we'd put up our food in them

Revenue agents confiscating a moonshine still, north Georgia, 1920s. The still is at left, dug into embankment. The alcohol content of steam from the still was raised by the addition of beer in the "thumper" keg at center; the steam was then piped under the cooling stream to condense it into whiskey. *Courtesy of Georgia Archives, Vanishing Georgia Collection, geo080.*

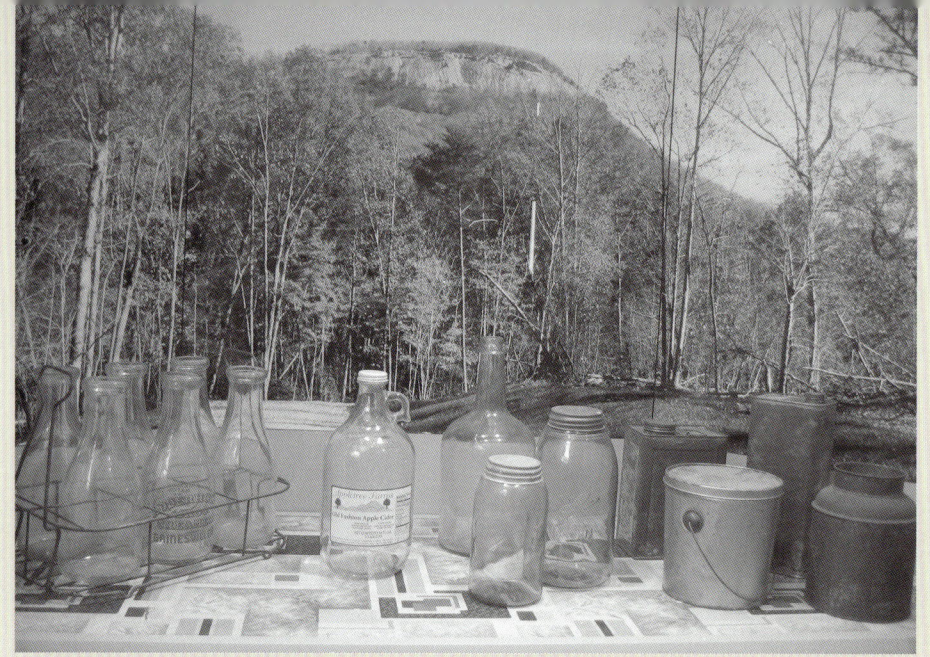

Factory-made glass and metal containers of the sort that began to replace north Georgia folk pottery in the early 1900s, Folk Pottery Museum display. *Photo: author.*

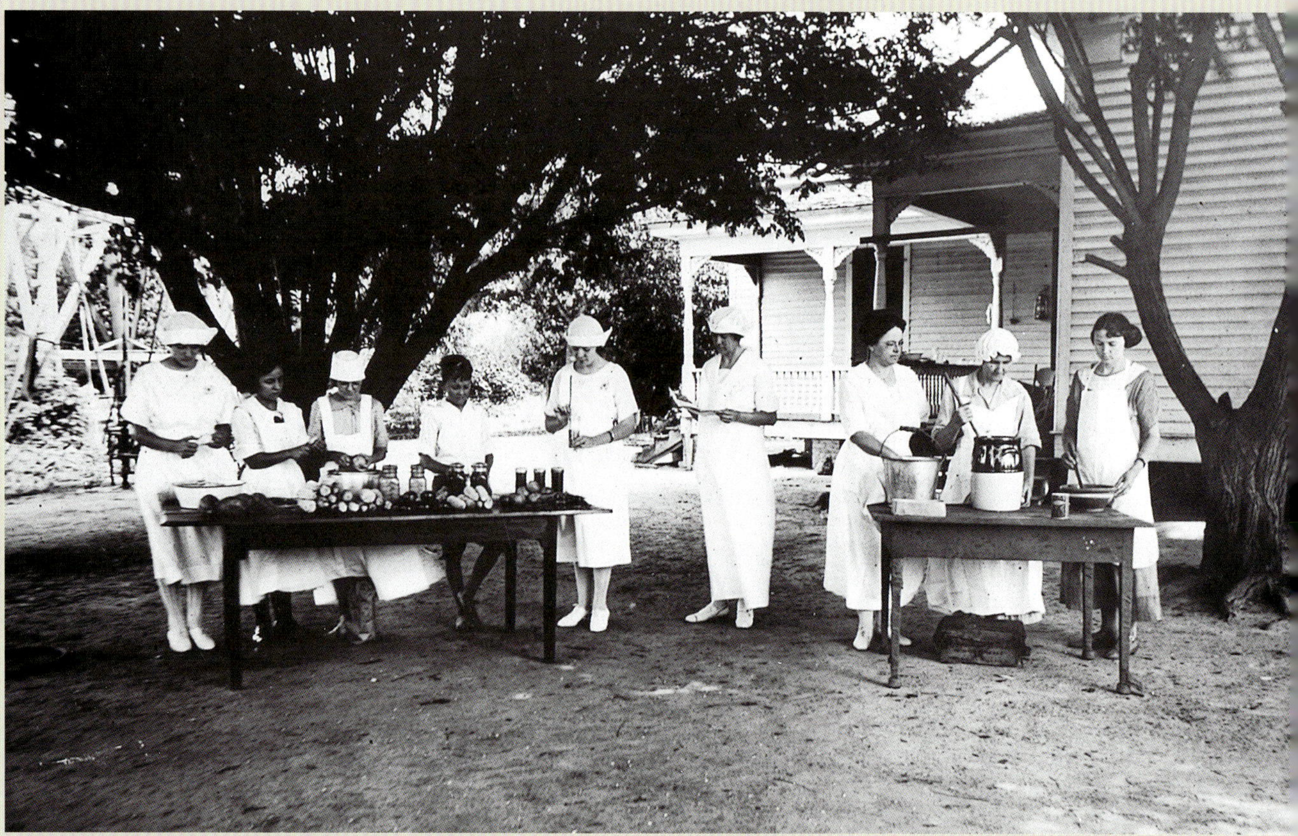

Home demonstration of canning and butter making at Sisters Community Club, Washington County, Georgia, ca. 1922. Photo: Little Studio, Tennille, Georgia; *courtesy of Georgia Archives, Vanishing Georgia Collection, was310.*

stone[ware] jars." But the later spread of glass jars—which could be sterilized and thus were more sanitary than clay jars—and instruction on their use by home demonstration agents, revolutionized home canning and made the clay jars obsolete.

Commercial Dairies

With the rise of commercial dairies in the 1920s, fewer and fewer north Georgians bothered to keep their own cows, and churns and jars made for home processing and cooling of milk and butter no longer were needed. Lanier Meaders's former grade-school teacher had a smokehouse full of old dairy wares on her farm, including churns by Lanier's uncle Wiley, collecting cobwebs and mostly broken by the 1970s.

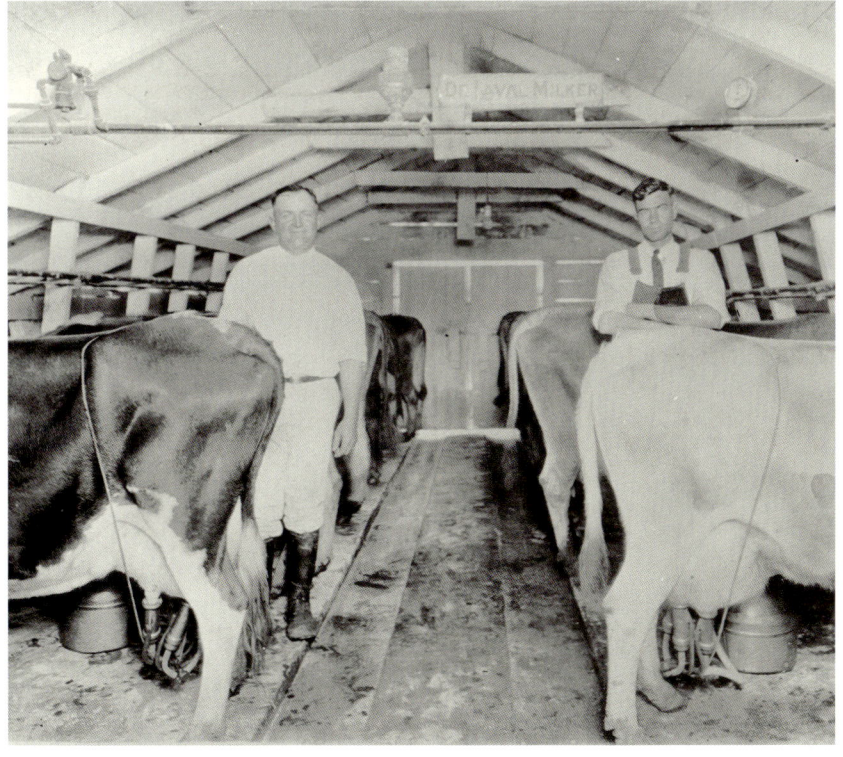

H. H. Cobb Dairy complete with milking machines, Oconee County, Georgia, 1921, marking the beginning of commercial dairies and the decline of home dairying with associated pottery. *Courtesy of Georgia Archives, Vanishing Georgia Collection, oco003.*

CHAPTER 8

New Markets

Keeping Their Hands in Clay

With the erosion of their customer base in the 1920s and 1930s described in the previous chapter, north Georgia folk potters had to make some serious choices if they were to keep their hands in clay. Only Cheever Meaders of Mossy Creek clung to the old ways, dropping the price for his wares to three cents a gallon during the depression until a growing crafts market took up the slack. For the rest, it was either find another path in clay or another trade altogether. New strategies were developed, all requiring changes in the way those potters approached their work. But none of these strategies involved a total break from the older tradition.

Garden Pottery: The Gillsville Story

Georgia folk potters had always made a few flowerpots, supplying containers for brightly colored plants to beautify their neighbors' porches. Gillsville potters who survived the depression saw an opportunity in the craze for potted plants and lawn ornaments as America's suburbs blossomed after World War II. Since the roots of plants must "breathe," the best horticultural vessels are made of porous red clay. Customers expect to pay less for unglazed pottery, so greater volume is needed to turn a profit. To meet that challenge, Middle Georgia Pottery at Lizella geared up as early as the 1920s to mass-produce flowerpots with machines and molds.

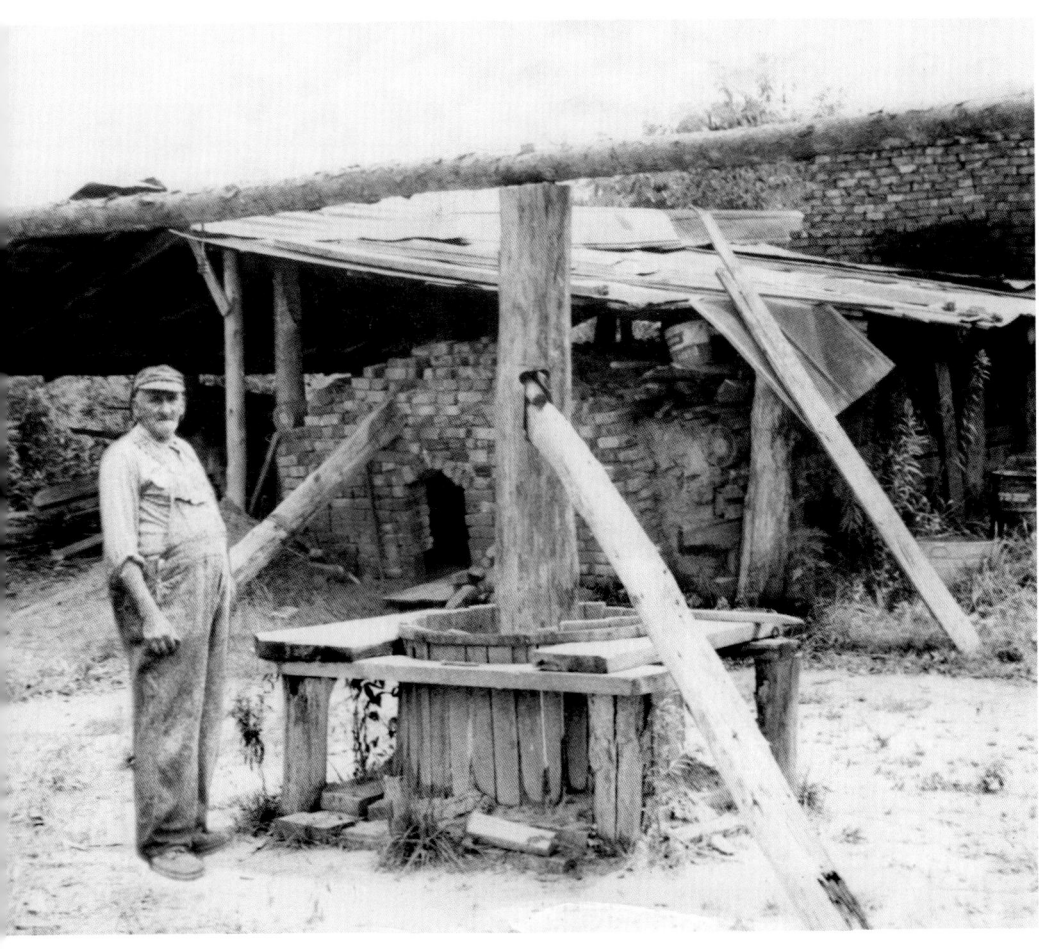

Cheever Meaders at his "mud mill," Mossy Creek, ca. 1960, about the time it and the mule that turned it were retired and replaced by an electric-powered clay mixer built by Cheever's son, Lanier. *Courtesy of Emory Jones.*

Gillsville potters, however, chose not to invest in such equipment but to channel their throwing skills into larger-scale production. They accomplished this with an expanded work force, mechanical clay preparation, motorized wheels, and large-capacity kilns. By keeping the shaping hand based, they could more flexibly develop new planter styles and sizes. Marketing also has a lot to do with Gillsville's reputation as the country's gardenware capital. Hewell's and Craven's have retail shops that include a large line of factory-made imports, and they maintain a wholesale network of garden-supply companies served by locally based coast-to-coast truckers (in 2007 Craven's closed its outlet in Commerce due to a depressed market).

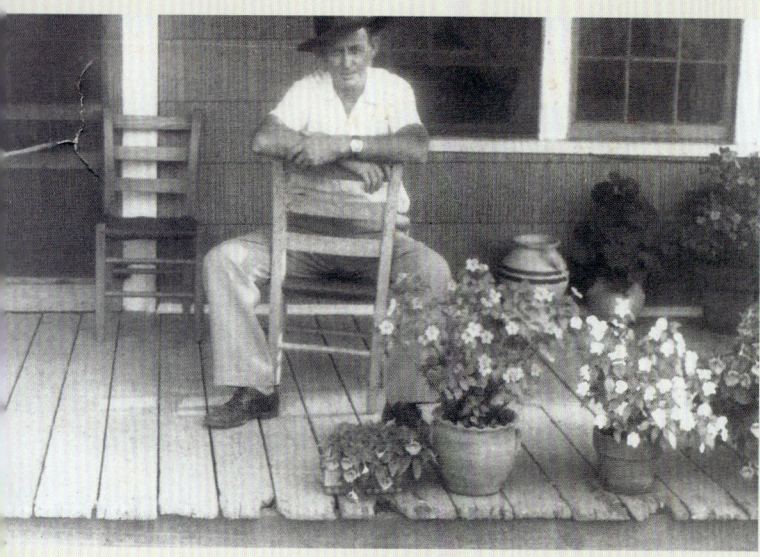

Potter William Patrick ("Pat") Ferguson on the porch of his Gillsville home ca. 1955 with planted flowerpots, some of which he probably made. *Courtesy of Ferguson family and Anthony Souther.*

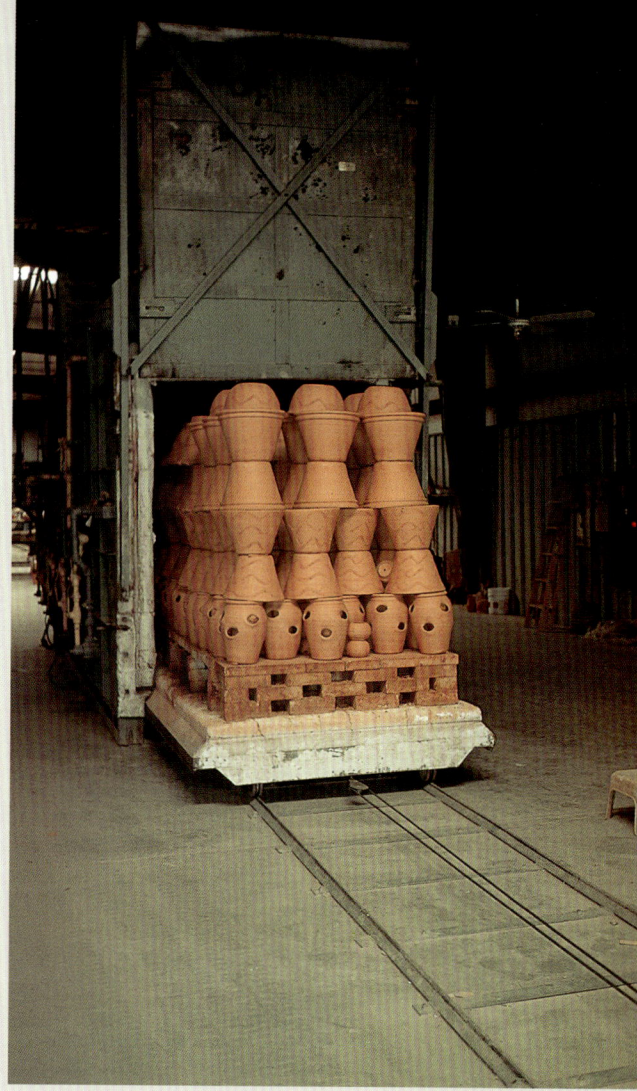

Computer-controlled, gas-fired shuttle kiln with a carload of garden pots being winched out, Hewell's Pottery, 1990. *Photo: author.*

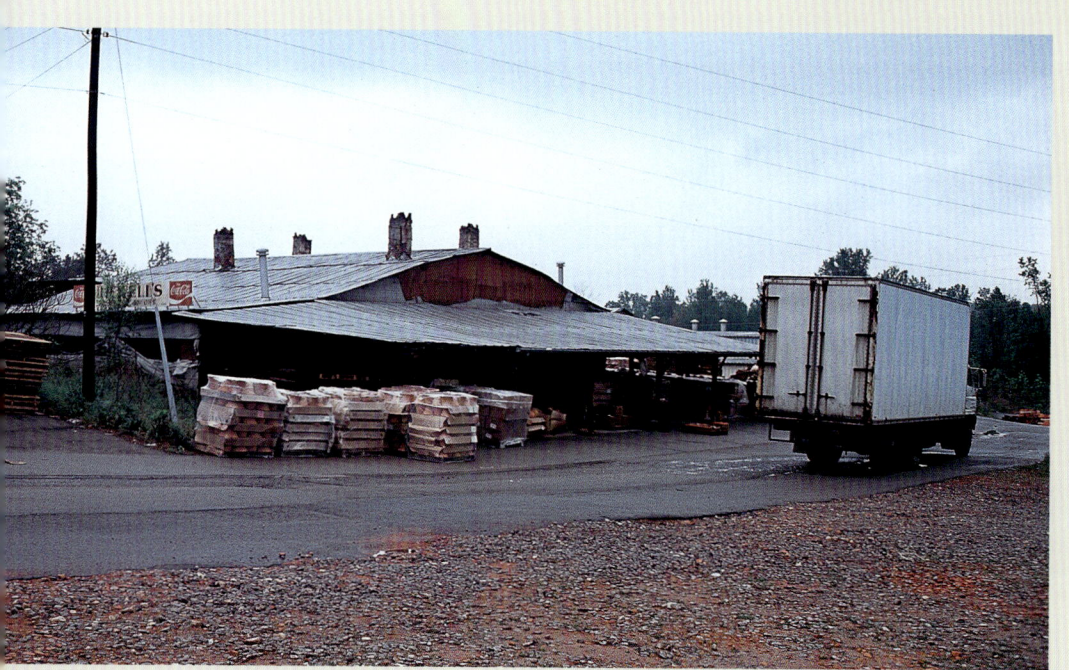

Shrink-wrapped pallets of garden wares at Hewell's Pottery ready to load onto a truck for sale to garden centers, 1990. In the background is the original four-stack downdraft kiln built in 1965 after the operation was moved to its present location.
Photo: author.

What's Old Is New Again: Collectors

The craft of north Georgia folk pottery is now kept alive by a collectors' market. This clientele, which arose mainly in the last decades of the twentieth century, consists of both outsiders and insiders to the potters' rural society: city dwellers, suburbanites, and, increasingly, countryfolk who attend, and buy at, shows like the Hewells' Turning and Burning festival. Although Meaders pottery was being collected as early as the 1950s, major interest in Georgia folk pottery was first stimulated by two 1976 exhibits: The Meaders Family of Mossy Creek at Georgia State University's Art Gallery, and Missing Pieces: Georgia Folk Art, a Georgia Council for the Arts traveling show that included a broad selection of pottery. Published information fuels any collecting field, and a substantial number of articles and books, including *Brothers in Clay*, have featured or included north Georgia folk pottery. The folk art, antiques, and crafts markets have all recruited new collectors, whose needs are served by outlets ranging from sales festivals such as the Hewells' to Internet dealers.

Buying face jugs from Lanier Meaders, Mossy Creek, 1983. Meaders pottery has been collected since at least the 1950s. Lanier had no showroom as such; wares were sold from the workshop or, as here, from the ground after unloading kiln. *Photo: author.*

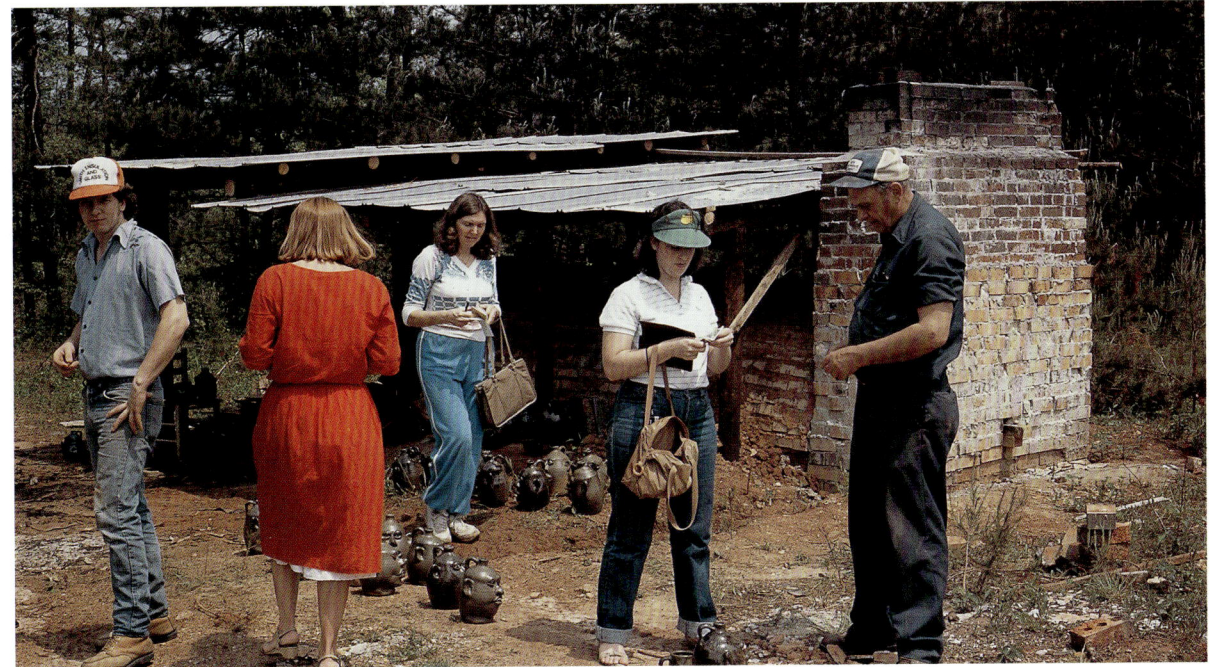

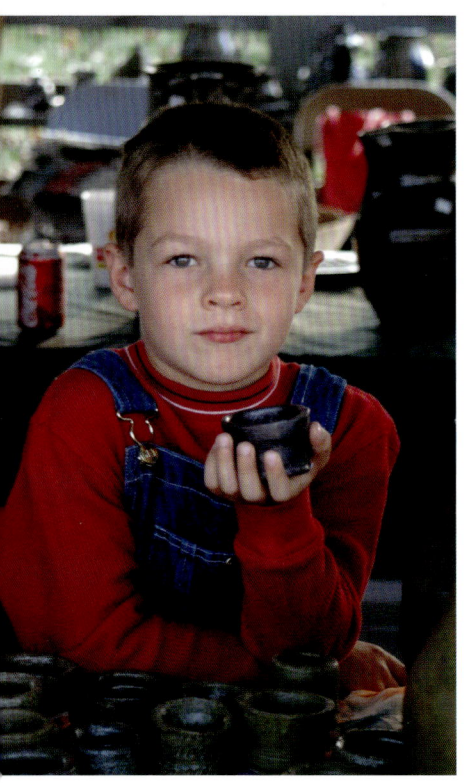

Six-year-old Eli Hewell selling his work at his family's Turning and Burning festival, Gillsville, 2004. He has since graduated from cylinders to face jugs. Some collectors like to follow a potter's development as part of their acquisition strategy.
Photo: Laura M. Drummond.

What is it, exactly, that attracts these collectors? The nostalgic "country look" in home decor and the investment value of a well-chosen collection are certainly factors. Rural collectors like to live with icons of their own heritage of which they now are justifiably proud, reminders of what has been lost—and gained—by modernization. Some collectors value, as much as the pots, the experience of visiting the active makers. And finally, collectors respond to the visual power of Georgia folk pottery—the organic beauty of older functional wares and the artistry of pieces made for this appreciative new market. Whatever their reasons, collectors now are the primary support group for north Georgia's folk potters, allowing the present generation of traditional clay craftsmen to carry on a trade their northern counterparts abandoned a century or more ago.

Earlier potters made special items, inscribed or ornamented beyond their run-of-the-mill line, only on a very limited basis, often as presentation pieces to mark events such as weddings. With the recent shift in clientele and the accompanying emphasis on visual appeal, makers are encouraged to exercise artistic talent rarely called for in the past, and as a consequence they can charge more for a smaller output. At the same time these potters, to remain folk, must balance creative expression and the desire to please their patrons with staying true to their inherited tradition.

Making Faces (on Jugs)

North Georgia's oldest not-strictly-utilitarian pottery tradition is the face jug. Jugs with applied faces were made around 1900 as occasional novelties by Charlie Ferguson, whose ancestors may have brought the idea from South Carolina where both African American and white potters made them. William Hewell likely picked up the idea from his Ferguson in-laws at Gillsville, then introduced it to Cheever Meaders at Mossy Creek. Cheever passed the tradition to his son Lanier, who made face jugs big sellers in the folk-art marketplace. His success prompted his young friend, Chester Hewell of Gillsville, to revive the Hewell face-jug tradition, closing the circle of influence. Virtually every southern potter, folk or not, has since tried making faces—on jugs.

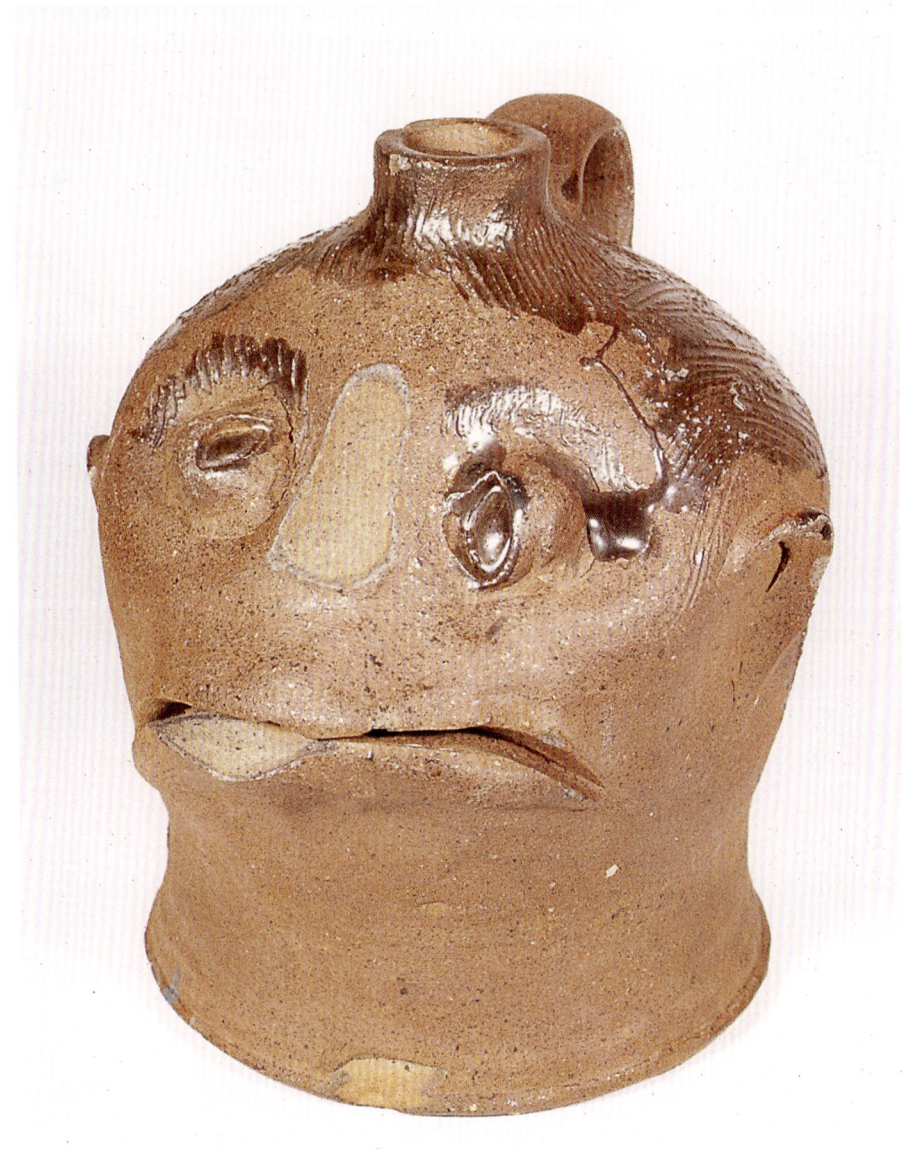

Face jug attributed to Charles P. ("Charlie") Ferguson, Gillsville, ca. 1900. His face jugs, the earliest known for north Georgia, typically are unglazed except for Albany slip highlighting hair and eyes. Although unmarked, this is by the same hand as one inscribed "Henderson 1902" (Charlie worked as a turner for shop owner James Henderson). As well as this standard jug form, he sometimes put faces on his variation of the monkey (field) jug. H. 7½ inches. *Photo: author; FPM collection.*

Face jug, William J. Hewell (signed "Bill" on base), probably Mossy Creek, early 1900s, Albany-slip glaze. He likely learned about face jugs from his Ferguson in-laws at Gillsville, then introduced the idea to Cheever Meaders while working in White County for Daddy Bill Dorsey. His rather flat faces have realistic (not exaggerated) features; as with Ferguson face jugs, some have hair scratched with a comblike tool. H. 8¼ inches. *Photo: David Greear;* FPM *collection.*

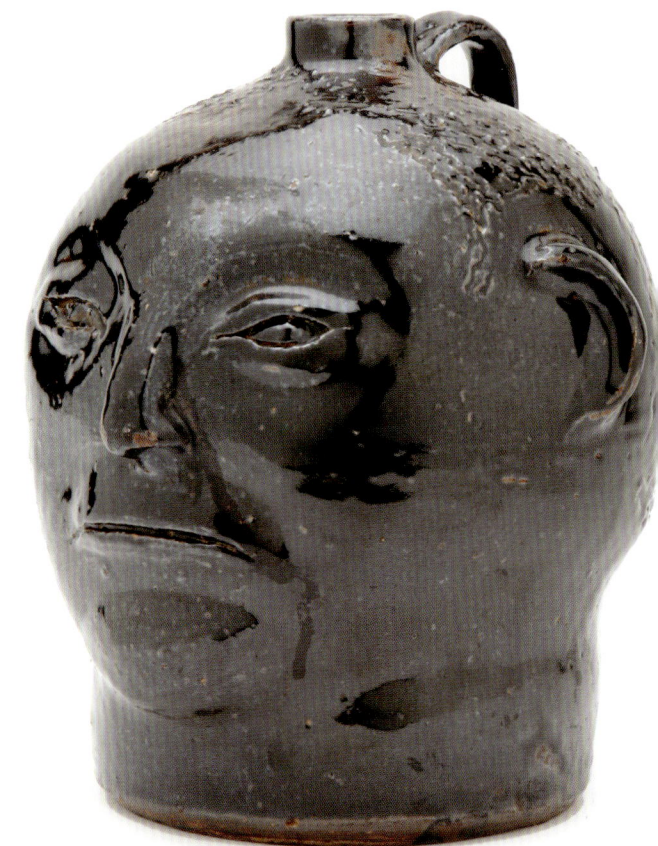

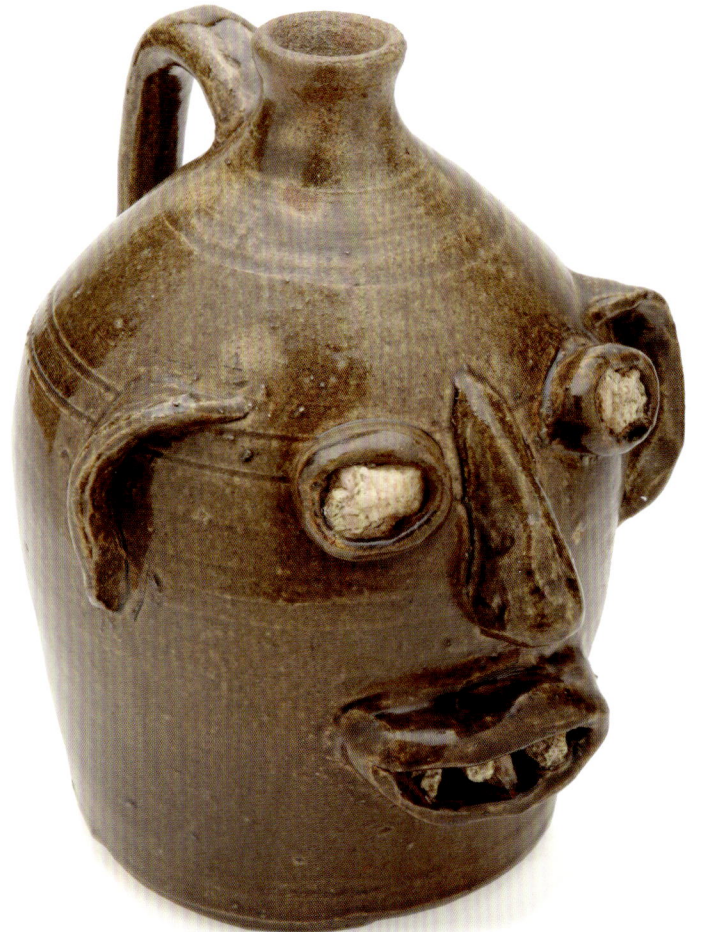

Face jug, Cheever Meaders, Mossy Creek, 1953, modified alkaline ("Mossy Creek green") glaze. Cheever, who said he learned about face jugs from William Hewell, made only a small number at the urging of customers, declaring, "Don't like to make 'em. Time I get it decorated and fixed up, I could turn two or three [useful] pieces." His are quite basic, with features, including quartz eyes and teeth, laid onto an unsculpted wall. H. 9 inches. *Photo: David Greear;* FPM *collection.*

Face jug, Bobby Ferguson, Gillsville, 2001, colored glaze. A descendant of Edgefield-trained potter Charles H. Ferguson, Bobby made some face jugs in the monkey form (a water jug with stirrup handle across top and angled, off-center spout), similar to some by his father Pat, grandfather Charlie, and antebellum Edgefield potters. His glazes carried on the colorful trend begun by Pat in the 1930s. H. 11¾ inches. *Photo: David Greear; FPM collection, gift of maker.*

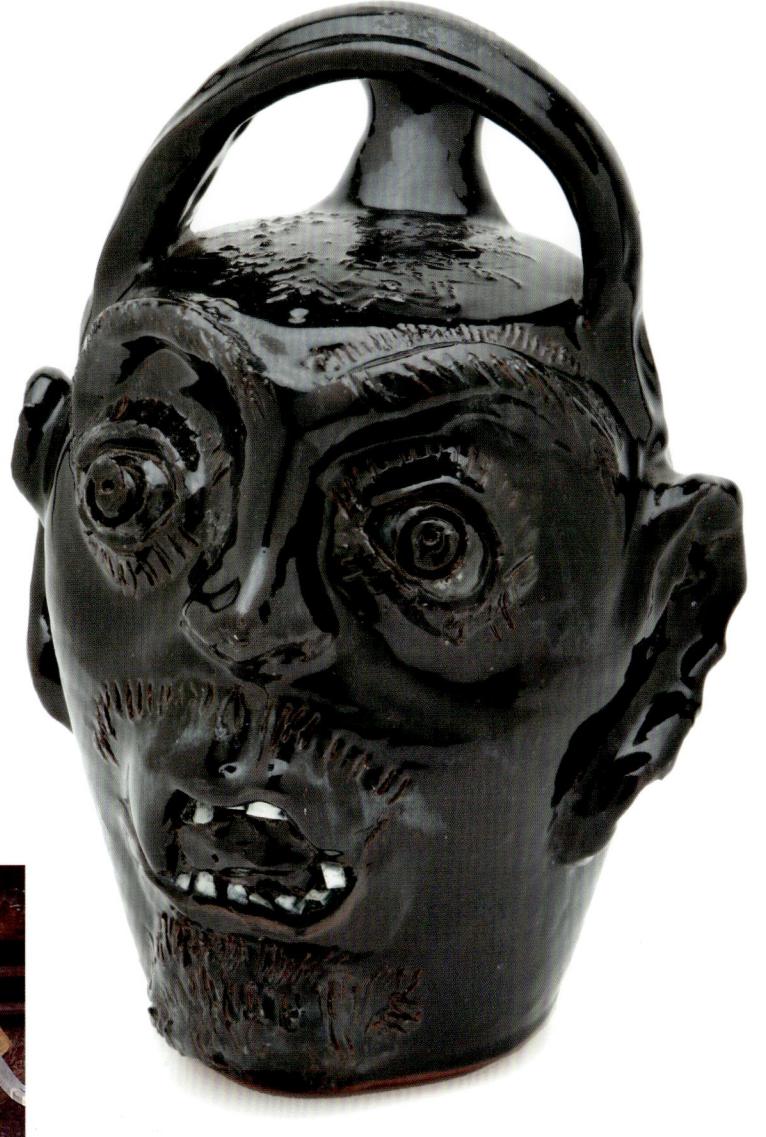

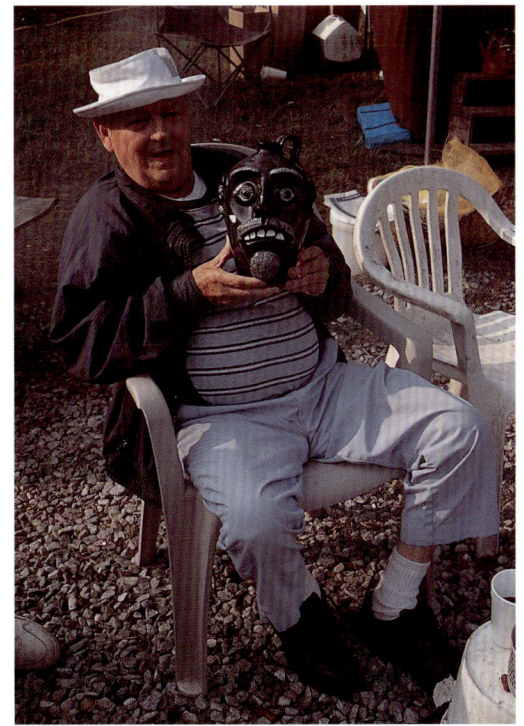

Bobby Ferguson, Gillsville, 2004 (less than a year before his death). A grandson of Charlie Ferguson, Bobby was at least the third generation of the family to make face jugs. *Photo: author.*

Lanier had mixed feelings about his face jugs: "They're about the ugliest thing a person could make. Seems like the more useless I make something the more they'll trample each other to get to it." But the 1967 sale of his face jugs at the Smithsonian's first Festival of American Folklife showed him that they'd bring more income than other wares, and by the 1980s he was making little else. In his twenty-five-year full-time potting career Lanier produced thousands, no two identical; they became so much a part of his identity that he chose "Jughead" as his citizens band radio handle. His sense of humor and creativity revitalized the face-jug tradition, making it an emblem of southern folk art.

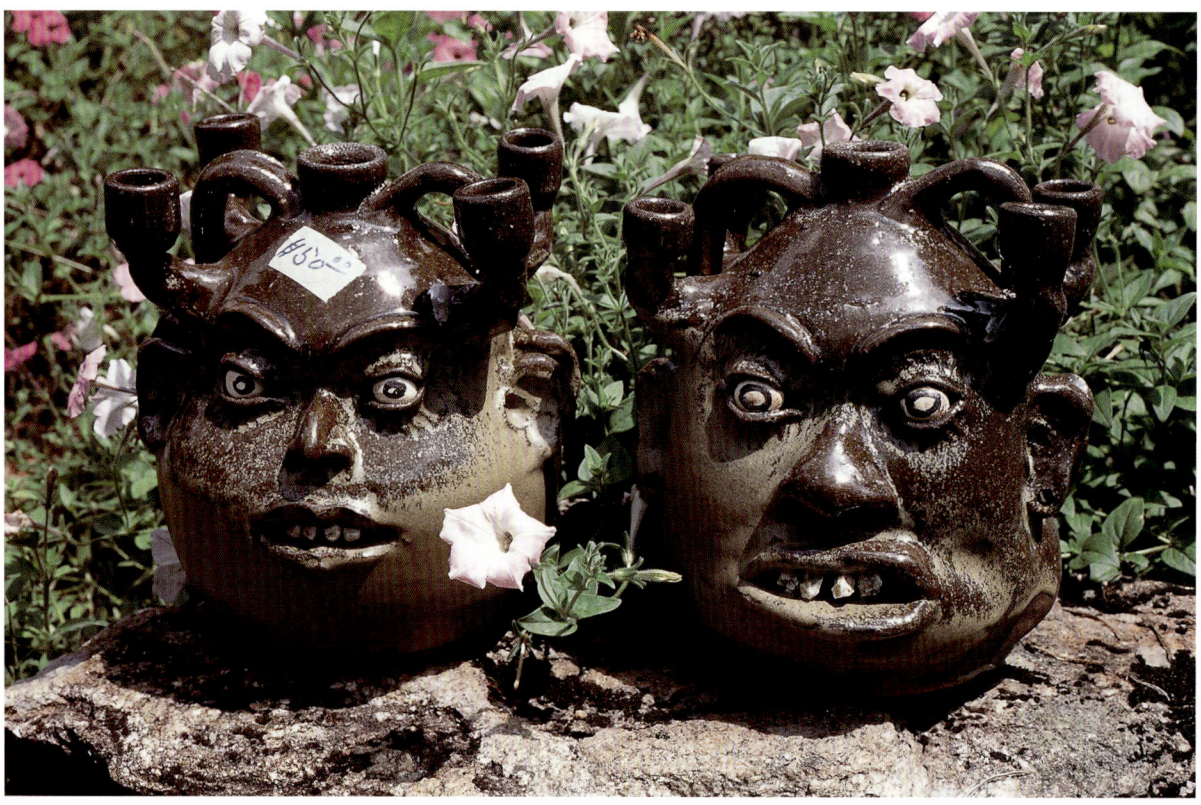

Candelabra face jugs, Lanier Meaders, Mossy Creek, 1977, modified alkaline glaze. In 1975 Lanier began making two-faced jugs, dubbing them "politician jugs" after watching the televised Watergate hearings. To some he added hornlike candle holders—just the thing for a dining-table centerpiece, seance, or black mass! Note his $50 price tag; today each would sell for several thousand dollars. H. 10 inches. *Photo: author.*

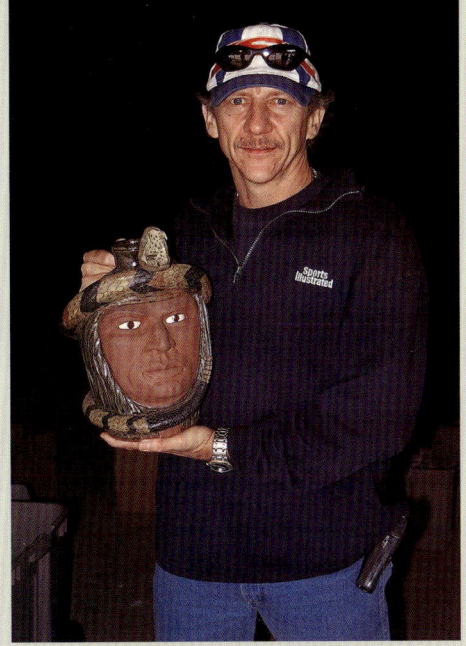

Melvin Crocker of Lula with partially ash-glazed Indian head-and-snake jug, 2003. He never learned to use the potter's wheel when he worked at Wilson's, so his brother, Dwayne, turned this jug for Melvin to sculpt and decorate. The unglazed red clay was used to advantage for the face; the realistic rattlesnake's mouth is lined with white clay, its scales picked out with plastic drinking straws.
Photo: author.

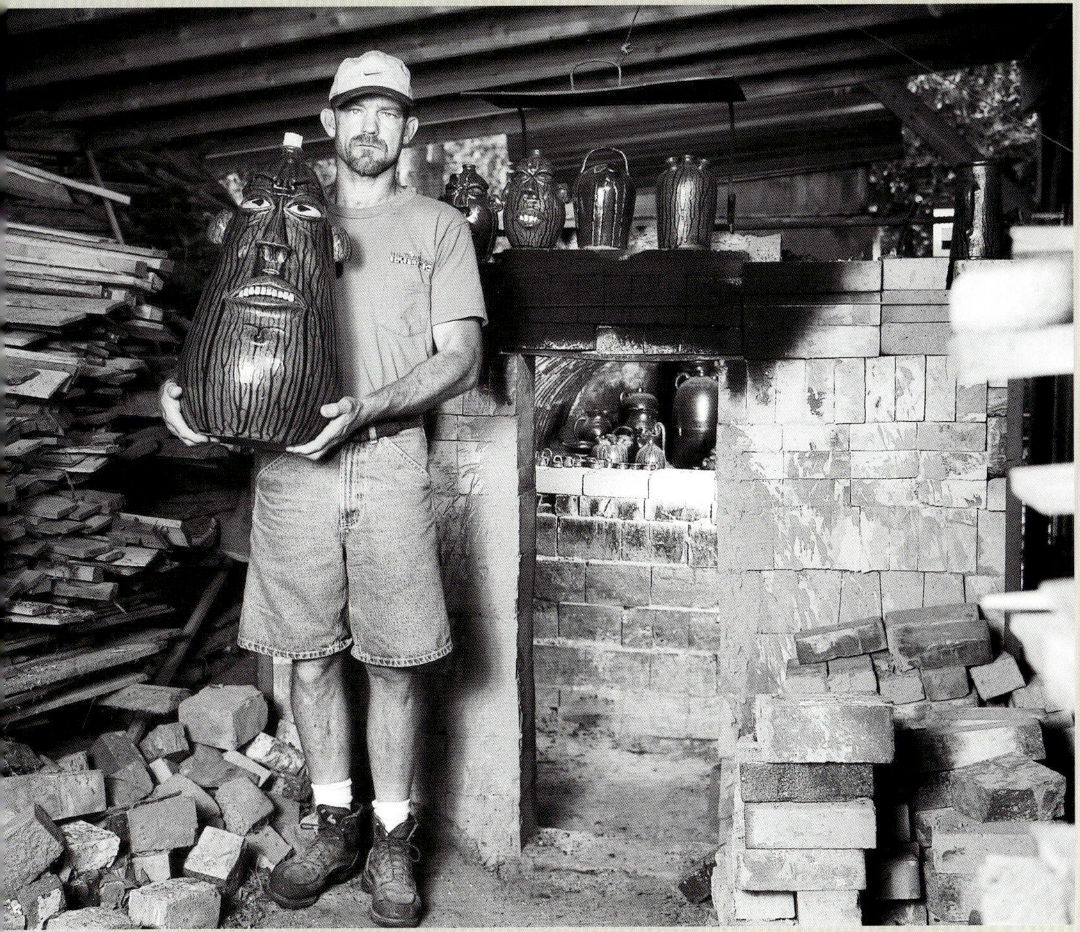

Wayne Hewell with big ash-glazed face jug at his wood-burning tunnel kiln, Lula, 2001. The son of Carl Hewell, Wayne was trained at Hewell's and Craven's before setting up his own shop.
Photo: Chris Swanson.

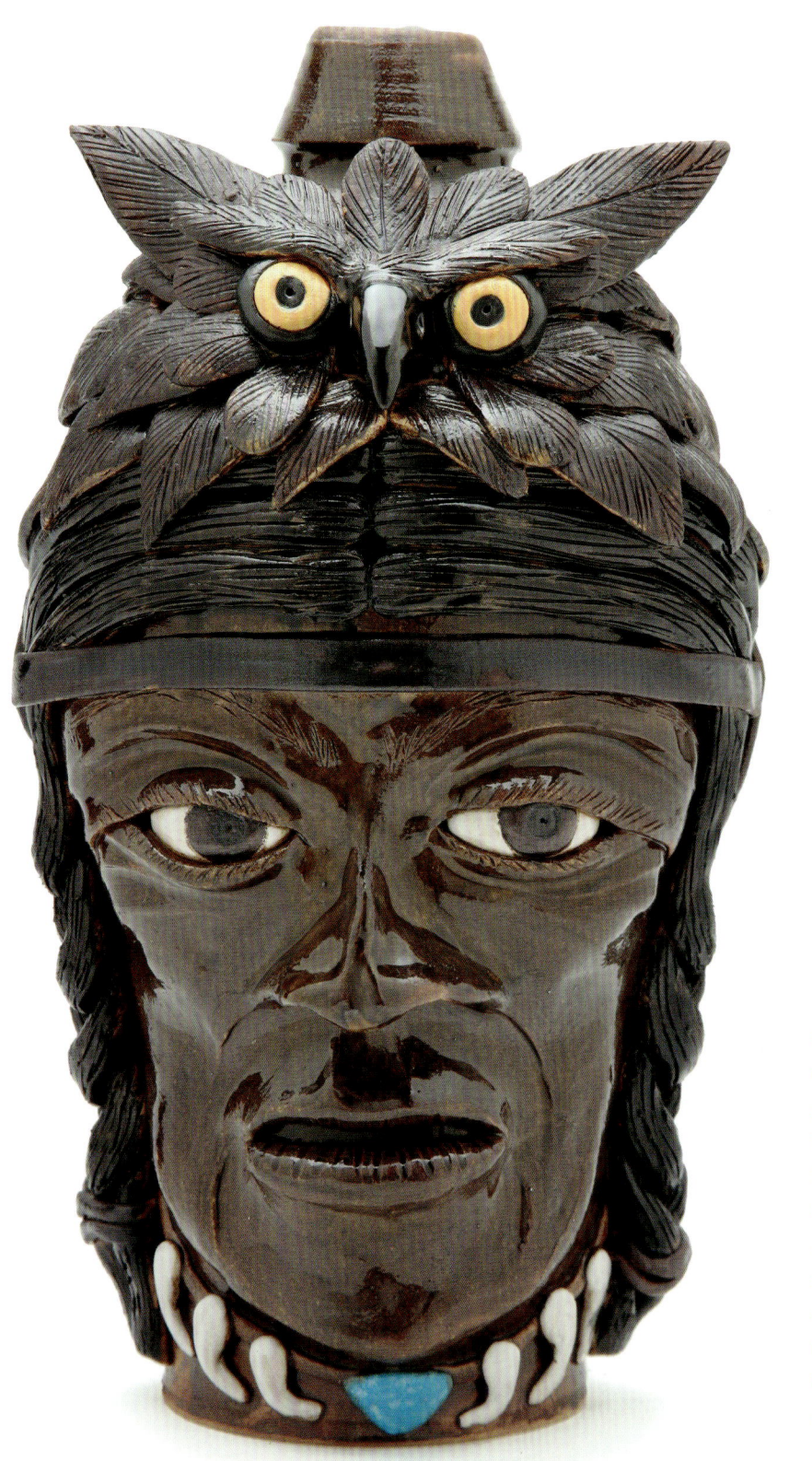

Indian-head jug, Lin Craven, Cleveland, Georgia, 2001, colored glazes. An elaboration of the face-jug idea, this is from a series featuring Native American animal totems. Coming late to folk pottery seems to have given Lin, who apprenticed with Bobby Ferguson at Gillsville, greater freedom in interpreting the older tradition. H. 12 inches. *Photo: David Greear; FPM collection.*

Decorative Wares

Flowers, grapes, snakes, roosters—today's north Georgia folk pottery is alive with images from nature and farming, reflecting the rural society to which the makers still belong. One pioneer of pottery decoration was Cleater Meaders of Cleveland, who in the late 1920s made vases with the outside left unglazed to be painted later according to the purchaser's desire, perhaps influenced by the hobby of china painting as popularized in William Lycett's Atlanta studio, which opened in 1883.

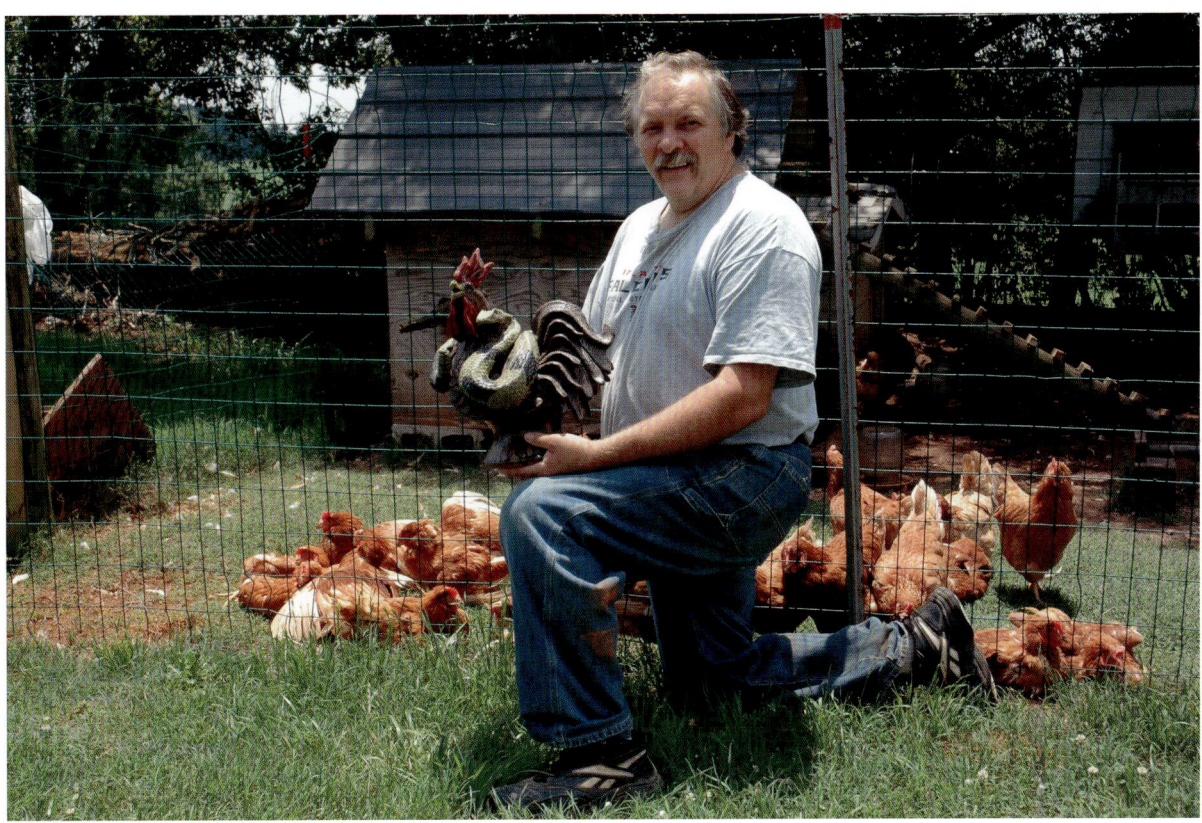

Dwayne Crocker posing with ash-glazed rooster-and-snake in front of his live "models," Gillsville, 2005. Like other north Georgia folk potters, Dwayne draws inspiration from his rural surroundings. His fondness for fowl (he has since turned his chicken coop into a virtual poultry theme park) may account for his lively sculpting of them in clay. *Photo: Kirk Elifson.*

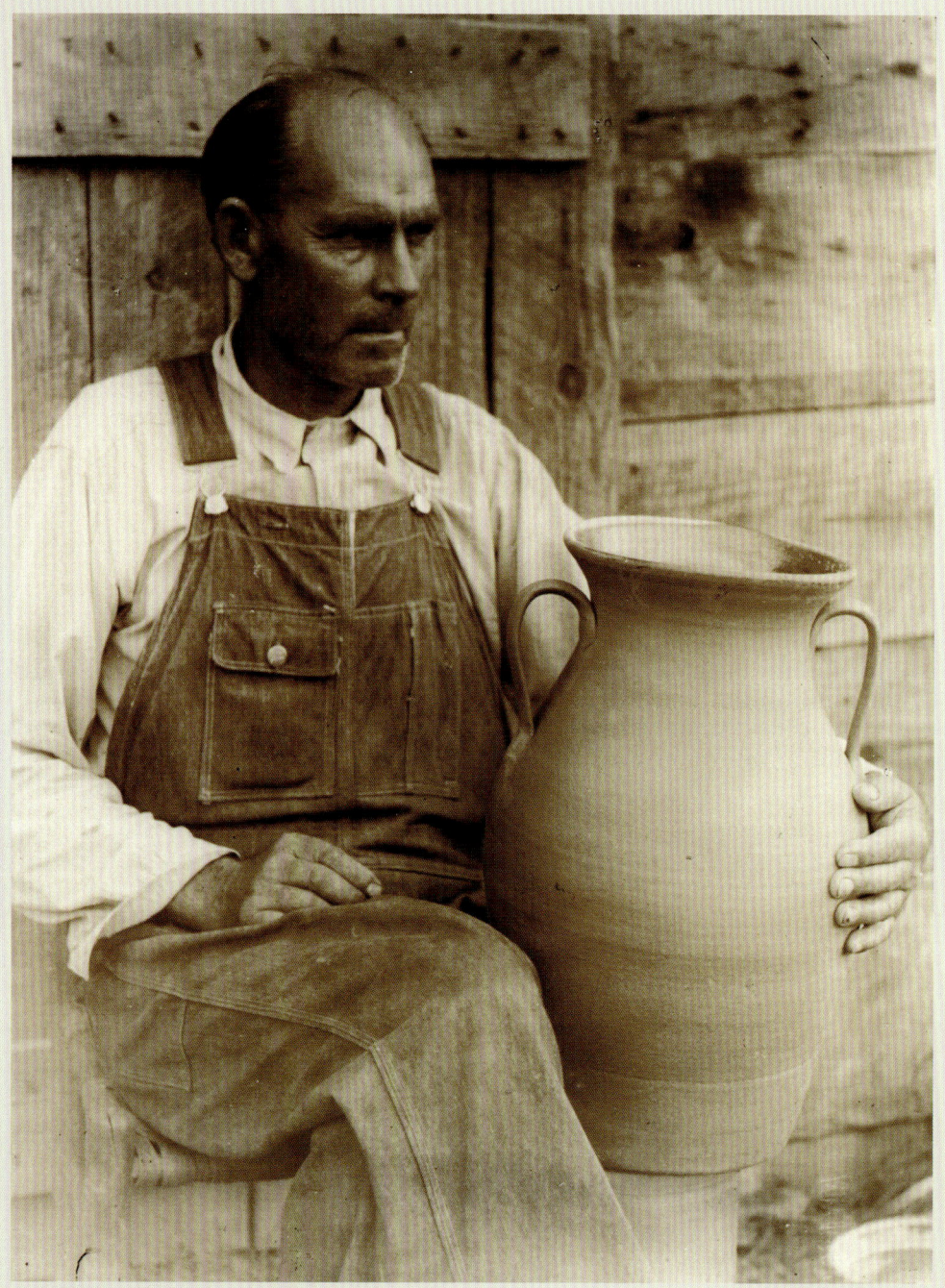

Cleater Meaders Sr., Cleveland, Georgia, ca. 1930,
holding a type of vase he developed for more urbane
customers, unglazed outside so it could be painted.
*Photo: Doris Ulmann, used with special permission from
the Doris Ulmann Foundation and Berea College Art
Department, Berea, Ky.*

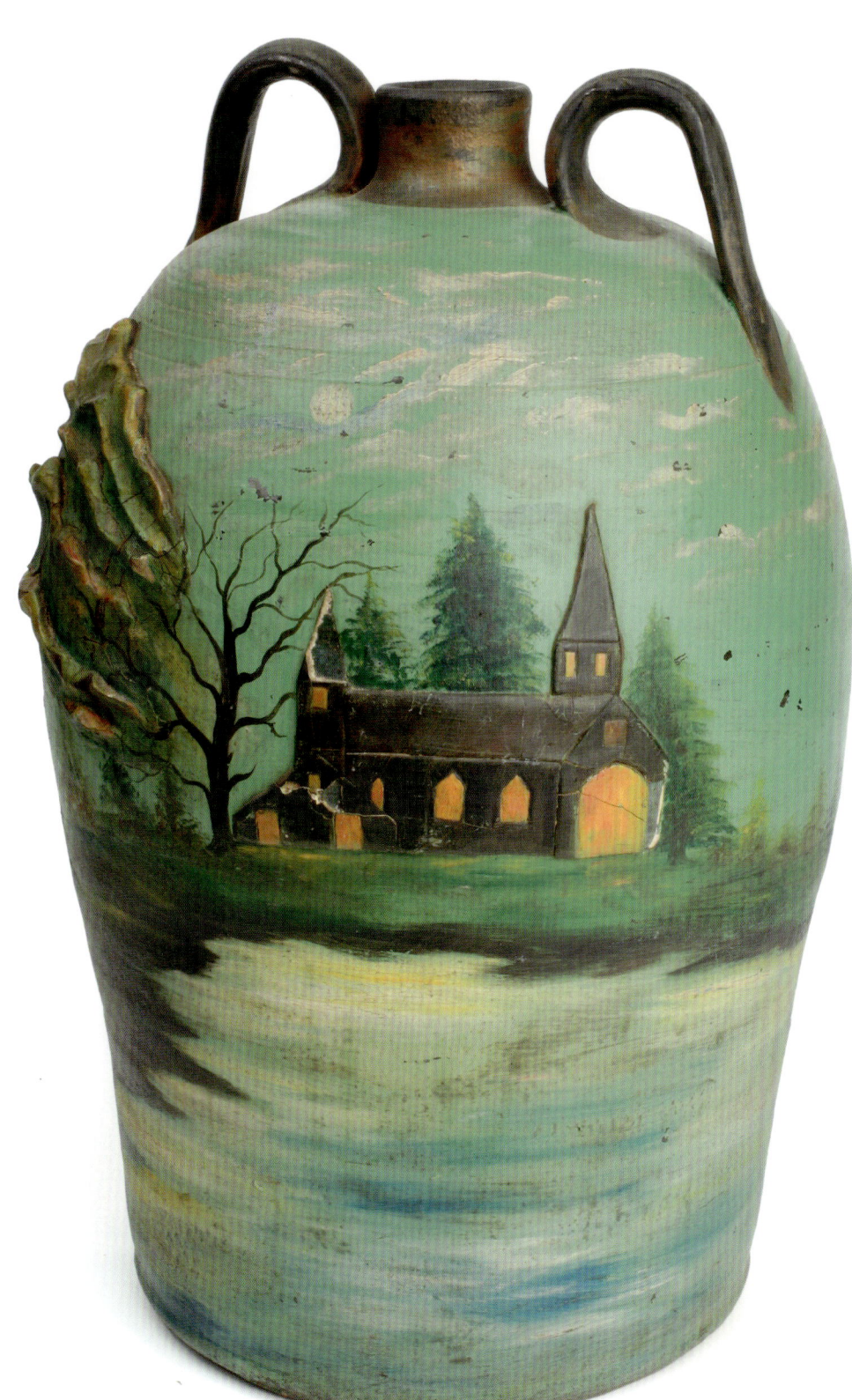

Five-gallon syrup jug, Cleater Meaders Sr. and anonymous artist, Cleveland, Georgia, ca. 1930, Albany-slip glaze. Cleater is said to have hired an Athens, Georgia, artist to decorate some of his wares for well-to-do tourists with painted scenes such as this plaster-relief country church. H. 17½ inches. *Photo: David Greear; FPM collection.*

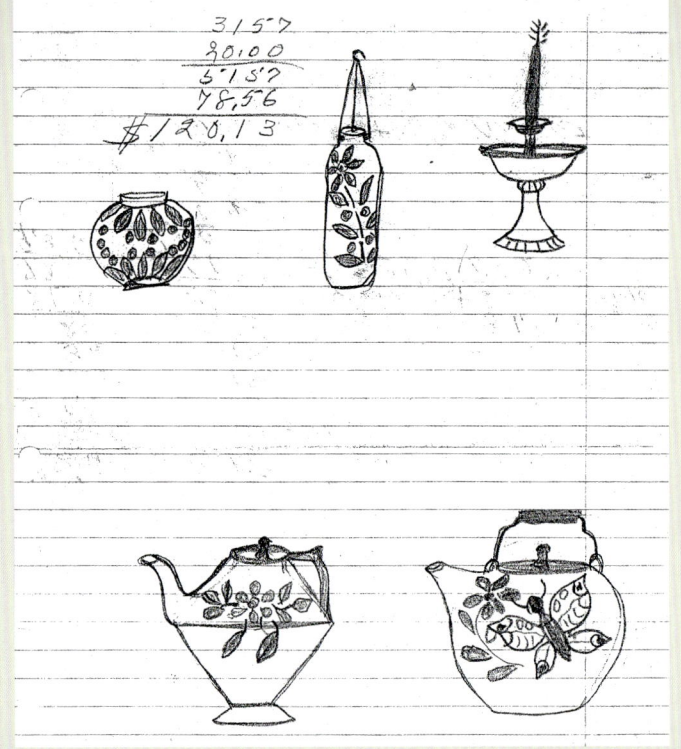

Pottery design sketches by Arie Meaders,
Mossy Creek, 1950s or 1960s. *Courtesy of
Atlanta History Center Folklife Collection,
gift of Betty Jean Meaders.*

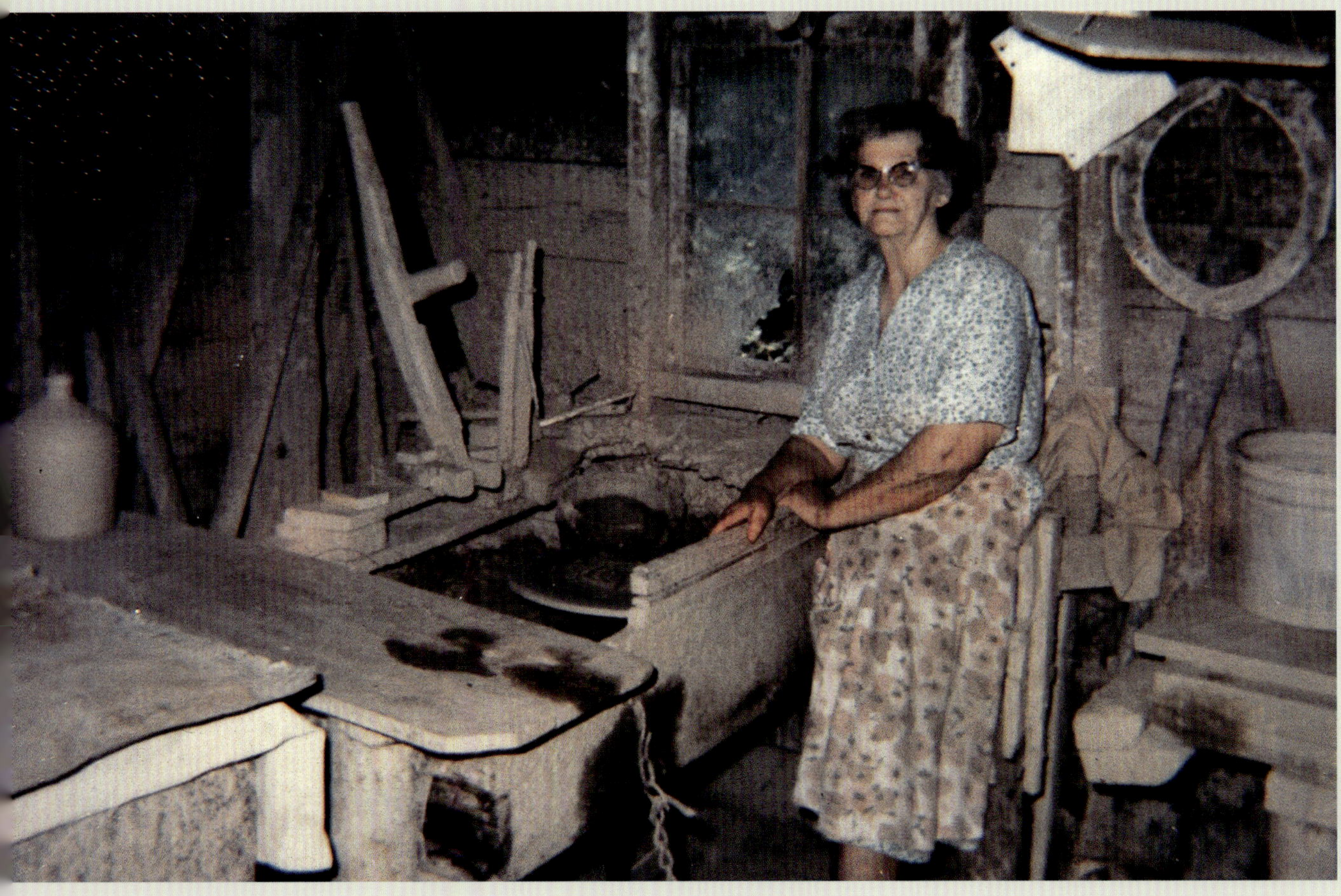

Arie Waldrop Meaders, Mossy Creek, late 1950s, about the time she
taught herself to use the potter's wheel during the temporary "retirement"
of her husband, Cheever. *Snapshot courtesy of Arie Meaders.*

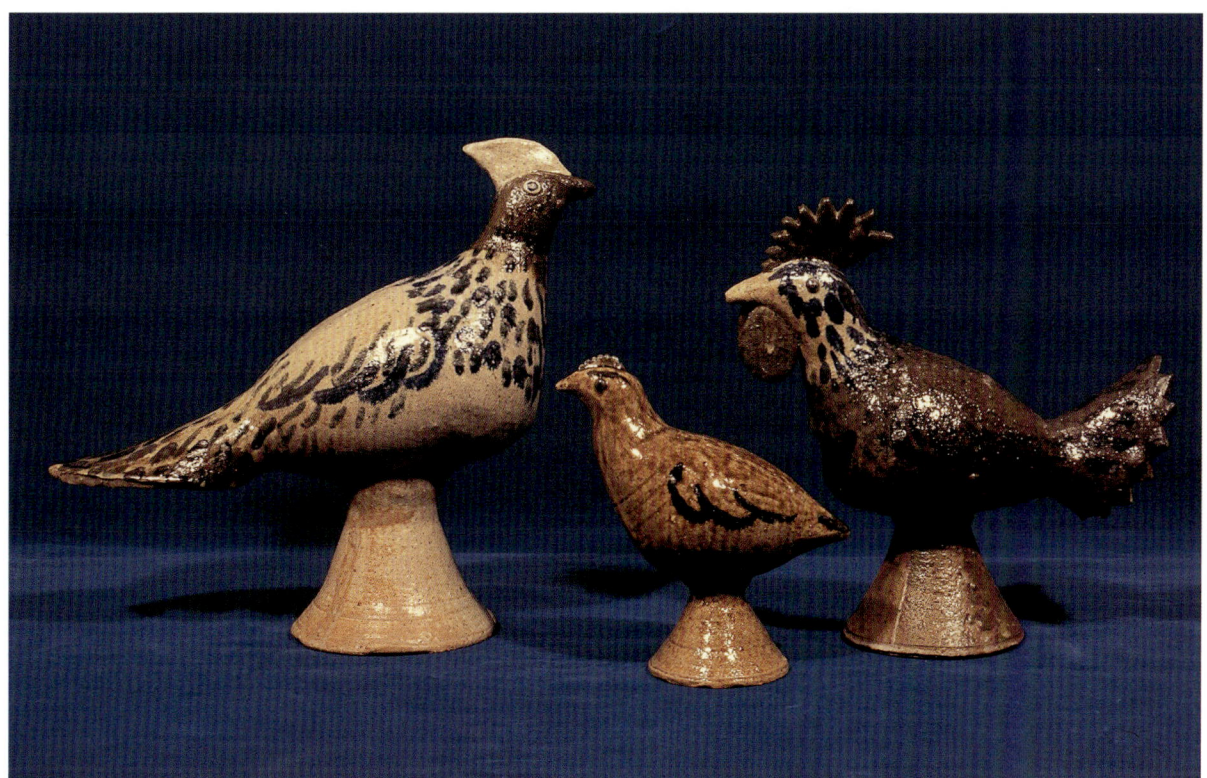

Northeast Georgia's premier clay artist, however, was Arie Meaders. She began by using minerals from ceramics supply firms to paint and glaze pottery thrown by her husband, Cheever, who, she explained, "couldn't make the things that I could vision in my mind." Having learned to use the wheel in 1957, Arie then created her own line of colorful wares. Her favorite "spar" (feldspar-based) glaze, often colored light gray with zinc oxide, served as backdrop for her grape clusters, dogwood blossoms, and remarkable wheel-thrown birds and animals.

The grape vases of Arie's son Lanier and nephew C.J., the roosters of her son Edwin and a later generation of others, the tree-stump ornaments of grandson David, and the artistic work of brothers Michael, Melvin, and Dwayne Crocker all owe a debt to the decorative tradition begun by Arie Meaders.

Pheasant, quail, and rooster, Arie Meaders, 1968, spar (feldspar-based) glaze with oxide colors. She formed birds by joining three wheel-thrown, cone-shaped segments, two for the body and one for the base. H., L–R: 12 inches, 7¼ inches, and 10½ inches. *Photo: author; author's collection.*

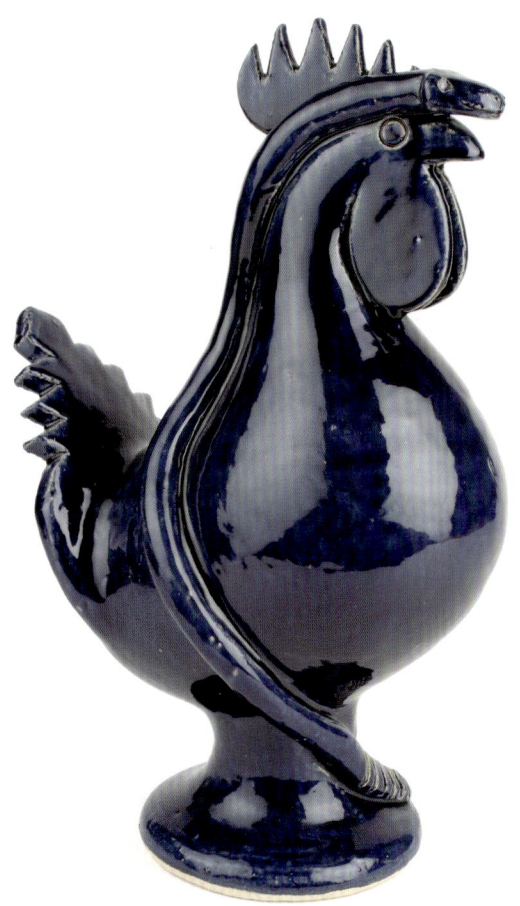

Rooster with snake, Edwin Meaders, Mossy
Creek, 1996, colored glaze. When Lanier's
youngest brother, "Nub," retired in 1970
from a poultry-processing plant, he built a
small shop at his home up the road from
Meaders Pottery. With guidance from their
mother, Arie, he was soon specializing
in wheel-thrown roosters like those she
developed; his have a streamlined elegance.
H. 16 inches. *Photo: David Greear;* FPM
collection.

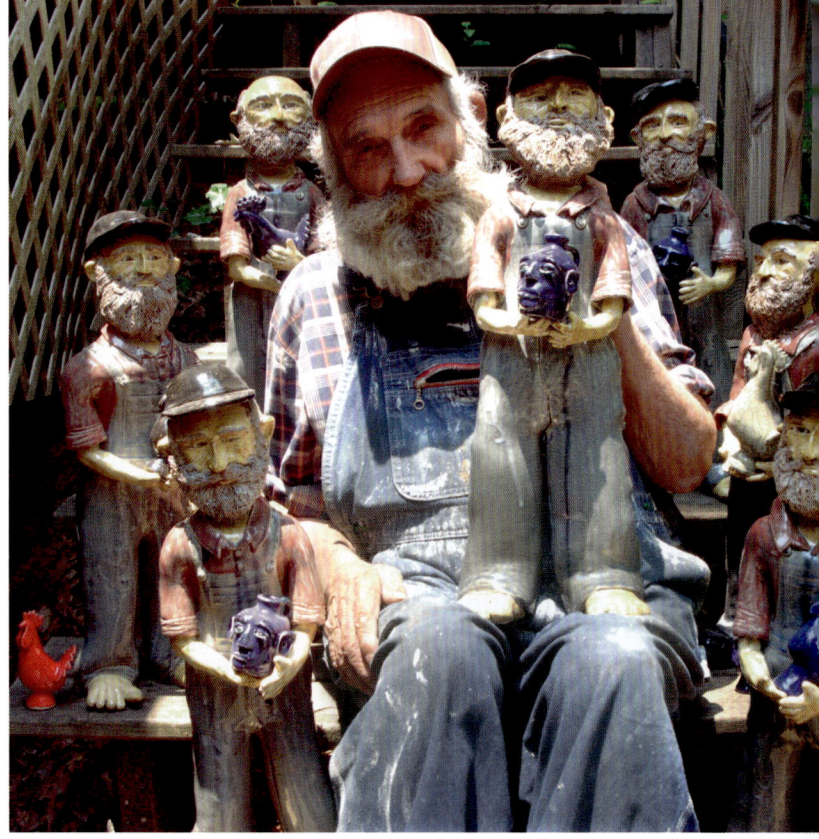

Edwin ("Nub") Meaders, 2005, surrounded by Lin Craven's clay portraits
of him from her Meaders potters series acknowledging that family's
contributions to the north Georgia tradition. *Photo: Emory Jones.*

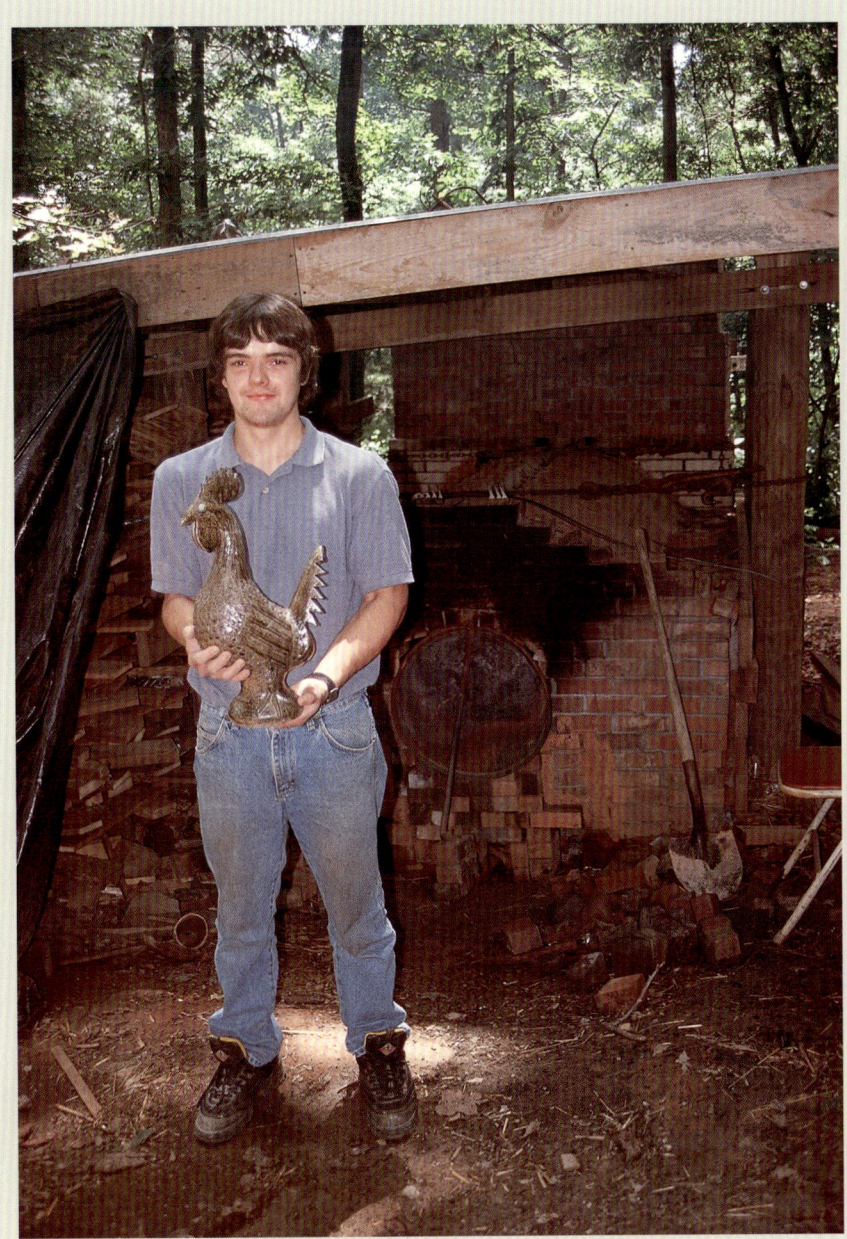

Clint Alderman with ash-glazed rooster at his wood-fired tunnel kiln, 2001, before he moved from White County to Hart County. As a young man he fell in love with Mossy Creek pottery and informally apprenticed with Edwin Meaders. *Photo: author.*

Rooster, Charlie West, Cleveland, Georgia, 2001, colored glazes. Trained in the gardenware tradition at Sims Pottery, Charlie then worked with Todd Hewell before setting up on his own in 1998. Roosters and lamp bases are his specialties; made of earthenware clay, their lower-firing glazes can produce vivid colors. H. 20¾ inches. *Photo: David Greear;* FPM *collection.*

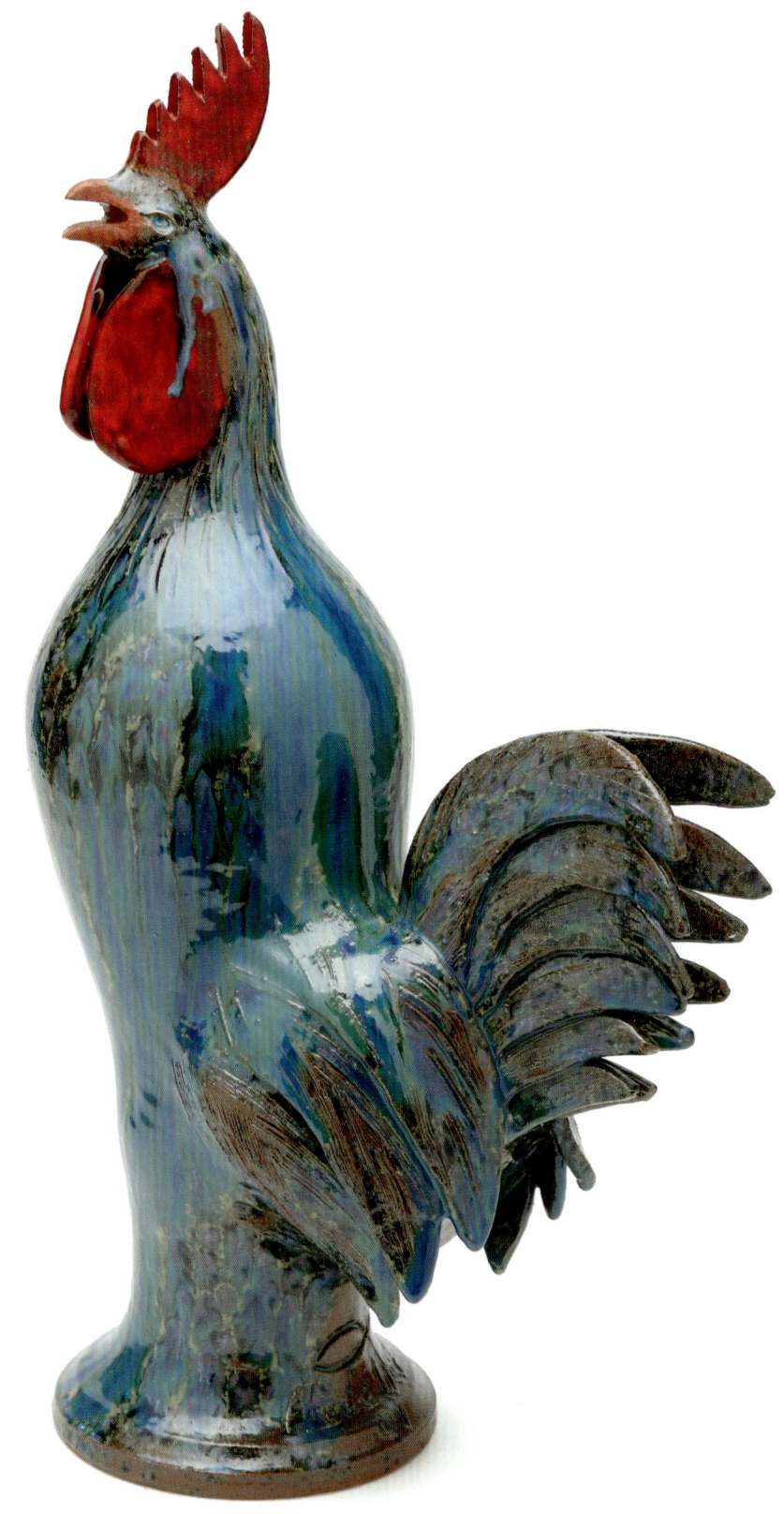

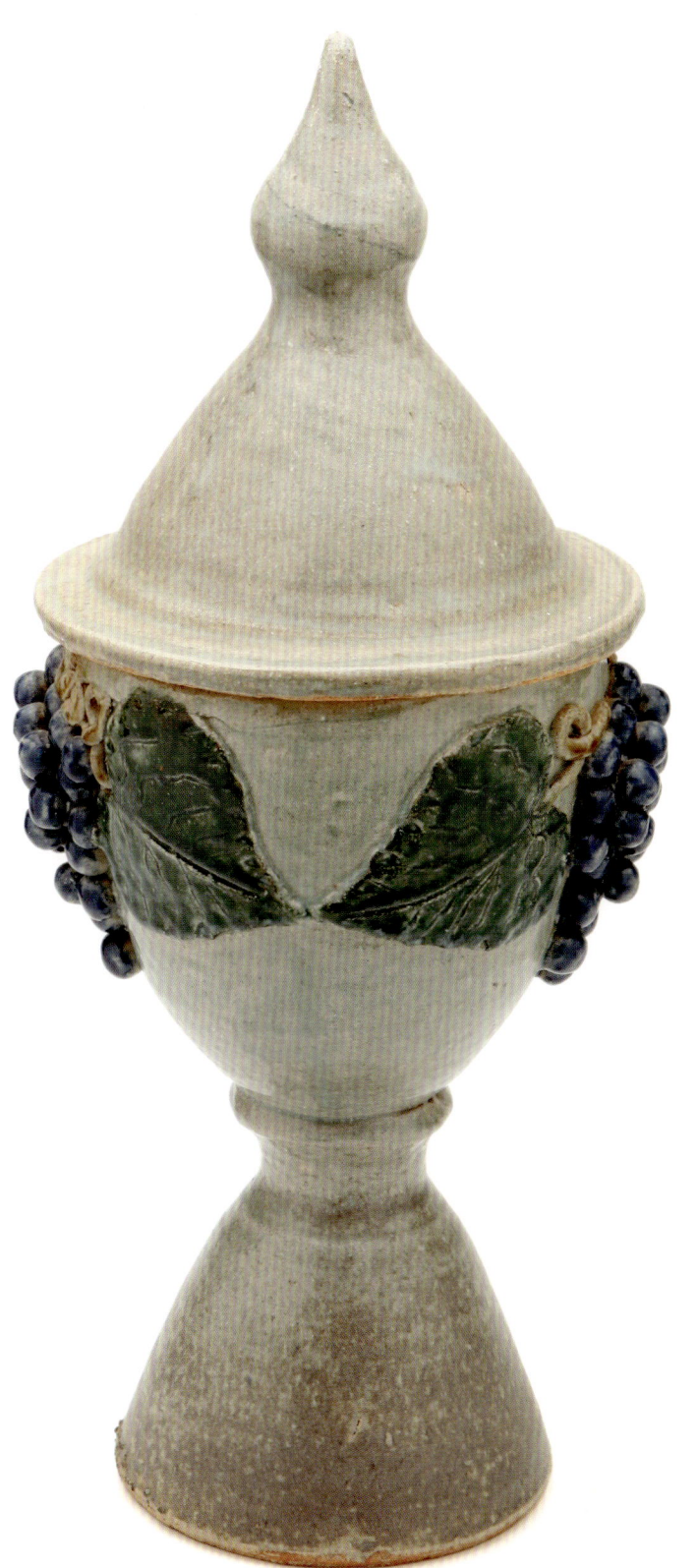

Funerary urn, Arie and Cheever Meaders, Mossy Creek, 1966, Bristol-type spar (feldspar-based) glaze, applied and painted grapes. This collaboration was turned by Cheever and designed and decorated by Arie, who sketched her ideas to help her husband visualize unfamiliar shapes. H. 19 inches. *Photo: David Greear; FPM collection.*

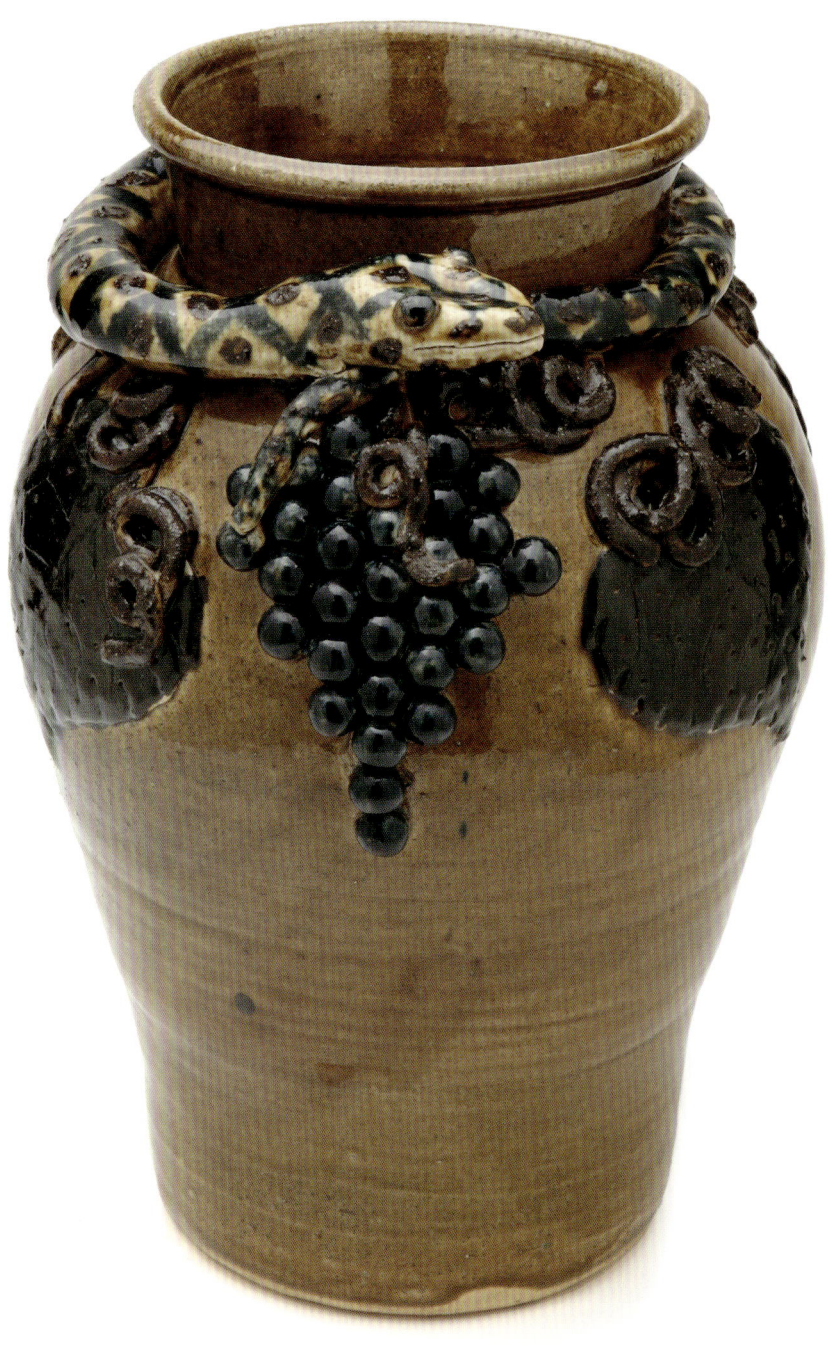

Snake-and-grape vase, Lanier Meaders, Mossy Creek, 1978, alkaline (modified lime) glaze. He made only a few of these, combining his mother's grape motif with his own snake idea. He used her favorite white clay from Cooley farm for greater contrast. H. 13⅛ inches. *Photo: David Greear;* FPM *collection.*

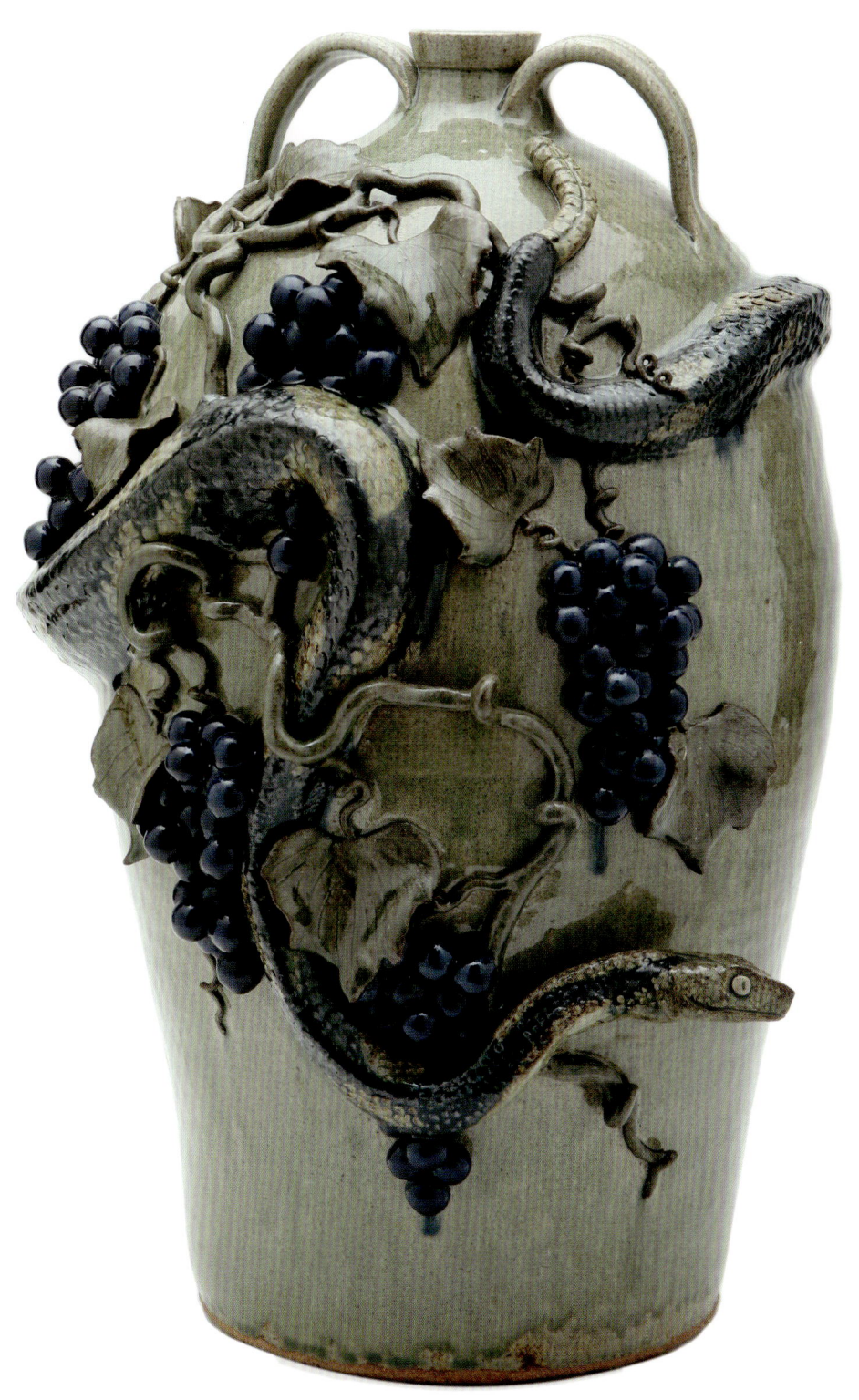

Six-gallon snake-and-grape syrup jug, Michael Crocker, Lula, 2003, alkaline (flint) glaze. Trained in the gardenware tradition at Wilson's and Craven's, Michael's appreciation of Mossy Creek wares is evident in this Arie and Lanier Meaders–inspired piece. He achieved a full relief effect by not flattening the leaves and vine to the jug wall. H. 22 inches. *Photo: David Greear; FPM collection.*

CHAPTER 9

A Home for North Georgia Folk Pottery

In 2001 I was invited to join a small group planning a museum devoted to northeast Georgia folk pottery. I'd heard vague rumors about the project but not who was behind it. The group offered me the position of curator, which meant developing a story to interpret an existing collection in a historically and culturally meaningful way, selecting the objects and images to support that story, and writing the text for section panels, object labels, and illustration captions. My first response was "Thanks, but no thanks"—I was still recovering from curating the six-hundred-object Atlanta History Museum permanent exhibition, Shaping Traditions: Folk Arts in a Changing South, and had decided that it would be my last big exhibit. Further, I knew that it took long-term commitment and substantial financial resources to pull off such a project, having seen the similarly ambitious North Carolina Pottery Center at Seagrove struggle with raising funds before it finally opened in 1998. I agreed, however, to attend the next meeting, where all would be revealed.

There I met benefactors Dean and Kay Swanson, who had sold their northeast Georgia telephone company and wanted to use some of the proceeds to "give back" to their part of the state. Since they knew of the area's reputation for its pottery tradition, the idea of an institution to celebrate it seemed natural to them, so they bought a core group of wares for their proposed museum from the huge collection of potter Michael Crocker of Lula. Also at that

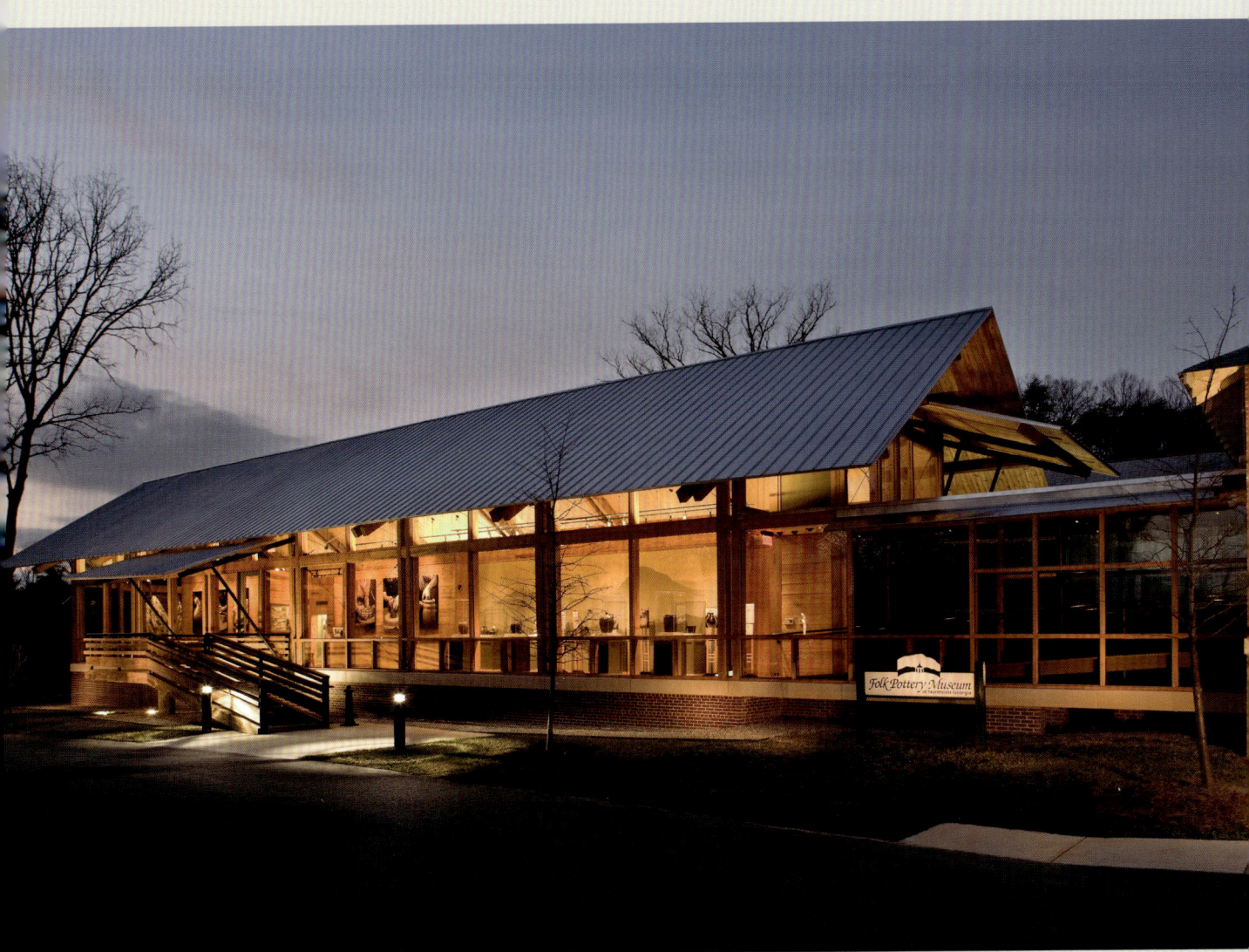

Folk Pottery Museum of Northeast Georgia at dusk,
Sautee Nacoochee Center, 2006. *Photo: Paul Hultberg;
courtesy of Bob Cain.*

meeting were architect Bob Cain of Atlanta and exhibit designer Dale Brubaker of Decatur, both of whom had impressive track records. To fulfill their vision the Swansons were committing over $4 million, including an endowment to maintain the museum, so fund-raising was not a concern—a big factor in my decision to join the museum project.

There were still key issues to resolve, the first being the location. With the living tradition concentrated in both the Gillsville and Cleveland areas, building the facility in either center could be seen as slighting the other and would necessitate the additional expense of land acquisition. The ideal situation would be for an existing nonprofit organization at a nearby but "neutral" site to host the facility, and the Sautee Nacoochee Community Association, near Helen in the White County hills, fit the bill. After presentations to, and deliberations by, the membership, it was agreed to build the museum there as an addition to their center.

A number of construction companies in Atlanta had experience with public buildings, but the Swansons wanted to support their area's economy by hiring a local firm, and Hartley Construction of Gainesville was finally selected. Bob Cain's ambitious design posed a challenge to the small company, but with local builder Jim Johnston as coordinator the work was largely completed, despite weather and other delays, in time for the Labor Day 2006 opening. In 2008 the building received an Honor Award of Architectural Excellence from the Georgia Chapter of the American Institute of Architects.

The museum's exterior was inspired by the Meaders Pottery's massive kiln shelter as seen in a historic photograph.[1] Inside, natural materials—oak beams supporting the cathedral ceiling and yellow pine flooring and paneling—predominate, and an expanse of windows offers views of the surrounding countryside. The main floor includes 3,200 square feet of exhibition space for approximately 175 pots.

Flanking the reception foyer, the walls of which display paintings of old-time pottery making at Mossy Creek by well-known north Georgia artists John Kollock and Linda Anderson, are four exhibit galleries. The first illustrates old-time production methods, including a workshop replica with working treadle wheel for demonstrations, an "exploded" model of a "tunnel" kiln, a video of the pottery-making process—from digging clay to unloading the kiln—by members of the Meaders family, and a case displaying glaze ingredients and their appearance on examples of fired pottery.

The second gallery illustrates the original uses of north Georgia's functional folk pottery with scenarios that place the wares in early-twentieth-century settings: farm kitchen, smokehouse, springhouse, and whiskey still (photographs of the first three appear in chapter 6).

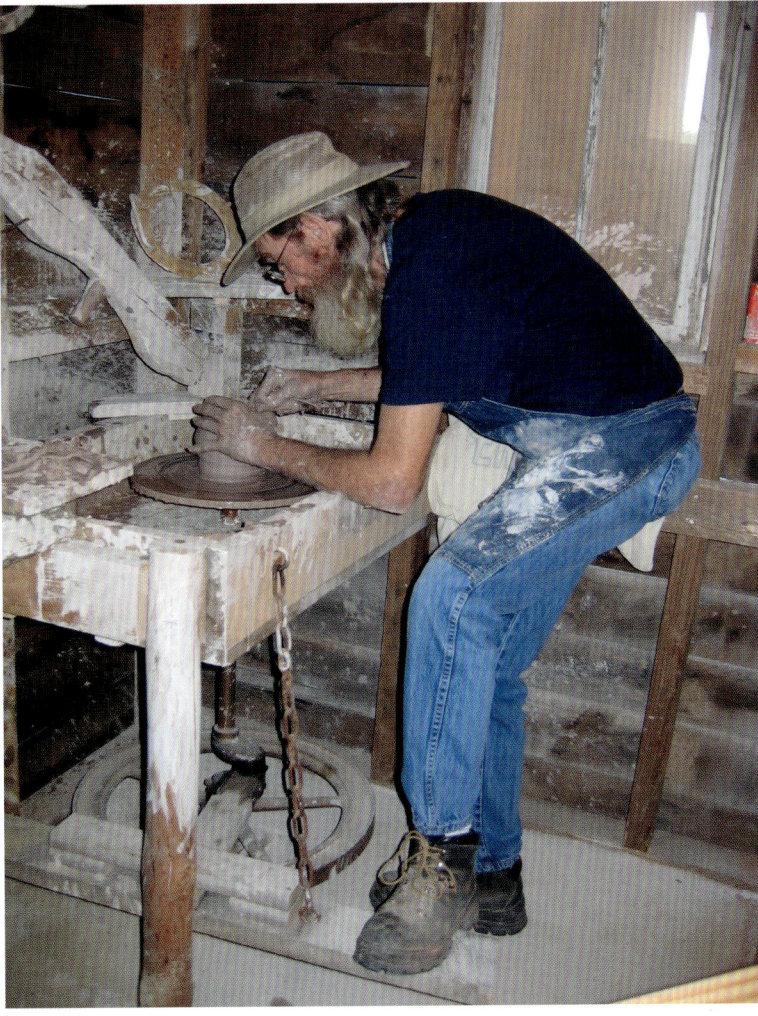

David Meaders demonstrating the treadle wheel in the Folk Pottery Museum's workshop replica, 2007. *Photo: author.*

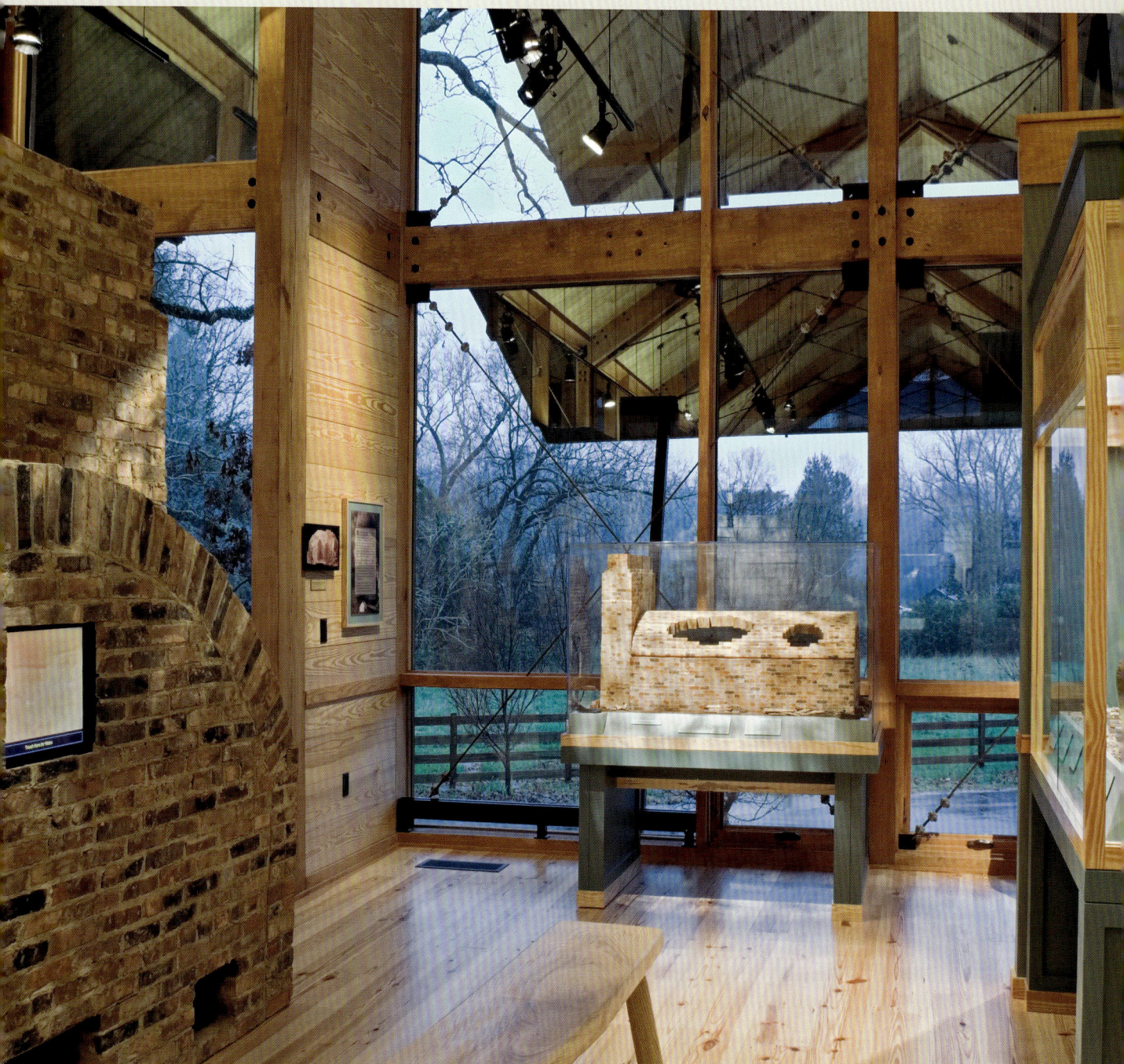

Part of the pottery-making gallery, Folk Pottery Museum, 2006. Meaders pottery-making video is running in the foreshortened kiln replica at left; tunnel kiln model is at center. *Photo: Rob Karosis; courtesy of Dean and Kay Swanson and Bob Cain.*

The third, and largest, gallery displays the bulk of the museum's permanent collection. It begins with a definition of folk pottery, using both traditional and nonfolk (mass-produced and studio) wares to illustrate the difference. The rest of this gallery is organized geographically and chronologically. Older wares of the three upper-Piedmont centers and the few mountain shops are followed by features on the Meaders and Hewell "clay clans" and the early-twentieth-century changes that prompted north Georgia folk potters to shift their emphasis to horticultural and decorative wares. On the walls are quotes by the potters themselves expressing their attitudes toward these developments. There are two large cases of face jugs, one showing the growth of Lanier Meaders as an artist and the other filled with old and recent examples by others. The last cases exhibit a piece by each of today's traditional potters, arranged by their different kinds of training, with their photographic portraits grouped together on the wall. Visitors moving through this gallery will see a transition from the green and brown earth tones of the utilitarian wares to the more colorful wares in the last section.

The fourth gallery is located in the corridor that runs along the museum's front windows and connects the building to the Sautee Nacoochee Community Center. This space is devoted to annual changing exhibits of traditional ceramics borrowed from other collections, private and public. The early exhibits featured wares from beyond north Georgia, including those with connections to the area: the old Edgefield District of South Carolina (probable source of the alkaline-glazed stoneware tradition and training ground of pioneer Jug Factory potter Charles H. Ferguson); and North Carolina with its varied earthenware and stoneware traditions, including those brought to Mossy Creek by that center's pioneer potters. The third year's loan exhibit, on international folk pottery, displayed ceramic traditions from as far away as Japan, Germany, and Britain, with some glazes and forms similar to those of north Georgia. Future exhibits in this space may feature north Georgia families or individual potters only touched upon in the permanent collection.

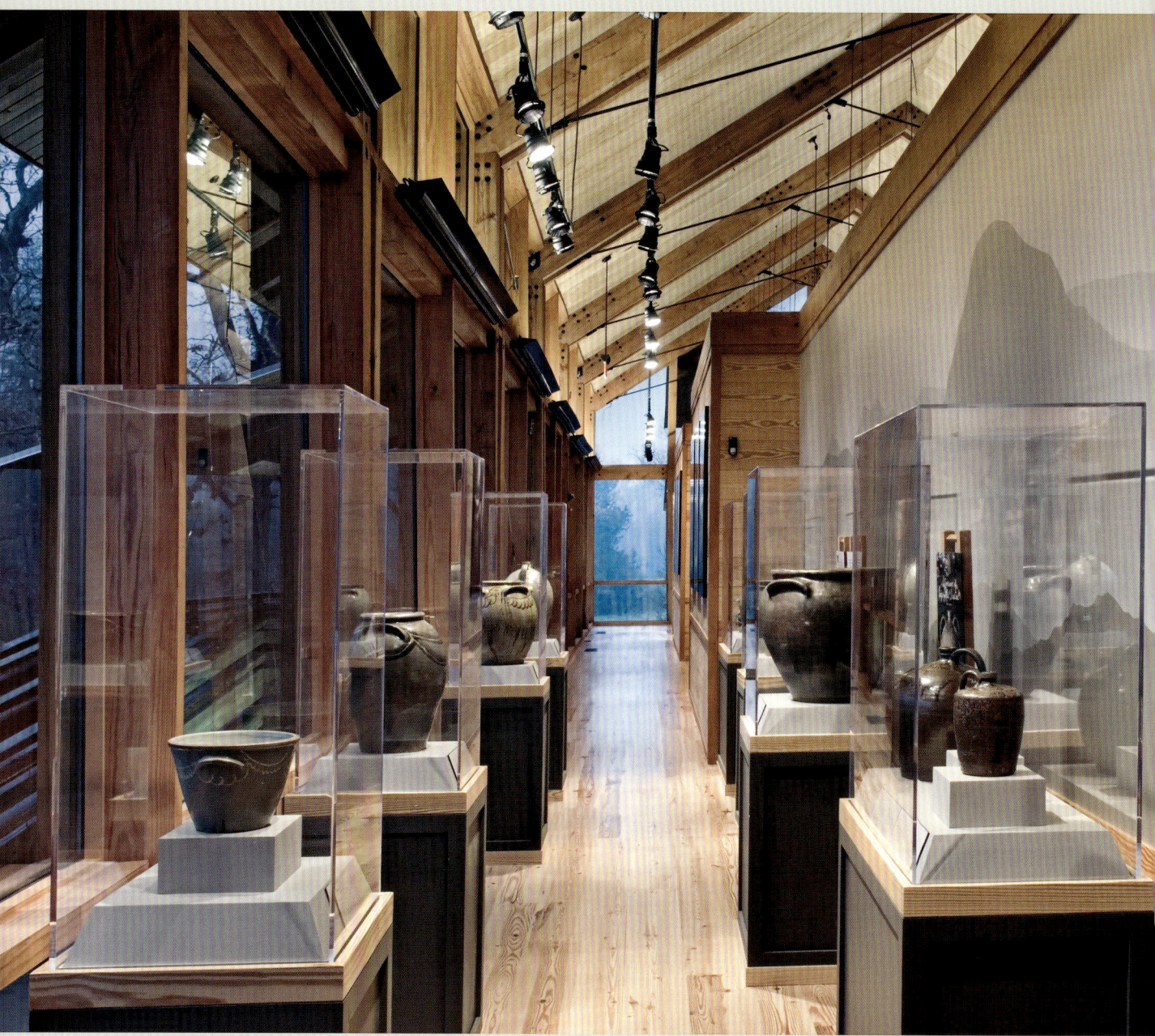

The Folk Pottery Museum changing exhibits gallery, 2006. In the
museum's first years this space featured ceramic traditions beyond,
but still related to, north Georgia, in this case stoneware of antebellum
Edgefield District, South Carolina, on loan from the collection of
Mr. and Mrs. Levon Register. *Photo: Rob Karosis; courtesy of Dean and Kay
Swanson and Bob Cain.*

The chief mission of the Folk Pottery Museum of Northeast Georgia is education. However, promotion of the active traditional potters, many of whom struggle to sell their wares in an increasingly difficult economic climate, is another important goal. To that end a Folk Potters Trail brochure was developed, with maps and contact information for potters who wish to be included. The museum thus makes a positive contribution to cultural tourism in Georgia while supporting one of the state's most distinctive folk arts and joins a small number of other institutions throughout the world devoted exclusively to traditional ceramics.

CHAPTER 10

The Living Tradition

North Georgia Folk Pottery Today

In previous chapters I described the historical development of north Georgia's pottery tradition to explain how it came to be what it is today. It is now time to explore in detail the living tradition, including a census of the area's active folk potters and interviews in which potters representing various facets of the tradition tell their own stories.

The only Georgia potter to have kept alive the old alkaline-glazed stoneware tradition into the 1970s was Lanier Meaders. Hewell's Pottery, meanwhile, had continuously maintained the old hand skills in the later gardenware tradition. The interest in folk pottery generated by Cheever, Arie, and Lanier encouraged others of that family to return to the craft and motivated a new generation to learn from older potters. But to some extent north Georgia folk pottery also was transformed by Arie's and Lanier's artistic contributions. Before, folk potters were "production" potters who made useful farm wares day in and day out; the emphasis today, as we've seen, is on decorative wares for collectors.

That simplistic contrast is complicated, however, by a distinction that exists for today's folk potters between those who are still essentially utilitarian craftsmen who channel their turning skills into the old useful forms—however much ornament they sometimes add—and those who follow the later trend established by Arie: decoration for the sake of decoration. Among the former are Harold Hewell, a superb potter who has done little decorative work, his equally skilled grandson, Matthew, and his nephew, Wayne. Inherent in these three is the value system seen earlier in Cheever Meaders and his nineteenth-century predecessors: that of the potter who strives to make the best "working" ware as efficiently and consistently as possible. Some of the current products, such as pitchers and mugs for beverages, are still used to serve the container functions for which they were designed. The hardest-working wares being made these days, though, are the plant pots of Hewell's and Craven's.

Grace Hewell, like Arie Meaders before her, married into the tradition, and Lin Craven also came to it late. The greater freedom of interpretation this permitted them, along with a generic feminine artistic vision that Grace's grandson, Matthew, refers to as "bright ideas," may explain the decorative thrust in the clay work of these three women. But how to explain the attitudinal difference in the work of brothers Michael and Dwayne Crocker, both of whom had the same gardenware training? Michael, the elder of the two, certainly can decorate (as shown by his snake-and-grape syrup jug illustrated in chapter 8), but his execution of the old useful shapes is incomparable. Michael's passion for the old north Georgia wares and admiration for the subtle beauty of their forms and glazes seem to be integral to his personality. Dwayne is also expert at the wheel, but his emphasis on detailed sculptural work falls more into the decorative camp established by Arie Meaders.

Recent experience with potters I had not previously known brings into sharper focus the realization that folk potters seldom work in isolation but are in contact with one another within particular circles of influence, resulting in the sharing of ideas beyond their initial training. Increasing this contact in recent years are events promoting north Georgia pottery such as the Mossy Creek Pottery Show at Mossy Creek Campground (begun in 1992 to mark the centennial of the founding of Meaders Pottery), Hewell's Pottery's Turning and Burning festival (begun in 1993) and other concurrent Gillsville venues on the first Saturday of October, and the North Georgia Folk Potters Festival at Banks County Middle School in Homer (begun in 2000). These events have helped to break down any parochialism within each of the two active centers (which is not much, given that they are separated by only a thirty-minute drive). New ideas (actually variations on older themes, such as cigar stubs in face-jug mouths and snakes combined with roosters) are now rapidly picked up and adapted to the borrowing potter's personal style.

Even without such gatherings, there is a tendency for potters to visit one another, arising from curiosity about what others are doing combined with a sense of occupational kinship and resulting friendships. One summer in the early 1980s I accompanied the Hewells to Vale, North Carolina (a distance of more than 200 miles from Gillsville), to visit folk potter Burlon Craig. Chester exchanged face jugs with Burl and learned from him the Catawba Valley technique of melted-glass decoration, which the Hewells use to this day. Burl, in turn, had earlier visited Lanier Meaders and borrowed his idea of wheel-thrown wig stands, while Burl's older face jug tradition, learned from mentor Harvey Reinhardt, may have been introduced by Lanier's uncle, Casey Meaders, who settled at Catawba, North Carolina, in 1921. Those North Carolina connections continue in the present, with three of our Gillsville-area potters—Dwayne Crocker, Wayne Hewell, and Steve Turpin—visiting Hickory to exhibit their wares at the annual Catawba Valley Pottery and Antiques Festival.

Automobiles certainly have facilitated such contact, but even before their advent potters communicated with each other, sometimes at a considerable distance. The documents on which historians depend so heavily are scarce for our potters, but a letter has survived from potter James Gunter of Forsyth County, Georgia, to Mossy Creek potter Azel W. Davidson (a son of Frederick). It is dated March 15, 1858, shortly after Azel left White County to join his potter brother, Abraham, on Sand Mountain, DeKalb County, Alabama (he would subsequently die fighting for the Confederacy in 1862). It states:

> You say that Mr. Lee wants to turn for me. I want him and another one. Tell Mr. Lee to come and see me and I will give him employ at some price. My rule is to give one and a half cents [a gallon] for large ware and two cents for small ware. You tell Mr. Lee to come and see

me and you come with him and lets see what we are adoing [*sic*]. I have made four blasts [kiln firings] since Christmas and it is as nice ware as you ever saw.[1]

Along with opportunities for greater interaction, another recent trend is the increased involvement of women in this male-dominated craft. The loosening of gender roles in all strata of life in the United States, including southern folk culture, is traceable to the Women's Liberation movement that began in the 1960s. Again, however, there are historical precedents. Perhaps the first to break that gender barrier for north Georgia folk pottery was Sarah Gunter, widow of Allen Gunter's youngest brother, James (uncle of the James Gunter quoted above). She is listed as a potter in the 1860 census for Hall County and would have been working at the shop of her brother-in-law, Allen, near Oakwood, twenty miles west of Gillsville. At the same location, Lydia Foster appears as a potter in the 1900 census. Then there were Eli Hewell's daughter, Catherine, who worked at Gillsville with her husband, Charlie Ferguson, in the early twentieth century; and Jean Henderson, who worked at the Gillsville shop of her uncle, Barney Colbert, in the 1930s. Of north Georgia's deceased women folk potters, the greatest contributions to today's tradition surely were made in the 1950s and 1960s by Arie Meaders.

Among the living folk potters interviewed later in this chapter are three generations of women: Grace Hewell, Lin Craven, and Jamie Ferguson. But there are others working as well, including several of the Meaders family, and at least one who is coming along: Grace's seven-year-old great-granddaughter, Susannah Hewell. Of Grace, Lin, and Jamie, the only one in the interviews who addresses her role as a female folk potter is the oldest, Grace, and it is not in political terms (a sense of kinship with other groundbreaking "sisters") but as an expression of pride in personal achievement. There may, however, be a hint of feminism in Grace's delight in helping to train Susannah: "I'm gonna have me a girl a-making pottery!"

Some of today's folk potters grew up in a continuous family tradition; others acquired their throwing skills in the garden pottery tradition or through one-on-one apprenticeship with a master traditional potter. "Folkness" can be a matter of degree; some practicing folk potters have stronger ties to the local tradition than others, and not all make pottery full-time. But all have learned at least some of their skills and designs from other traditional potters, drawing on the ceramic heritage of their native northeast Georgia and contributing to it in turn.

Census: Active North Georgia Folk Potters

Folk culture is dynamic, not static; as new traditional potters come on the scene and their work evolves, others die, retire, or take a hiatus. I've made every effort to include below all active north Georgia folk potters and brief descriptions of their current work, but changes will have occurred by the time this book appears. Consider this census, then, a work in progress; my apologies to any traditionally trained potters who were inadvertently omitted. I've organized this list by the three types of traditional training just described as a way of emphasizing what, in my opinion, is a key factor in defining a folk potter; within each category, potters are arranged alphabetically. The categories of training, however, are not always clear-cut; Hewell's Pottery, for example, is a family business that, since the 1940s, has emphasized the making of garden pottery. The locations given are the nearest post-office towns; if someone in the census has an interview included later in this chapter, that is indicated at the end of the summary.

Family Training

Mary, Stanley, and Jamie Ferguson, Gillsville
  These are the three current generations of a seven-generation pottery family tracing back to Edgefield District, South Carolina. Mary is the widow of Bobby Ferguson, Stanley is their son, and Jamie is Stanley's daughter. Brightly colored face jugs, Rebekah pitchers, roosters, pigs, and spider jugs are among their specialties. Interview.

Harold ("Bull"), Grace, Chester, Nathaniel, Matthew, Eli, and
Susannah Hewell, Gillsville

These are the four current generations of a seven-generation pottery family with roots in Jug Factory (Barrow County). Chester
is the son of Harold and Grace, Nathaniel and Matthew are
Chester's sons, and Eli and Susannah are Matthew's children. In
addition to unglazed garden pottery, the Hewells make both utilitarian and decorated alkaline-glazed wares, including Edgefield-
style slip-trailed stoneware (a result of their family connection
to the Fergusons), fired in their wood-fueled kiln. They host the
annual Turning and Burning festival on the first Saturday of
October. Interview.

Todd and Marissa Hewell, Gillsville

Todd, a grandson of Harold's brother Jack, began at Hewell's
Pottery. He makes such items as Upside-Down face jugs; his
wife, Marissa, makes figural sculptures, some influenced by her
Latin American heritage.

Wayne ("Sweet Boy") and Kevin Hewell, Lula

Wayne, a son of Harold's brother Carl, received his training with
his cousins at Hewell's Pottery. He uses an ash glaze, a clear glaze
to show off the two alternating colors of clay in his "swirl" ware,
and colored glazes; wood-fired face jugs and pitchers are among
his products. His son Kevin sometimes works with him.

Benjamin Ray ("B.R.") Holcomb, Lula

B.R. began at the Gillsville shop of his father, Samuel Rayburn
("Ray") Holcomb, which closed about 1945; he occasionally
makes ash-glazed face jugs at Hewell's Pottery.

Chris Holly, Gillsville

A son-in-law of Bobby Ferguson, Chris learned from Bobby and
Stanley and works part-time at their shop making brightly colored devil jugs and skulls in the Ferguson style.

Clete Meaders, Hoschton

Clete is the son of Cleater ("C.J.") Meaders Jr. and works at
the old-fashioned shop he built in Jackson County. Specialties

include sculptural, ash-glazed face jugs and roosters fired in his wood-burning kiln. Interview.

David and Anita Meaders, Lula

David is the son of Reggie Meaders, one of Lanier's brothers. He and his wife Anita work in the Meaders home area. Specialties include wood-fired, alkaline- or spar-glazed "jugheads," tree stumps, and roosters. Interview. In memoriam: Anita died July 21, 2009.

Edwin ("Nub") Meaders, Cleveland

Edwin is Lanier's youngest brother and, like his siblings, began under their father Cheever at the original Meaders Pottery, down the road from Edwin's home and small shop. Known as the Rooster Man, he specializes in alkaline- or blue-glazed roosters, but also makes big-eared face jugs.

Jessie Meaders, Cleveland

Jessie is the widow of Jack Meaders, who was a son of Caulder, one of Cheever's brothers. She makes whimsical flying pigs and "snowpeople" using colored glazes. Her son Jeffery also made pottery for a time.

Mildred Meaders, Annette Meaders Boswell, Mike Boswell, and Mary Meaders Adams, Cleveland

Mildred is the widow of Cheever and Arie's oldest son, John Meaders. Their daughters, Annette and Mary, and Annette's husband Mike, also make pottery, some of it fired in John's wood-burning kiln; grape-decorated pieces and two-headed chicken bowls are specialties. The family hosts the Meaders Homeplace Celebration show and sale each May across the road from the original Meaders Pottery.

Reggie and Flossie Meaders, Cleveland

Reggie is a brother of Lanier and the father of David; he and his wife Flossie make ash- and spar-glazed face jugs, hogs, and owls as specialties. In memoriam: Reggie died August 22, 2009.

Ruby Meaders Irvin, Cleveland

Ruby is a sister of Lanier, thus a daughter of Cheever and Arie. One of her specialties is white-glazed speckled chickens.

Whelchel Meaders, Cleveland

Whelchel is a son of L.Q., one of Cheever's brothers; he occasionally makes ash-glazed face jugs and utilitarian wares.

Gardenware Training

Billy Joe and Mike Craven, Gillsville

Joe is a "skipped-generations" potter from one of the South's oldest clay clans, so he had to pick up the craft at Hewell's Pottery, learning to turn under Harold. He went on to found his own gardenware business, Craven's Pottery, in 1971, which remains a training ground for upcoming folk potters. Joe still occasionally makes Pat Ferguson–style face jugs; his brother Mike makes decorative glazed pottery.

Dwayne Crocker, Gillsville

Dwayne and his older brother Michael began at Wilson's near their family home in Lula, then refined their throwing skills at Craven's in Gillsville before opening their own shops to make glazed wares. Dwayne makes lively roosters and cartoonlike face jugs, using both ash and colored glazes. Interview.

Michael Crocker, Lula

Michael's Georgia Folk Pottery Center is a former chickenhouse converted into workshop, office, and storage space for his enormous collection of historic north Georgia wares. For a time he worked with brother Melvin, who decorated Michael's turned pieces. Inspired by the older Mossy Creek tradition, Michael makes both functional and decorative alkaline-glazed wares.

Michael ("Bugsy") Perdue, Lula

Mike is a grandson of Gillsville potter Hugh Dorsey Perdue and great-nephew of shop owner Dave Perdue. Trained at Sims, Hewell's, and Craven's, he now has his own part-time operation and makes face jugs, grape-decorated pieces, and utilitarian ware with ash and colored glazes.

Jeff Standridge, Gillsville

Jeff received his training at Hewell's and Craven's. His specialty is ash-glazed face jugs, which have an old-time look.

Steve and Abby Turpin, Homer

Steve's twenty-seven years at Craven's included a stint as manager of their Handmade Division. He began making glazed wares at home and now works on his own full time. He uses both ash and colored glazes; specialties include roosters and Siamese Good-and-Evil face jugs. His daughter Abby has been learning from him. Steve manages the North Georgia Folk Potters Festival in June at the Banks County Middle School in Homer.

Charlie West, Cleveland

Charlie began at Sims, then worked with Todd Hewell before setting up on his own. He specializes in brightly colored earthenware roosters and lamp bases.

One-on-One Apprenticeship

Clint Alderman, Hartwell

Clint informally apprenticed with Edwin Meaders and also was mentored by Michael Crocker. His technology, forms, and glazes hark back to the older White County tradition, including a wood-burning kiln. Ash-glazed roosters are one of his specialties.

Roger Corn, Lula

Roger apprenticed with Bobby Ferguson. Among his thin-walled products are distinctive face jugs with bow-shaped open mouths, elongated noses, and dark (nonalkaline) glazes.

Lin Craven, Cleveland

Like her cousin Billy Joe Craven, Lin is descended from one of the oldest southern "clay clans," but her White County branch of the family stopped potting before her time, so she apprenticed with Bobby Ferguson at Gillsville. Using colored glazes on a white stoneware body, her work is sculptural and innovative but includes traditional forms such as ring and face jugs. Interview.

Rex Hogan, Cleveland

A descendant of Mossy Creek potter Riley Hogan, Rex learned the basics of the craft from Mildred Meaders and her daughter, Annette Meaders Boswell, as well as from Whelchel Meaders. He combines wheel-throwing and handbuilding to create sculptural roosters, other birds, and face jugs.

Kevin ("Turkey") Merck, Buford

Kevin learned basic skills from Wayne Hewell, Jeff Standridge, and Mike Perdue. He uses alkaline and colored glazes—often sparingly to highlight the natural clay—on his detailed face stumps, animal sculptures, and character jugs inspired by popular culture.

Pat Shields and Janice Hall Shields, Danielsville

Pat and Janice apprenticed with Bobby Ferguson and also worked with Jerry Brown at Hamilton, Alabama. At their Georgia Mudcats Pottery in Madison County, they mix their north Alabama clay in a mule-turned mill to produce wood-fired face jugs and a range of other wares with colored glazes.

The Turners Talk: A Selection of Interviews

This sampling of recent interviews with living practitioners represents those different learning backgrounds and a range of perspectives on the tradition in which they all participate.[2]

The Hewells of Hewell's Pottery, Gillsville

Hewell's Pottery, located on State Highway 52 west of town, is hard to miss, marked as it is by a large sign and stacks of garden pottery and yard ornaments. Of the potters interviewed for this book, the Hewells are the only ones who keep regular business hours (although some of the others are full-time potters). The family has been handcrafting pottery continuously since at least the time of the Civil War. The modern practices in their businesslike sales shop and production plant are balanced by visible evidence of their deep appreciation of old ways of doing things in the rural South, in particular pottery making: a wood-burning tunnel kiln for their alkaline-glazed stoneware and an old-fashioned workshop with mule-turned clay mill outside. The latter two structures were built to demonstrate the "old-timey" approach to the craft at the annual Turning and Burning festival the Hewells have hosted since 1993.

While rooted in the same family tradition, each member's work reveals his or her own personality and ability. Harold is a "bigware" potter, although ill health has slowed him down in recent years; his glazed pitchers demonstrate his superb sense of proportion and turning control. Matthew is an equally fine potter who expresses his faith by adding the Christian fish symbol to his name on the bottoms of his glazed pots; of particular note are his melted glass-decorated and recent Edgefield-style, slip-trailed wares. Nathaniel tends toward smaller wares with delicate handles; he manages the computer side of the business. Grace enjoys decorative work; her face jugs are distinguished by bits of clay added for chin and cheeks. Chester is the innovator, always dreaming up new ideas and strategies to keep the business afloat in hard times.

The following conversation was recorded on the porch of their hilltop general store with these members of the family: Henry (born in 1924); his brother, Harold ("Bull," born in 1926); Harold's wife, Grace Nell (born in 1933); Harold and Grace's son, Chester, manager of Hewell's Pottery (born in 1950); Chester's youngest son, Nathaniel (born in 1976); and Nathaniel's older brother, Matthew (born in 1972).[3] Raised in the family business, Henry studied ceramics briefly at what is now North Georgia Technical College in Clarkesville, then made a thirty-year career in the U.S. Marines, after which he returned to Gillsville and worked at pottery for fifteen years before retiring; he now pursues woodworking as a hobby. All other family members interviewed are active potters.

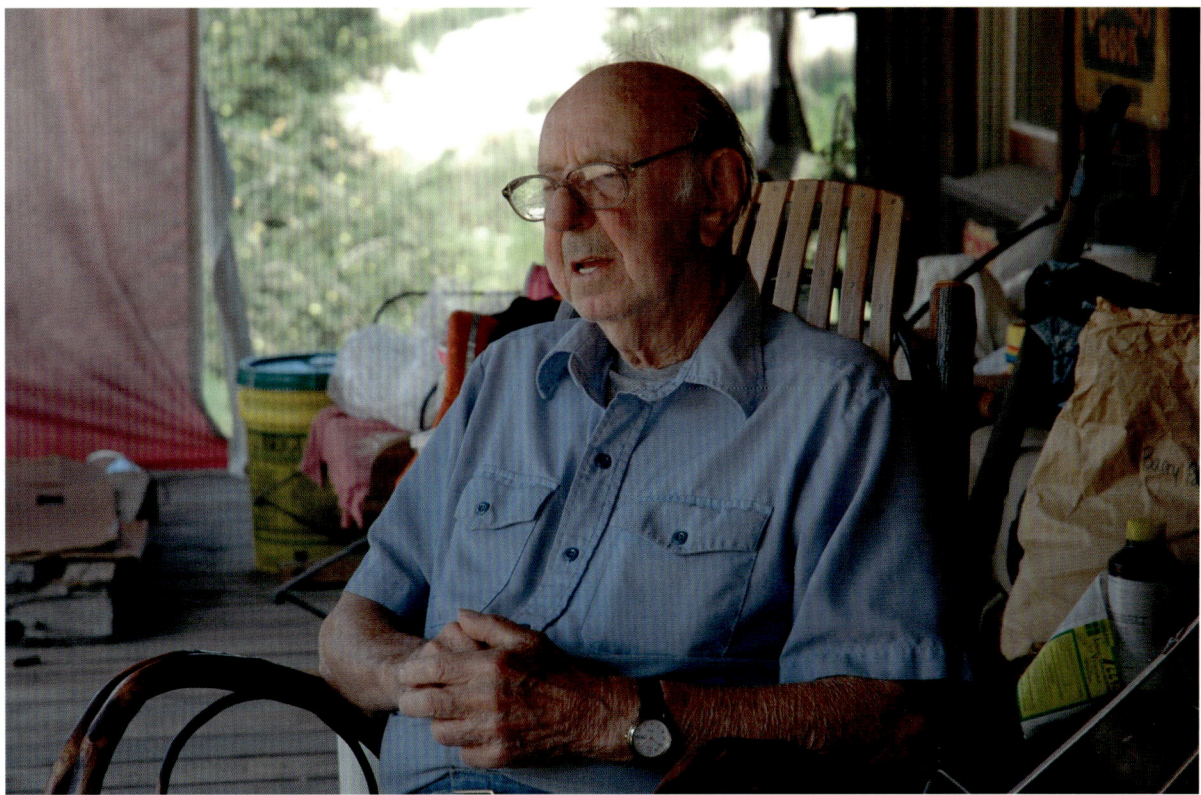

HENRY

I can remember working at a very early age [at the old shop, about a mile from the present site]. All of us as we grew up, by the time we were five or six years old we were doing *little* chores around the place. We ground clay with a mule, pulling around in a circle at the clay mill. And at five or six, you'd be out there keeping that mule moving. Mules are not stupid; if you walked away, he stopped. So you had to keep him moving, and that was one of my functions, at least until I was a teenager. Then, as the clay was ground, you helped to take it out of the mill. You got it out by bending your gut over the side of that tub and grabbing it with your hands and lifting it out. Then we blocked it up as big as you could handle, which would probably weigh, oh, thirty, forty pounds. We put it against our tummy and walked that thing into the shop where they kept it damp covered with wet burlap bags to keep it from drying out and getting

Henry Hewell, 2008.
Photo: Kirk Elifson.

hard. I've ground lots of it, get it inside where it could be used; it was pretty tough work.

We were working out of an old log shop which my father [Maryland] had built himself. He didn't cut the timber, but he laid the logs and helped scalp 'em down. It was a pretty open building; they calked [Henry uses his ex-Marine term here] it with red dirt (not the same clay as they used for pottery, they wouldn't use good clay to calk that shop), he just dug it out of a hillside. It periodically had to be patched—not altogether recalked—because the weather would wear part of the chinking out of the shop. It was fairly cool in there in the summertime; with the wet clay and the pottery drying on the racks there was a certain amount of moisture, and it was well shaded. I *guarantee* it was cold in the wintertime! They did have a stove, sometimes burning wood, sometimes coal. The back side of the shop would be very cold anyway, and you'd have to take extra precaution to keep the wet pottery from freezing and actually destroying it.

Well, you had those chores that kept you busy, and of course there was school. So learning to turn for a kid like I was, if you found a few spare minutes, of *course* you were interested: you lived with [pottery], you grew up with it, that's what everybody there did. So you got on a wheel that somebody wasn't using, your brother's or your father's—well, not your father's, nobody messed with that! You'd probably get started at six or seven, trying some. Now, that kid over there, Eli, they had him started [at age two]. But nobody took those pains with us to say, "You're three years old and we're gonna teach you how to turn." No, you did this mostly on your own, until you could actually make a little something, like a half-gallon or one-gallon pitcher, whatever. When I was ten or twelve years old I could make little pitchers or jugs. They were glazed with Albany slip at that time; this would have been the [mid-]'30s. I remember one of the Wilson boys was moving [selling] the pottery for us; he would take those little jugs and stuff. I was getting maybe a nickel apiece for 'em; maybe he sold 'em for a dime, made a little profit off of it! If I had twenty or thirty of 'em, he'd put 'em in a box and take 'em off. He got rid of 'em, all right.

My father did a glass glaze, and this was an excellent glaze. Now, Albany slip, if you put kerosene in [pots glazed with it], the kerosene might seep through; but the glass glaze, you can put acid or anything in it. For a period of time, possibly in the early thirties, everything was glazed with the glass: utility vessels such as milk pitchers and jugs for syrup, churns for butter and the pickling that was done to a great extent in the mountains north of here. . . . Father came up with an item called a glass beater. He acquired [broken bottles] from the Nehi Bottling Company in Gainesville and hauled them by pickup truck and just dumped them in a pile. He had built a steel tray— four foot long and eight or ten inches wide and about that deep— and filled that with the broken glass. And he had four trip hammers driven by a gasoline engine (up until 1936 we had no electricity in this area). They was nothing but two-by-fours some ten foot long, had a steel bar at the end of each one; they was lined up at such a distance apart. And the engine drove a shaft that had pins sticking out of it, and these were the triggers. They picked up the two-by-fours and lifted them fourteen inches. Then the pins would rotate out of the way and the steel bars, weighing maybe fifteen pounds, bounced down on this glass. It did this over and over again until it beat the glass into a very fine powder. We sifted the glass through a household sifter and mixed it [with water] into a slurry with a little bit of clay and ashes. Then it was poured into and around the outside of the pottery and fired to quite a high temperature.

HAROLD ("BULL")

[The Hewells] stayed here [in pottery] from the first to the last, didn't give up when times got hard; we thought it was hard for everybody, so we just kept going. I'd say for sixty years we've majored [done the best] in sales. I've traveled extensively in the eastern United States—didn't go west of the Mississippi much—and we just kept selling and selling and selling. I was on the road generally every week; I'd be out on the road two–three days, [often] on the weekends. Didn't have a lot of weekends free! I was earning a living and a little extra; it took that encouragement to keep you going. I've been

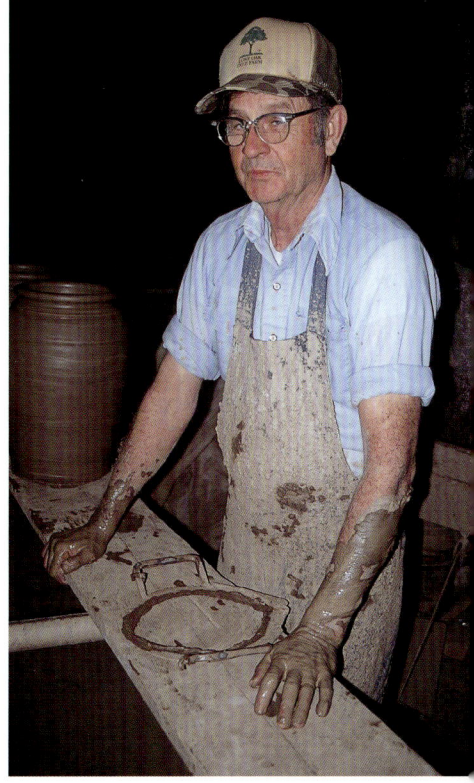

Harold Hewell taking a breather while turning garden pots, 1992. *Photo: author.*

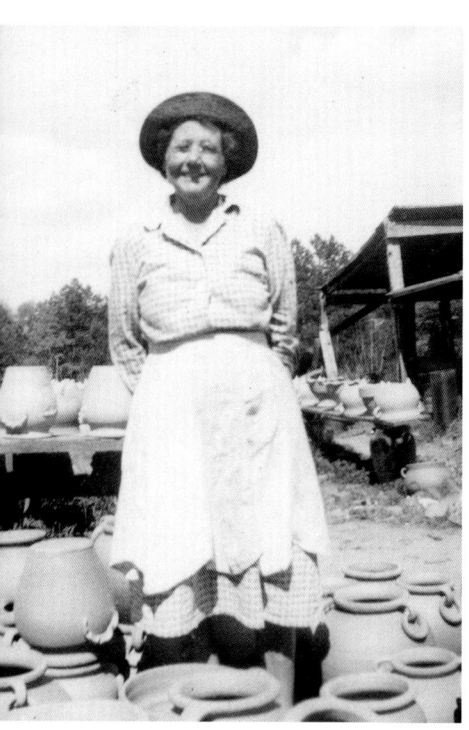

Ada Hewell, ca. 1954. She helped her husband, Maryland, by preparing clay and adding ear (lug) handles to churns. *Courtesy of Hewell family.*

clear to Boston; we went to Missouri with a lot of stuff. I remember the hard times [Great Depression] in the thirties, I remember well! They'd carry those loads [of pottery] out and exchange it for goods that we could use back home. Merchants wouldn't want to turn loose of no cash, so they'd barter. We still had cows back then, so they'd swap for cow feed.

I remember the glass glazing; my mother [Ada] helped a lot with that. My daddy [Maryland] built a machine to crush broken bottles with. You had to get the glass *fine*, see. At first he used a gas engine, and then when the [electric] power came he got an electric one-and-a-half horsepower motor, and he used it for everything. He was a fast worker, but an impatient man. He was as fast a turner as I ever saw, and made good ware. But he wanted things done quick—but good! Them two things don't mix much! Mom also made [clay] balls for Daddy, cutting 'em on a wire—that's a man's work. And she "handled" one side of the churns [with "ear" or lug handles].

[Hewell's Pottery] was automated as much as possible to do handmade stuff. In other words, the ball-making was eliminated; we use a pug mill now. Still a lot of work about getting the clay to the pug mill. It's changed from making churns to garden pottery, and that came about at the end of [World War II], gradually. While the war was going on you couldn't make enough churns, they'd just buy everything [a temporary return to self-sufficiency]! But once the war was over it begin to taper off rather sharply. People began to make a little more money; taking care of a cow just to get a little milk and butter wasn't worth the hassle. So you didn't need no churns. Now, I sold a good bit of that [churns] in my early travels, but I begin to see right away that we had to get to the garden ware. It came about just as soon as we got back home from the various services, around '46.

[The Brown potters, based in Atlanta] were all easy to work with. The earliest one, his name was Horace Brown [father of current folk potter Jerry Brown of Hamilton, Alabama]. I was a kid when he worked there [at the old shop]. Later on, I hired Otto, then [in 1956] his boy came to work with us, Jimmy Brown. We liked them very well. They finally went to Bethune, South Carolina. They've all done passed on now. Pat Ferguson did a lot of that face jug work. Pat was in and out of it. He was an excellent turner, and a *fast* turner, but he didn't like clay work. He became an excellent man in the building trade. They said [his father] Charlie was the kind of guy that loved to pull jokes on people. They said he dismantled an old-time wagon and then put it back together up on [a farmer's] barn rooftop! I can remember the old wives' tales about him; he must have been something!

GRACE NELL

Harold and I honeymooned up at Cherokee, North Carolina, in 1949, and as soon as we got back I told him that I wanted to work in the pottery. And he said, "Well, you don't know how."

They had toted all the pots to a big old shade tree outside the shelter where it would be cool. Harold and Mrs. Hewell [Ada] was a-working on log planters. And I stood there a little bit and watched them do that, and they both was so slow I couldn't hardly stand it! And I said, "Let me try that."

And Harold said, "Aw, you don't know how to do this, Grace."

And I just reached over and sort of punched him and says, "*Just step aside* and let's see how good I can do!" Well, he stepped aside and I got ahold of them things. They both just stood there and looked at me. I took the job away from both of them! I mean, I went to doing it *that* quick. He never did no more finishing, and she never was out there to help, because *I* could do it. I wanted to learn, and I did. I've always been a striver; anything that I set my head to do, I *will* do it.

My daddy was a Wilson, and Hallie Wilson [a potter who trained at Hewell's] was Daddy's cousin. But I didn't grow up around the pottery, I just married into it. I'm the head [honcho] of the women potters, because when I got married, I never heard of a woman potter. I had a mother-in-law and three sisters-in-law that was raised in the pottery, but not a one of them could make pots. . . . See, I would do that finishing, handling and legging pots, cutting [pockets in] strawberry jars. We was out there one day [in 1950] putting in a kiln

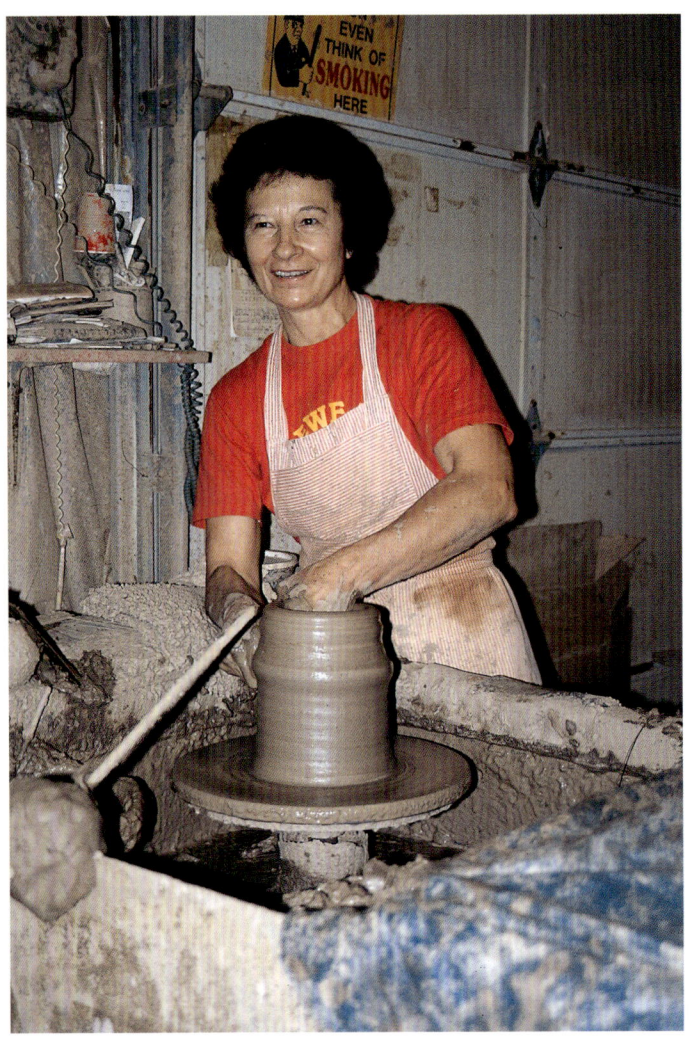

Grace Nell Hewell, 1992.
Photo: author.

of ware, and [Harold] made a smart remark to me of some kind, made me sorta mad. I said, "Well, toodly-doodly, I won't do nothing but go in yonder and make me a pot!"

And he laughed and said, "You can't do that."

I said, "Yeah, you say I can't do this, I can't do that; I'll show you what I can do." So I went in the shop, and there was one boy a-making pots in there. And so I says, "I want to make a pot." And I just got me a little ball of clay and went to a wheel. And I says, "What do you do with this clay?" See, I hadn't even watched them, 'cause I was so busy doing all that other.

He said, "Hold your hands and make the ball round."

I said, "Okay," and done that. I said, "Now what do you do?"

He said, "Well, pull it up."

And I said, "Put your fingers on it?"

And he said, "Yeah."

So I pulled it up. I said, "Now what do I do?"

He said, "Take you a chip [wood or metal rectangle for smoothing pots, known as a "rib" to studio potters] and form it."

So I did that. And that's all the coaching that I had right there. I made the first pot that I tried, and I would go back in there every day. The more I made, the more excited I got. And it just tickled Harold to death. He said, "I'm not gonna say that you can't do nothing else!"

One day, Lanier Meaders and [his father] Cheever come to get some glazing; see, they bought [Sadlers slip] glazing from Harold and Daddy Bud [Maryland]. I was just a-working [in the shop]; I mean, I was *really* working! And Cheever said, "My, my!" Said, "How I would love to have you" [to help in his shop]. He said, "I'd give a dollar for you!"

And see, I was just seventeen years old. And it just tickled me to death; I just died laughing. I went to Harold and I says, "That old man come in there and said, 'How I'd love to have you; I'd give a dollar for you!'"

And Harold, he looked at me and laughed, and he says, "Well, I'll tell you right now, it'll take more than a dollar to get you!" . . .

[Harold was in the navy reserves, and in 1951 he was called to duty in Korea for fifteen months.] I stayed on, and me and his daddy and mama [Maryland and Ada] run the pottery. So when he come back out of the navy, see, we still had our pottery. If I'd a-been like a lot of seventeen-year-old girls, I wouldn't have gone to that shop and worked every day; but I didn't miss a day. Another time that I kept the pottery shop going was when it burned down, burned to the ground [at the present location in 1969; the fire is thought to have been started by a careless worker's cigarette]. The fire rangers cut the shop away from the [four-stack downdraft] kiln; we would never have been able to build back if they hadn't saved our kiln.

That night we went down there and looked at all the [roof] tin laying there; it was really terrifying. And Harold says—he was so pitiful—he says, "Well, I'll just go get me a job somewhere; you can just stay at home."

And I says, "No. Tomorrow we're gonna come back here and pull that tin out. And we're gonna go to building back just as quick as we can."

He says, "Well now, you don't have to do that, Grace, if you don't want to."

I says, "That's what I want to do. I don't want the pottery going dead; I want to keep it going."

A lot of people said, "Well, it was just an old shop."

I said, "Yes, but that is our living!" . . .

I worked the whole time 'til Chester was born. I crawled in the kiln the day he was born that night. And then I came home from the hospital, stayed around the house for three weeks, and went back to work. I carried my baby with me from the time he was three weeks old. I raised him in the shop. And [Grace's great-granddaughter,] Susannah, I'm learning her to make pots too; I'm gonna have me a girl a-making pottery! She comes to me and says, "Pot, Granny. Pot, Granny."

I decided to see how many number-two gallon hats [for jack-o-lantern "punkins"] I could make one day [in about 1977]. So, we's in the old shop [rebuilt at their present location after the fire], and my wheel was in the corner. I started at 7:30 [a.m.]. We didn't have room for all the hats in there; there was two boys toting them out, putting them under the shelter. I put a cement block on the treadle of my [electric] wheel and lifted them off with my hand like that; never stopped the wheel! (But I did stop for dinner.) I'm the only one that can grab the pots off like that and set 'em down. I even put my [receiving] board right at my wheel where I could set 'em off. I could *make* one quicker than I could set it off! Just like a *machine*, setting 'em off, setting 'em off! Got done, and we counted them pots, and I was tickled to death! So we wrote that note [shown in a commemorative photo] that says I made 1,070 pots in one day. But that's not all I did that day! I cut forty bird feeders, and put handles on some pots, and then I went and jogged two miles that afternoon!

[On the source of her ideas:] The idea just springs up in my head. It's sorta like making a flower arrangement. I carve a lot on my pitchers; I don't have no idea what I'm gonna do, but while I'm sitting there I just carve it out. It's just all creative. I'd rather make bird houses and frog huts than to make strawberry jars, because I've made so many of [the latter]. Oh, I love to make a face jug! I make some that's got two faces on; I make some that's got three faces on. I make some that look like they've been on a drunk, sorta cocky looking. And it's just imagination. When I go to put that clay on there [for facial details], I fix them different. I love to fix them different.

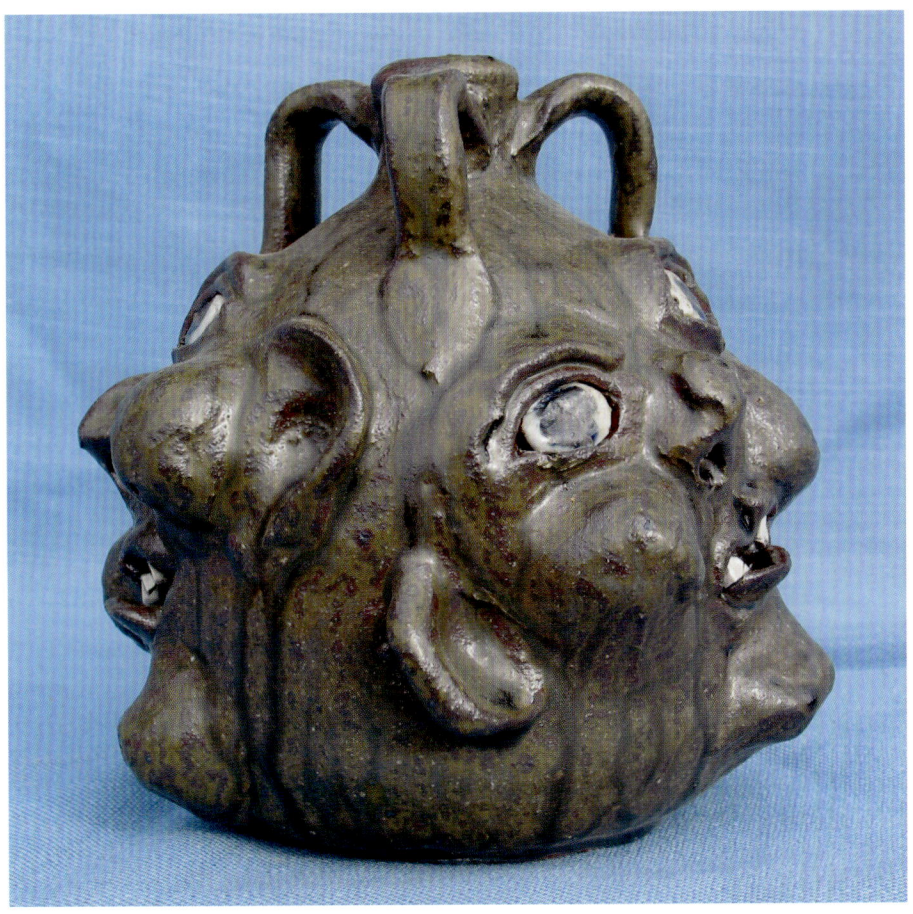

Three-face jug,
Grace Nell Hewell, 2004,
alkaline (ash) glaze. *Photo:
Laura M. Drummond.*

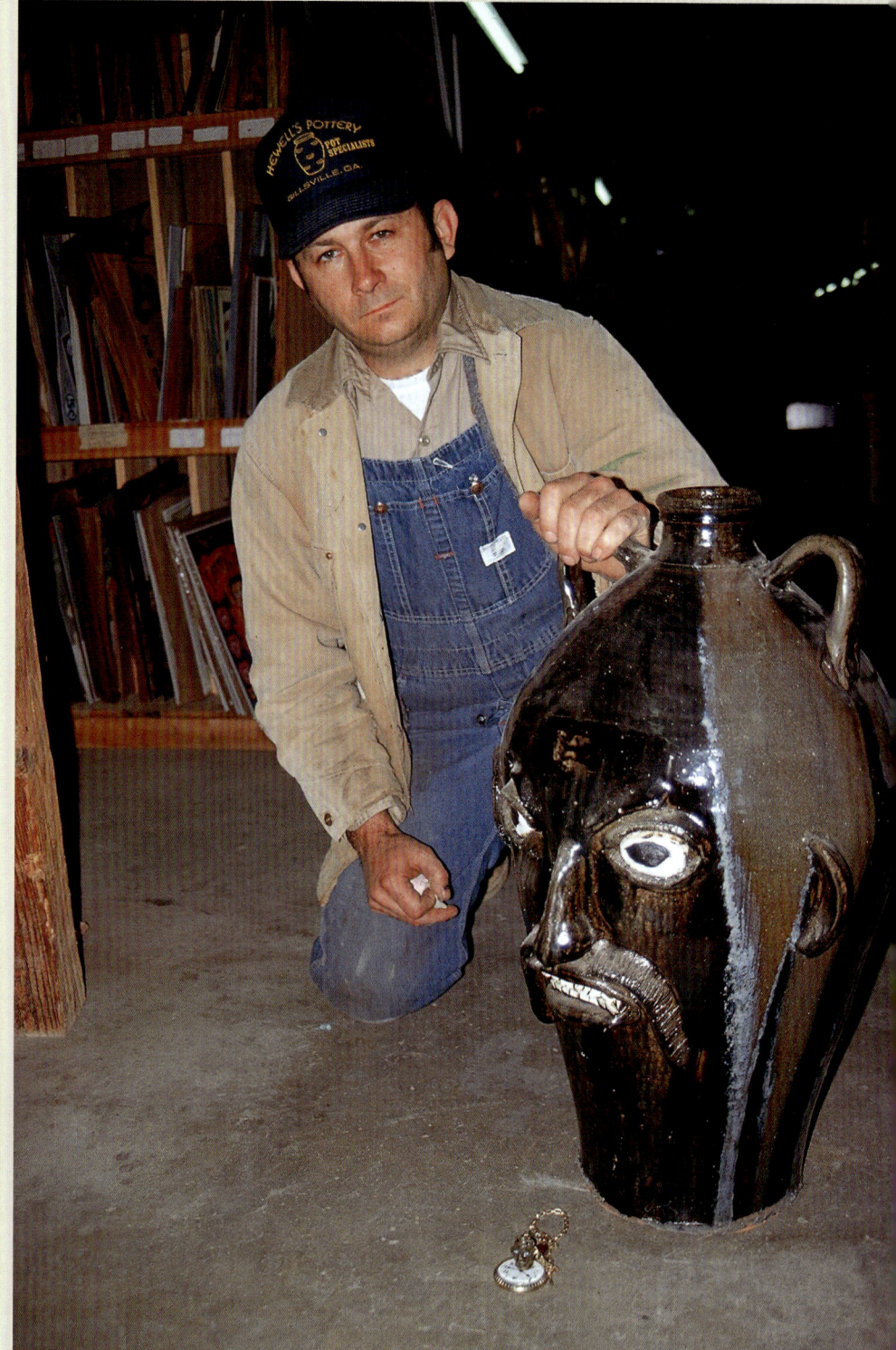

Chester Hewell with size range of his ash-glazed face jugs, from a height of 26 inches down to 1 inch (on pocket watch), 1992. He learned about melted-glass decoration (on big jug) from Catawba Valley, North Carolina, folk potter Burlon Craig. *Photo: author.*

[The greatest concentration of Gillsville shops occurred] in the middle 1930s to early forties. It tapered off 'til there wasn't nothing here except Daddy's shop. Supply and demand—elbows and rear ends! See, when times got more modern, folks got to where they didn't want to work. And I see that happening now. But, I see a thing happening that may turn it back to where they don't mind working: in hard economic times, folks will be more willing to work.

Things changed from all glazed stuff—almost, they always made a few flowerpots, not a lot—to terra cotta pots because of supply and demand, and [a potter] wanting to stay in the same type work he was doing, not willing to run up yonder and get a job at a cotton mill. They had to switch. It's like walking out into the ocean: if you walk one step every twenty minutes, you're not going to get very deep, but after a while you're going to be completely wet! That's how they changed [to garden pottery]: it was gradual. When they first started, they was making approximately half a kiln of glazed stuff, and gradually eased up, by 1953 or '54, to where they wasn't making but very little glazed stuff. In the early fifties, Williamsburg Pottery wanted us to make some little pitchers and jugs with a green glaze.

Where I started at was down at the old place. 'Nother words, as a young'un I remember going down there at night [in winter] to keep fire in the heaters to keep it warm where it wouldn't freeze. You had to haul wood, and you had to get up enough wood to burn day and night. We would go down there at night to put wood in the heater and check the pottery. They done it in shifts: Carl would put it in on the early shift, Daddy would put it in later about eleven, and Jack would put it in about three o'clock in the morning [Carl and Jack were Chester's uncles, brothers of Harold and Henry]. But they'd always have 'em an ax or some heavy piece of metal to heat up in the fire first thing when they got there, to warm that water up at the wheel—it'd have ice in it, and the clay'd have chunks of ice in it. It was hard on a person's hands; there was no way to keep their hands from ruining, working clay like that; they was always chapped. You'd have Vaseline and beef taller [tallow] to put on 'em, but you couldn't keep enough on 'em in cold clay.

When we moved up here in 1964, we were still using [wood] slabs to heat one shop where Carl worked, and we was using a coal stoker to heat the shop where Daddy and Mama worked. You had to tote that coal in every day to fill it. We was burning the [four-stack down-draft] kiln here with fuel oil. It cost about seven, eight cents a gallon; the highest it got up was a quarter a gallon before we quit using it. Fuel oil, you couldn't glaze nothing in there unless you done it in a sagger [protective clay box]; I reckon the sulfur in that oil would make the glaze crawl off. But I did do a little glazed stuff in that kiln in saggers—came out slick as a button.

Getting back to the old shop, you had to take a shovel and chop the clay up—beat the clods up—and wet that down where it was suitable to grind; couldn't have no hard chunks in it. I've seen my grandpa on Mama's side grinding clay and it raining bad. That clay's always slick around the clay pile. Had to take dry dirt and sprinkle it out on his path [so he wouldn't slip and fall], and then he'd run out there, fill his wheelbarrow up, and make it back in. Have to do that again next time he ground a mill. About 1949 Daddy and my grandpa, Daddy Bud [Maryland Hewell], bought an old [motor-driven] clay mill from Ceramo Company in Missouri. [Bud had introduced a gasoline-powered friction wheel as early as 1919.]

The old place started out as a log shop, and there was a barn down there. They started building onto that barn to make it a pottery factory, really, where they could get production: be room for 'em to work, wouldn't have to tote that ware outside as much. They added a front on that barn, that was Daddy Bud's turning shop, two people could turn in that—my daddy and Daddy Bud. Then on either side of that they built what I'd call a closed-end shed; Carl had a shop and Jack had a shop on the other side. And then they had a clay mill shack, we called it, that hooked onto that. And then they gradually built on a big shelter that connected to the kiln to put the pottery under, where they didn't have to worry about the rain.

I went to Lanier Tech in Gainesville to a welding school, and I worked in Atlanta about a year. The welding school probably paid the biggest dividend of anything around here, because, without having the ability to fix stuff, you in trouble when you got to call somebody in. My wife, San [Sandra], when we got married, she was working in Atlanta, and I worked [there] at a place called Engineered Steel Products about three or four months. Couldn't stand Atlanta, really! Always figured that I'd [come back to Gillsville and] be working here in the shop; just didn't know exactly when.

[On Hewell's Turning and Burning festival:] Where else can you go to see the kind of things that's here? In other words, I'm trying to dig up people and things. . . . Now, some of the people [who demonstrate and sell crafts at the festival] are not traditional, but they're doing it the old way. And we love for people to be able to see it done the old way. I would really love to have the Turning and Burning some day without a tent, without any cars in view, and just everything look like it would have been in about 1930. But it's hard to do that.

Hewell's Pottery Turning and Burning festival, 2001. The county fairlike ambiance includes boiled peanuts (the tub in front of kiln) and gospel singing in the white tent (in front of the current production plant). *Photo: author.*

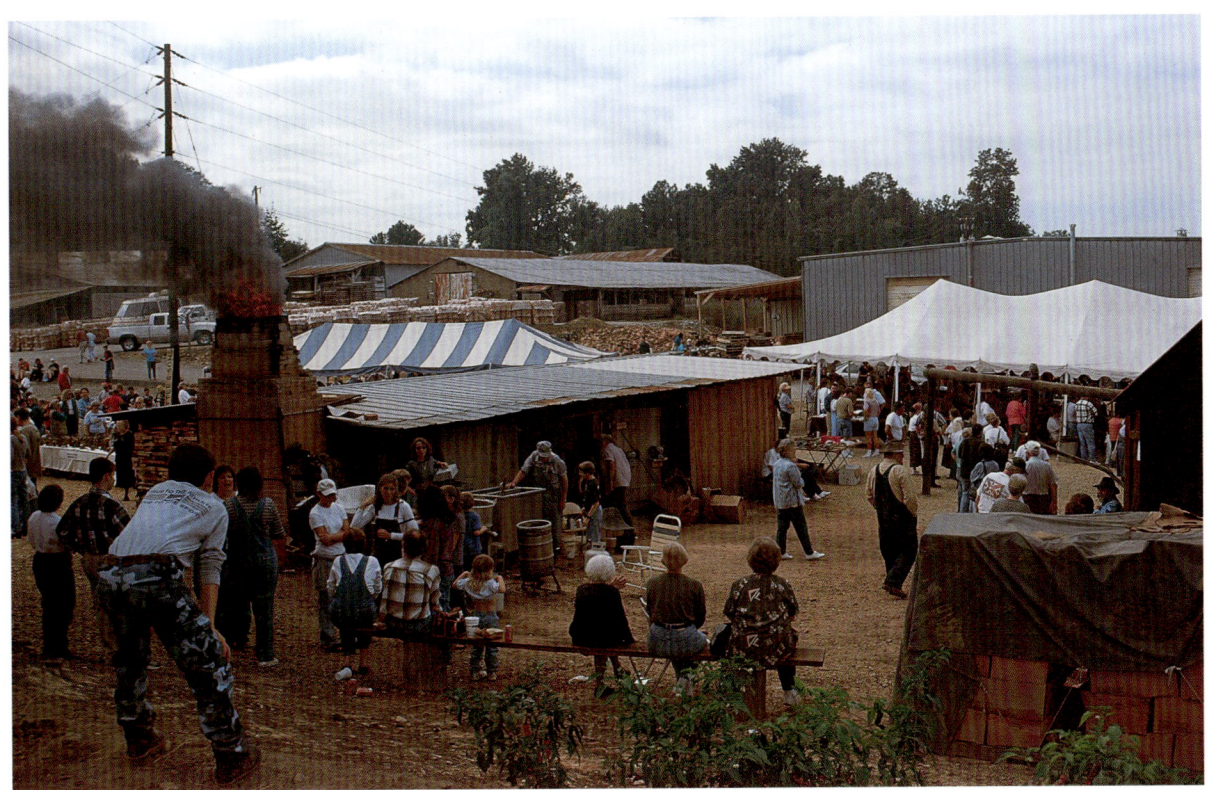

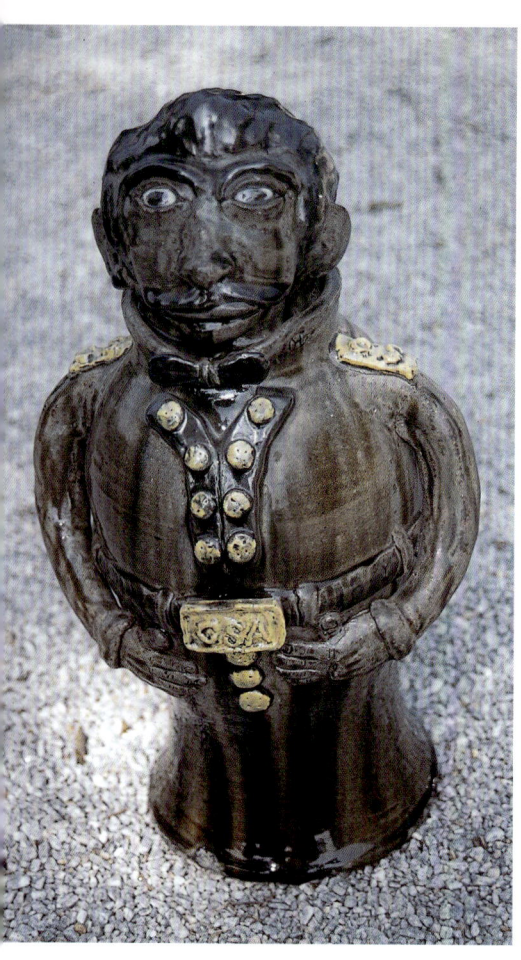

"Confederate Soldier," Chester Hewell, 1990, alkaline ("glass") glaze. Inspired by published illustrations of southern figural jugs, Chester has made a few nonfunctional sculptures depicting a character dear to his heart, complete with "CSA" belt buckle. H. 18¼ inches. *Photo: author; lent by maker to FPM.*

As far as old-timey ways, I could qualify as being a traditional blacksmith. I worked in a blacksmith shop with my grandpa, and I know enough to shoe a horse. I know enough to trim a horse's foot, and draw a piece of metal; I know enough to take a round rod and split it and make a hook out of it where it's got three or four [prongs] on it to dip a bucket out of the well. I know how to split a piece of flat iron to make a crowbar to pull nails with. So I *have* had *that* handed down to me.

[His response to declining sales a few years ago:] What you do in hard times: you gotta do what you gotta do to make things happen. We've been making some different-type pottery in the terra cotta (red clay garden pots): new shapes, new names. Such as "Tennessee" pots, that's a whole new line. [On the name:] I was coming through North Carolina when the idea came to me; "North Carolina" just didn't sound good! They're an open-top pot with pockets cut in it. We have improved our pockets and our clay. And [on] our strawberry jars, they're bigger and rolled out more, more plantable. We're still a-struggling; customers has died, and Wal-Marts has took over. But we're getting more people into it now because our pots look better planted—such a variety. And when you get a shape refined good enough to where you can recognize it anywhere—no mistake where it come from—you've done something.

[Sales of glazed wares are] off, but I think it's had a most definite turn. Not plumb to the good, but we are selling more of it now in the last four to eight weeks. [On the Hewells' improved Edgefield-style, slip-decorated stoneware:] I got to thinking about Charles Ferguson [a Hewell ancestor through marriage], who worked for Dr. Abner Landrum in South Carolina. I looked at some Edgefield District stuff over there [in McKissick Museum, University of South Carolina, Columbia], and I said, "I can do anything that he done." Thomas Chandler [antebellum Edgefield potter known for his slip decoration] was using a miller to mill his glazing. Lime and flint is hard to mill down to the finest texture to use in glazing, and he was doing that. So I got to thinking, I *had* everything I needed to do it here! The slip that goes on there [as decoration] also has to be milled. No doubt about it: you can't use lumps of clay big as the end of your finger to slip-trail with.[4] When I got home I called Matthew and told him we was starting on a new project! I figure that if someone else has done *done* it, how dumb can you be, you gotta be able to do it. It's a matter of setting your mind to it, and a little experimenting. I've had a ball mill from out of Ohio for many years, a-grinding my glazing. And we just bought a new ball mill; it'll hold twenty-five gallons. That's an unheard-of amount of glazing for anybody in this country [area] to grind. That'll last most potters five years; but as a general rule, I'll use maybe twenty gallons a month. That's a lot of glazing!

[Besides fine-milling the glaze and slip, the Hewells started burning their wood-fired kiln hotter—perhaps 2500°F—to improve the appearance of their slip-decorated wares.] The heat of the kiln brings the color out better. I've looked in that kiln lately and the jugs look like they're jumping up and down! (They ain't moving;

Chester Hewell's slip-decorated, alkaline-glazed stoneware in the style of antebellum Edgefield District's Thomas Chandler, 2008. The $350 price represents the high end of the Hewells' production; they've always kept their work relatively affordable. *Photo: author.*

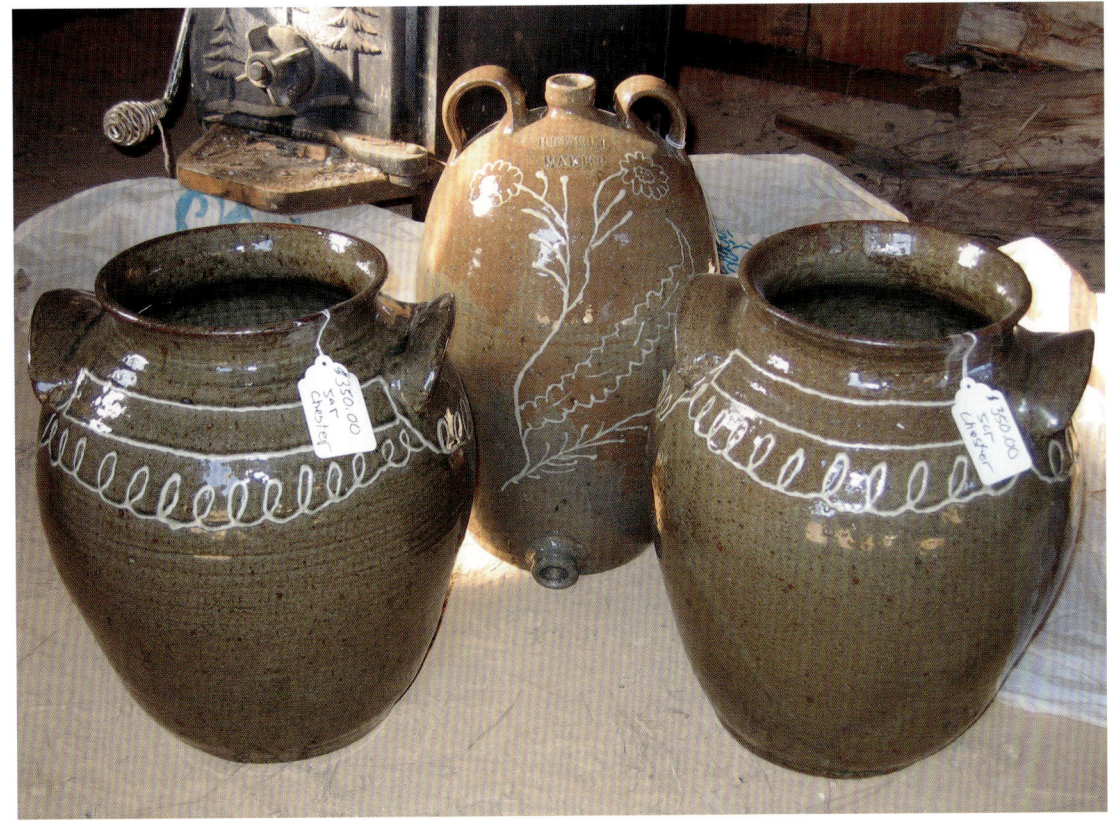

it's the heat.) Besides old Dave the slave [the now-famous en-slaved African American potter David Drake of Edgefield District], Thomas Chandler's one of my favorite people.[5] But some of the pieces that Chandler made, it's not as bright and pretty—it was underfired. [In the 1880s] W. R. Addington in our part of the country made some of the best stoneware ever made, bar none. It's stood the test of time and still looks good. He was having trouble with green wood, you can see it in the color of the glaze. But he'd hold that fire 'til even with green wood he got it hot enough through and through—'til it vitrified (I know that's a big old country word!) [became glasslike].

If our family hadn't continued, you wouldn't have no story to tell. It would have been over a long time ago. [The Meaders tradition] would have died out when Lanier died; they might have kept mak-ing a little, but as far as really producing and getting it out there to merchandise at a reasonable price to get people involved that had little or nothing to buy with, it wouldn't have never happened if we hadn't done what we was doing. I'm talking about old-timey [alkaline-glazed folk] pottery. [Hewell's Turning and Burning festi-val] most definitely *had* to have something to do with [the growth in public interest]. It bring on a craze of people as early as before daylight to get the good stuff. I've seem 'em have a feeding frenzy, like sharks, buying pottery, because they was scared somebody else was gonna get it (and we was toting it out and putting more out all the time!).

NATHANIEL

Everyone [in the Gillsville area] that is in pottery now in a tra-ditional sense, or "folk," their roots can be traced back to either Daddy [Chester] or Pawpaw [Harold]. In one way or another, their involvement in pottery will always lead you back to them. Like Mikey Perdue: he traces back to us. When he came here he knew how to center a piece of clay but he did *not* know how to turn. You've got Jeffrey Standridge, totally trained by Daddy. The Fergusons were out of it for so many years, I don't think they would have ever gotten back into it had it not been for seeing the money (what they *thought* to be money) coming in here. The Cravens: none of them [in later generations] knew—outside of [Billy] Joe, who was trained here.

MATTHEW

My family on one side has been doing this since the 1850s—on the Hewell side. Then on Daddy Bud's mama's side [the Fergusons], they go back to the early 1800s, a-doing it. A lot of people who have pottery in their families, they have skipped generations. My family don't have skipped generations; we're continuous potters from the 1800s to the present time.

The tradition just carries on with my two children. They've been going to the shop since the time they got big enough; couldn't even walk, they come to the shop. Eli [at age nine] can look up in the wood-burning kiln and tell you if the glazing is melting on the pots. So he done got a lot of knowledge about what's happening inside

Matthew Hewell, 2005.
Photo: Emory Jones.

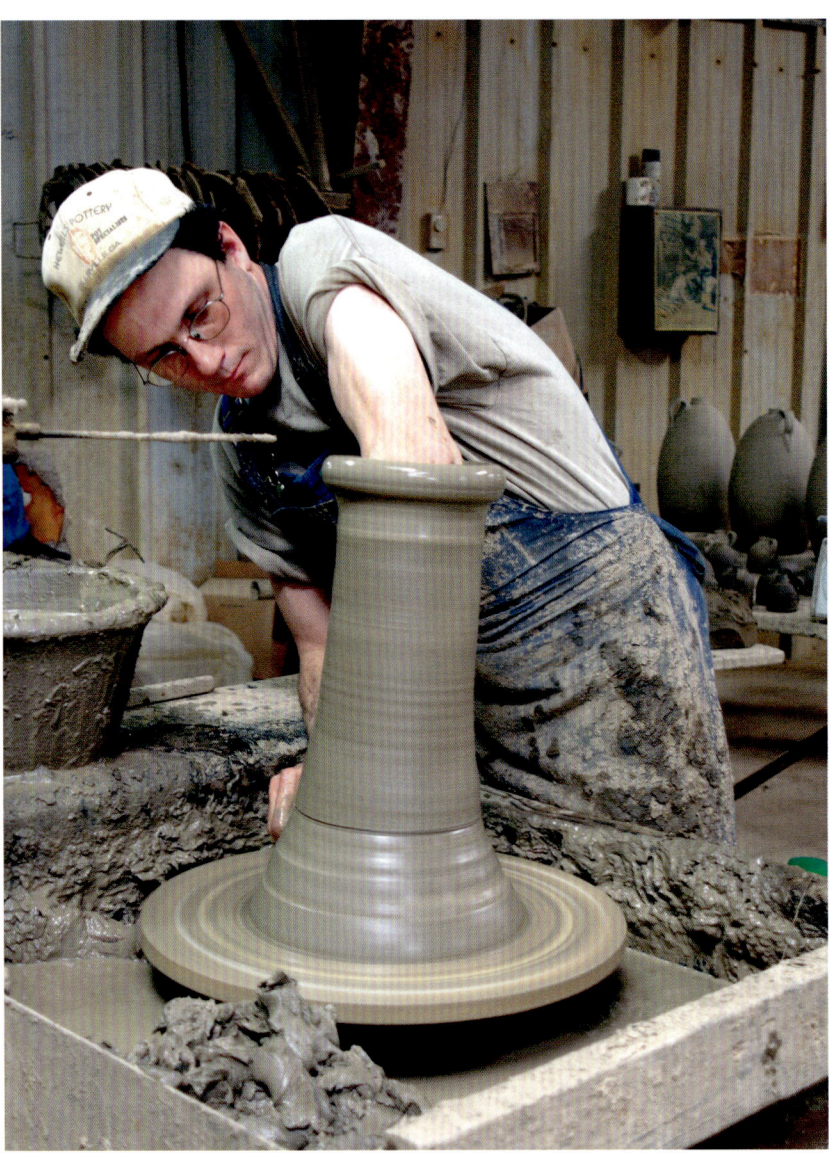

that kiln. That's a big part of what we're doing; he's got to know these things. He's got real good eyes; he can see objects in depth and get that in his mind. He ain't got all the pieces of the puzzle put together as far as producing bigger stuff, but he understands a lot about it, because he talks to me about it. One day we had a stacker [shoulder-type whiskey] jug out here that my great-grandpa [Maryland] had made, and Eli was looking at it with us. He went in the shop and made one! Wasn't nobody in there but him.

All of us as a whole has lost something. The knowledge that goes along with these crafts, whether it's pottery or farming or wood crafts, we're losing the knowledge. In time, we may need this knowledge again: may not always have these machines. I think it's sorta sad, because I hate to lose our history, and I think a lot of it has got lost in the transition to modernization. When I was a little boy, [great-]Grandma [Ada] Hewell would—every day, wasn't every once in a while, it was daily—she would tell me stories and how things was when she was small, and then when she married into the pottery business, about how things was with her and Daddy Bud, and things that her father-in-law, Eli, told her about how it was when he was a child. She give us a world of knowledge from back into the mid-1800s. I'd sit in her lap and she'd tell me stories, over and over. And I'm thankful for these stories now.

She was telling about—this was funny to me, still is—when Eli came to Gillsville [from Barrow County in the 1890s] with his son-in-law and brother-in-law all at the same time, Charlie Ferguson. Charlie didn't have no wagon, and Eli sorta felt sorry for him and brung him to Gillsville. [Chester's fuller variant of this family legend has Charlie jumping on the back of Eli's wagon just as it was leaving so he could marry Eli's potter daughter, Catherine.] Without Eli bringing him, the Fergusons would not have made it to Gillsville!

[On women in pottery:] Like Ms. Arie [Meaders] putting grapes and stuff on pots, I think a woman may have a little better eye [for decoration]; what Granddad [Harold] calls "bright ideas." On the other hand, Daddy Bud had a good eye; he could put grapes and stuff like that on pottery. But a lot of men can't get that in their mind, can't see it as good as a lady can. I can tell the ears my great-grandma

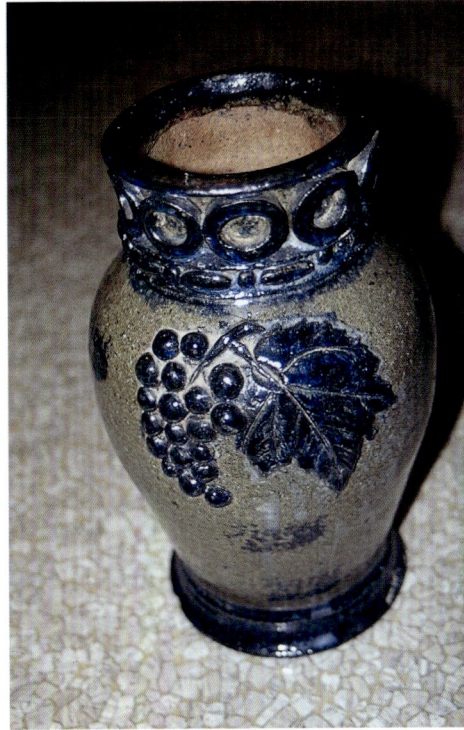

Vase, Maryland Hewell at J. D. ("Jug") Johnson's shop, Lanford Station, South Carolina, ca. 1923, alkaline ("glass") glaze over painted and sponged cobalt-blue, a precursor of Arie Meaders's grape decoration. *Photo: author; collection of Hewell family.*

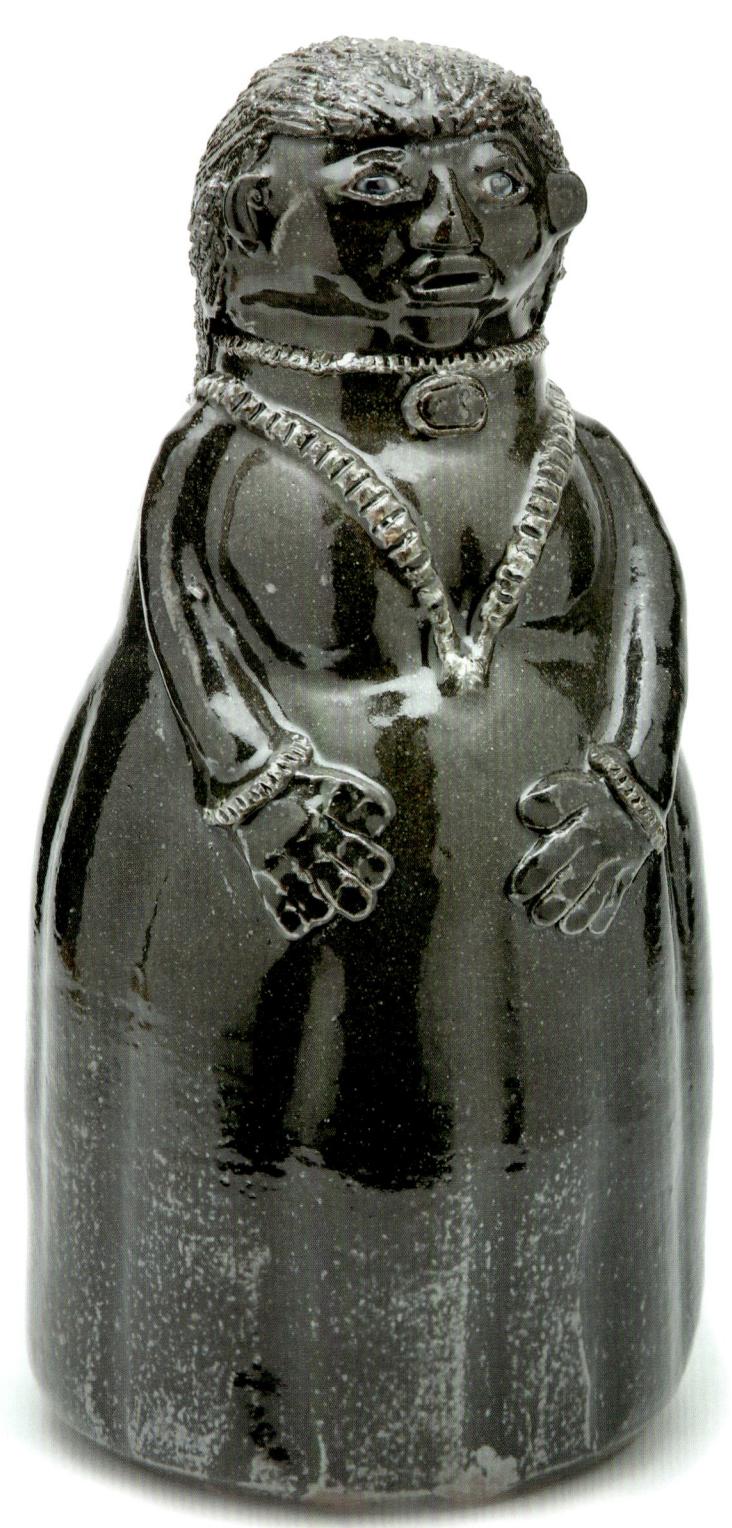

"Confederate Widow," Matthew Hewell, 2001, alkaline ("glass") glaze. This is the fifth Civil War soldier's wife figure Matthew has made, gender-balancing his father's Rebel soldiers. H. 18 inches. *Photo: David Greear; FPM collection.*

[Ada] put on churns by feeling it: you can grab ahold of one she put on there, your fingers don't feel like they're going to slide out from under it. It locks up under there; she done it just right. I've tried to make mine feel like hers; it's hard to do! She just had a knack about putting those ears on there.

Susannah is encouraging *herself*. She's got a lot of determination; she's a lot like Granny [Grace] in that way. She gets it in her mind she wants to do something, she's going to do it! Her brother's doing it, and she's not going to let him get one step ahead of her; she's going to outdo him if at all possible. She's a-practicing on making little cylinders right now. She's four years younger than Eli, so she's got a little ways to catch up.

We're not far from where we come from. We're still cutting wood and burning a wood-burning kiln, still making older shapes, we still go out and find the clay and mix it, make all our own glazes, don't buy that. If you've went to convenience, buying your clay already mixed up, using these electric kilns and little gas kilns, you're losing something there. I think, down the road, Eli'll be blessed because he'll have knowledge that a lot of these other potters won't have. We're still staying true to what our family's always done.

Eli, he pays attention to everything that we do, and Susannah will too. But right now, Eli's really involved, like I was. When Daddy burned the kiln, I would sit with him a little while, then I'd go spend time with my [great-]grandma. The gas kiln that we burned our flowerpots in, we'd burn it 'til midnight, and then my grandpa would take over and burn it the rest of the night. And me and Grandma would eat popcorn and she'd tell stories. I tell Eli—I don't want to swell his head up—I tell him, "Son, our family has stuck this out so long, we got all these stories." I tell him stories that Grandma told me, and Daddy'll tell him stories. And we bring all this history back alive. And down the road, he'll have a picture in his mind that'll go back 200-plus years. It's a real treasure to be able to pass it on to Eli and Susannah. And I want to see them pass it on to *their* families and still be able to make handmade pottery: churns and jugs, and the planters too, 'cause it takes all of it to keep it going.

Thinking about how long [the Hewells] have been making pottery: this is all we know, and this is all we've got. Without this clay running through our hands, we ain't got nothing else. This is where our love is, and it'll always be with us.

Cleater ("Clete") Meaders III, Hoschton

Born in 1956 to C.J. and Billie Meaders, and a cousin of Lanier, Clete is a younger member of another important north Georgia pottery family. He works on his own at his old-fashioned operation in rural Jackson County, about forty miles from the Meaders' home area in southern White County. Part of the year he works in construction as co-owner of cs Specialty Builders. Clete no longer actively promotes his pottery work, depending instead mainly on an established clientele. His artistic ability and sense of humor are evident in his ash-glazed, wood-fired wares.[6]

Dad made the statement about Lanier years ago: "Lanier done gone and put us in show business." I know the Meaders family is like a tree; it branches out and all that. But my history is only about Dad and, of course, Lanier was in it, and I knew Uncle Cheever well. But that's all I knew. The only [model] of a folk pottery shop and how to set it up was Uncle Cheever's shop, that was the only one. 'Cause Dad just had a wheel, and he would carry [his ware] up to Uncle Cheever's kiln to fire. You know, I took the Meaders pottery for granted. I never sat back in awe of it, because I was never *not* around it. When I first started in the pottery business people bought my stuff because I was a Meaders. Which was wild, because it wasn't any good! I was kind of cast into the limelight. When I was hit with that it took me several years to learn to deal with it. Because here I'm going from a regular old working stiff to somebody all of a sudden doing interviews!

I was born in Mobile [Alabama]; Daddy was working at Brookley Air Force Base until they closed it in 1966 [and the family moved to Warner Robins in middle Georgia, where Clete grew up]. He had this big garage in Mobile, and the back right corner was a pottery

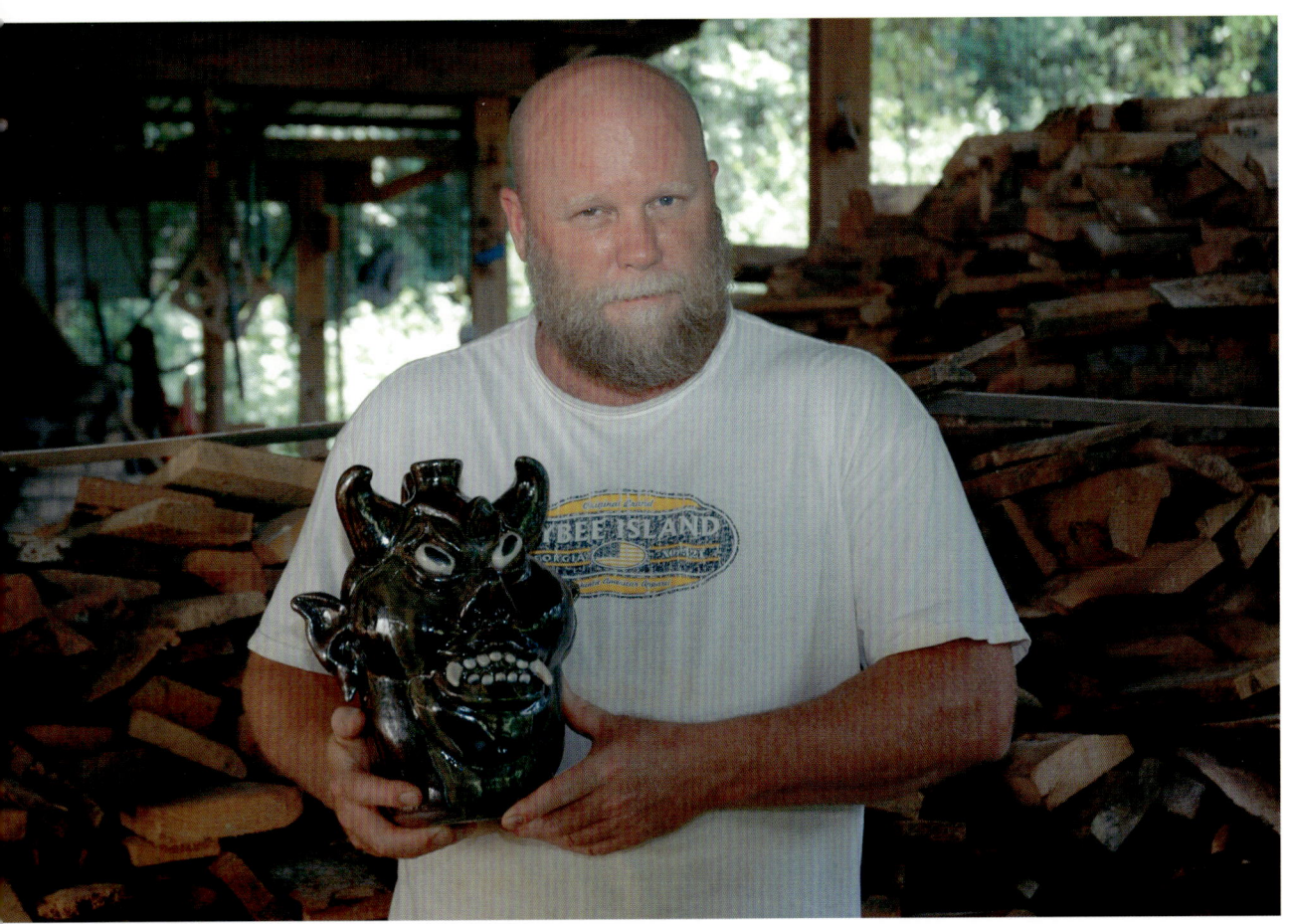

shop. And I'd sit on this plank just above his wheel and he would tell me stories; just sitting on that plank listening to my dad tell a story and kick that old wheel. Dad, as you know, was an excellent storyteller. So my earliest memories [of pottery making] go back to when I was four, I think. And that was when my first piece of pottery was made that's got my name on it.

I went into construction, and it took me out to Texas. When I was out there building a house for a fellow—boy, I got homesick. Man, I used to just dream about Lake Lanier. I told everybody, "This is the last one; I'm going home." When I was a kid we was going to Cleveland [Georgia] and we had a bad wreck in this area [near Hoschton, Jackson County]. That was very profound; it stuck with

Cleater ("Clete") Meaders III with ash-glazed devil face jug at his wood-burning tunnel kiln, 2005. His cousin, Lanier Meaders, and the Browns of Arden, North Carolina, also made devil jugs. *Photo: Kirk Elifson.*

me. So I come back here and I thought, "Boy, I really like the lay of this land." So I stopped to talk with this old man; he was whittling out there. I said, "I like it around here. Is there any place for sale?"

He said, "I'll sell you some land."

So I bought a bagful of peanuts from him and then bought five acres the same day! That was in '87. I was still building houses. And in late '90 I was contracted out onto a school, had to build seven or eight classrooms and a new lunch room. And the general contractor just starts screwing people royally. There was a [cinder-]block mason on the job with me. And I went to the general contractor to get my paycheck and he said, "We're not going to pay him; he never signed the contract, we can get out of it." And something flipped over inside of me. I never went back, and went into the pottery business that day! I decided then that I would never work for anybody else again. I asked myself, how can I be the most independent? Well, this was '91, and, you know, *Brothers in Clay* was "hot"; people were talking about it. So I started making pieces and carrying them to Cleveland to fire in Dad's kiln. I got five dollars for a face jug, but if it had a chin I got six! That's how I got started—out of rebellion, I guess.

A lot of times folks think you work for some inner landscape, you know. I've never done that. I'd probably love it [making pottery] to death—if I wasn't doing it! You haul the wood in June or July; we hauled wood all day yesterday, and that takes the shine right off a toy! And when you're totally dependent on it like I've been since '91—it's been a roller coaster. To me, it's a tool to make money. I used to kill myself down here, man; all the times I burned back in '95, more than once a month. My kids was babies, and I had responsibilities. And that's still what I think about: providing.

In my mind, folk pottery is avoiding modern conveniences and not for the novelty of being a folk potter. You practice these methods to achieve a certain end product. And they cannot be achieved with any other type of practice. If you go to a modern firing method, there is no ash to land on your pots. You see, once you burn all the sulfur and salt out of your clay, it becomes like a sponge. And your southern pine has a low flash point, and it scatters ashes and they adhere to them jugs. And it's just as identifiable as anything [on the finished product]. [Pause.] I guess I *do* have some family heritage, John, now that I think about it. But it ain't what Meaders pottery *is*, it's the *way we do things*.

. . . No, I don't still have a mule to mix my clay. I'll tell you what I found out: me and mules weren't meant to be together. I went through about four or five. (There's a good story about when I sold that last mule that was dead to an old bootlegger for twenty-five dollars.) I made the clay mill I use now out of an old butane tank I got from the junkyard and that reduction gear used to pull a chick-enhouse feeder. And this is how dumb I was: when I got done, Dad says, "You can *buy* a pug mill." I didn't realize that you could buy something that grinds your clay; I thought you had to make it! What

Pottery operation of Clete Meaders, 2005. At left is the retired mule-powered clay mill, with kiln shelter at right and workshop behind it. *Photo: author.*

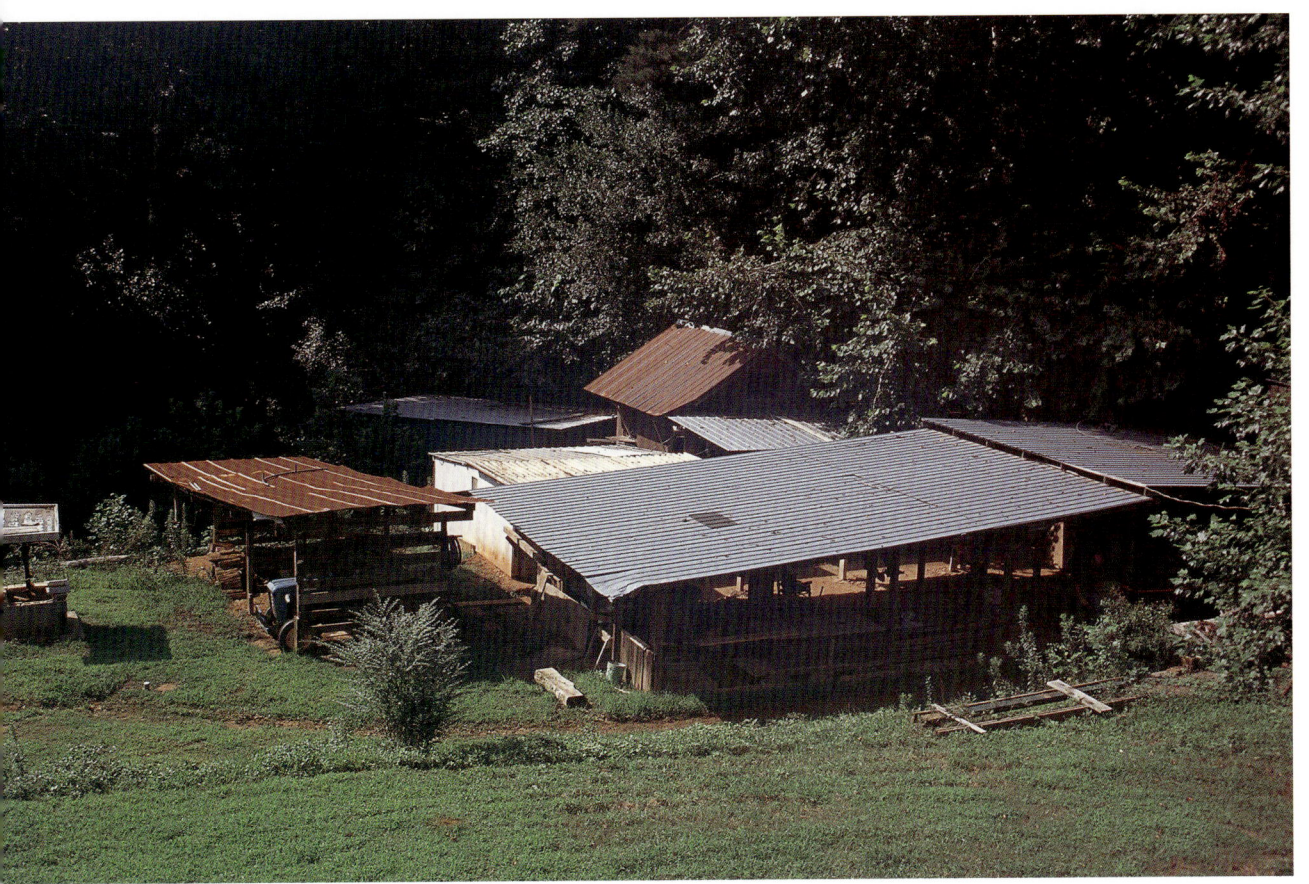

Dad always wondered: how in the world are you gonna run a folk pottery shop [full time] by yourself? Maybe he was giving me hints that a little modernization wouldn't hurt: start burning with gas, get an electric wheel, you know. But that seemed so foreign to me.

Dad used to call me all the time and ask how many gallons [of ware] I turned that day. That older generation that turned for a livelihood, you know, they were production potters. When I come into the picture it had already turned into art, which pays better than [functional] pottery! People now use Tupperware—I do, you know! And face jugs was the talk of the town; they were definitely collectible, you know.

I always had a knack for a face jug; I'm a pretty artistic dude. But my style is different from Dad's; I carry the *art*. My thing is what I do with the piece *after* I set it off the wheel; that's where I spend my time. I've never been that good of a turner; I've never concentrated on turning. Whereas Dad, it was nothing for him to make seventeen, eighteen face jugs a day, Lord-a-mighty! Me, you know, if I can average one a day I'm doing pretty good. But then again, my big jugs now bring four to six hundred dollars. I just flat gotten good at it. . . . One potter I held in admiration was D. X. Gordy [of Meriwether County, middle Georgia]. He just blew me away. He had more talent than any of us put together. When I seen his bust figure [self-portrait sculpture], that's the first time I realized, "This guy here is an artist."

You know, making a face on a jug, it's kinda like building something. I have like an architectural way of thinking; I'm really a carpenter at heart. I've learned a lot about making a face—and I've learned a lot about myself. What this kind of pottery taught me is patience. I'm out here in the morning early—before daylight. By ten o'clock my face jug comes to a stop because it starts to get bland; I lose that edge. I've learned to prepare, to do creative things at a certain time and knowing when that time is. I've got to have plenty of wood. My kiln gotta be in good shape. My clay gotta be worked up. Everything's gotta be behind me, where I've got an open path. When I've got those situations, and about seven pounds of clay [for a face jug], I'm real hard to beat!

[Clete's face jugs] have an animated look. I see things with kind of a twist, and that's probably where it comes from. I'm a pretty cartoonish kind of guy. I'm a cartoon fanatic; the *Simpsons* [on television] is the best thing going. I'm really captivated by creating an attitude. People ask, "Do you know what it's going to look like?" Well no, I never do. But I know what it's going to *be thinking*. I can get just as evil as the devil himself with them things. But you really have to push it out of me, because I'm not an evil guy—unless I'm mad about something.

[On Clete's "signature" pieces:] Well, I would say face jugs, chickens, and hogs, and then anything wildly obscure, like the Mother-in-Law Jug. It was a gallon jug that had, like, forty noses: just a nosey jug. So I called it the Mother-in-Law Jug. They were a hit. Then I had a chicken's body with a man's head. Those pieces come and go, and I'll get burnt out on them in a hurry. But my face jugs, they're my bread and butter. The chickens that I make now are $850. I burn every three months, and if I'm making chickens I'll make five or six in each batch. I really don't think there's any profit, 'cause you're going to lose stuff in that wood kiln. . . . I sketch everything. Everything I do, the whole kilnful, is sketched out. When I first started a kilnful of chicken heads, in other words, I sketched out Chicken Head Ed, Chicken Head Fred, Chicken Head Ted. So yeah, everything I do starts with a drawing—usually on a piece of wood.

Rooster, Clete Meaders, 2001, alkaline (ash) glaze. Incised "Aretha #28" on base, it shows the influence of cartoons and other mass media on his work. H. 14¼ inches. *Photo: David Greear;* FPM *collection.*

I have customers that are fiercely loyal; just collect *me*, you know. They like my style (and you can see my style, how it changes over the years). I've got some people in Florida that will buy everything I make. So I go to thinking, what would they want? Well, let me mix that in with what I can do, you know. So I come up with a theme, like the Hurricane [face] Jug series, which revolved around [hurricanes] Ivan and Charlie. The joy in what you do is really other people's joy. That's what they get; I don't. What I get out of it—what I probably couldn't live without—is meeting some real cool people. I found out that pottery collectors, they want to kinda hunt for it anyway; they don't want to get it off the shelf, you know. If a person is going to spend $1,000, $2,000 a month, they want to know you—and they should! We gonna go fishing, and we gonna talk. So that's what I mean by saying my pottery clientele is unique to me.

I can say that the old ways and the old trade and the old way of thinking is a dinosaur, and it's gonna be gone. I hate to see it go, but everything goes. Not so much the craft that we practice, it's the people who understand it, and I miss those folks. I'd like to hang out with them folks, and they're gone.

David Meaders, Mossy Creek

David (born in 1951) and his wife, Anita Warwick Meaders, live on the same property as his potter parents, Reggie and Flossie, below Mossy Creek at the end of Skitts Mountain Drive, just across the White County line in Hall County. Reggie is a brother of Lanier, which means that David is Lanier's nephew, Cheever and Arie's grandson, and a cousin of Clete. Anita works with him and is a fine potter in the Meaders tradition. For a while they worked at the original Meaders Pottery with Lanier's blessing when he was not there.[7]

Well, I'm just another one of the Meaderses making pottery, you know. [Great-]Grandpa John, they say, started it, then Granddaddy [Cheever] took the shop over, then Lanier, Daddy, John, and Nub [John and "Nub," or Edwin, are two other potter brothers of Lanier].

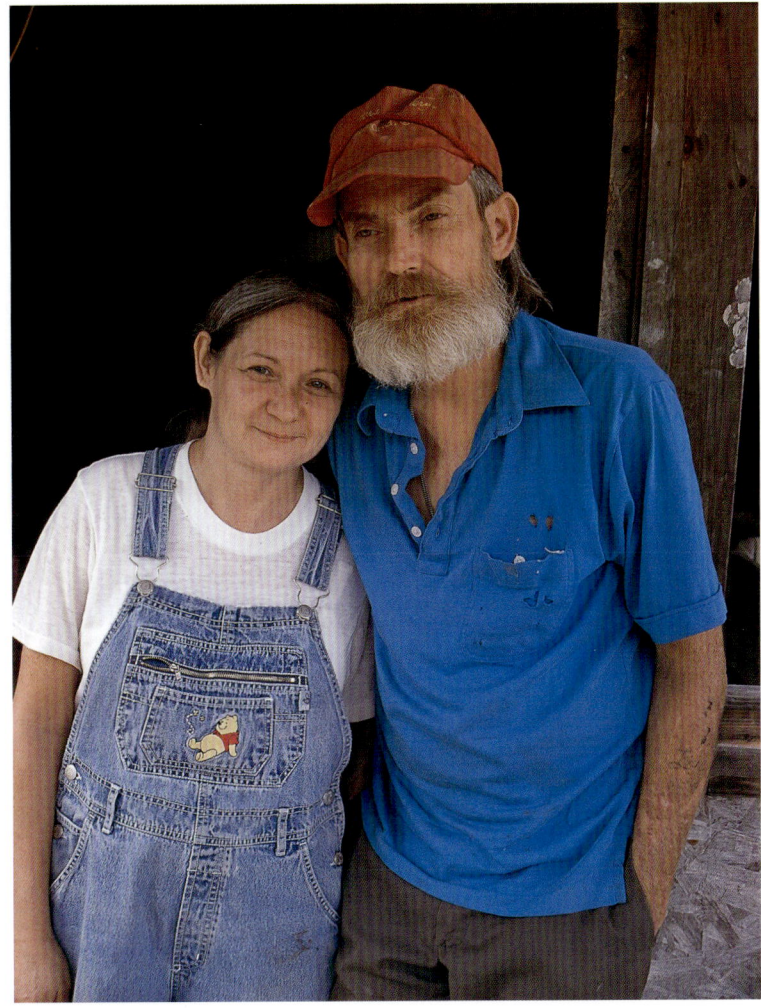

David and Anita Meaders, 2001.
Photo: author.

And now me, so that makes me the fourth generation. There's other members of the family that make pottery, but most of them started late in life. Anita and myself do this for a living, and Anita does the majority of it. I can't do a whole lot anymore; I got some health problems that hold me back. I'm just another one of the Meaderses, like Lanier said, "playing in the mud."

You know, this used to be fun when we first started. It quit being fun when it became a job! But if I didn't like doing it, I wouldn't. I've never done anything long that I didn't like. 'Course, it's hard work. Sometimes you get down to just beans and 'taters [potatoes] when you lose a kilnful of wares. I've thrown whole [ruined] kilnsful through these woods: fifty or sixty pieces, a month's turning.

When I was little I'd go up to Granddaddy's shop in the summer and stay a week or two, you know. And when it was school time I'd get off the bus there. I remember one time . . . our bus driver was Thomas Lee Hawkins. Thomas would stop and let me off [at Meaders Pottery], and Mama told him not to stop and let me off there no more. So we got near the shop one day and I told Thomas I wanted off. He said, "Your mama said you couldn't get off."

Well, we got nearer to Granddaddy's house and I got up next to the [bus] window and told him, "Now Thomas, if you don't stop I'm going to climb out of this window!" Well, he stopped and let me off. I got a good whipping for that one! But I played around at Granddaddy's.

Got to making little old pieces; I got to where I could turn a little cup, you know, something like that. Along about age thirteen or fourteen the ways of the world intrigued me more than pottery, and it took me 'til '82 to come back, and then the only reason I come back was to make a little money at it. Nub's really the one that showed me about pottery. I had a chicken ranch, and in the evening, when Nub got finished [his pottery work for that day], I'd go there and do my turning. He's the one that taught me the basics, taught me about glazes, and I took off from there. I built me a wheel out of junk parts. Then I got the bright idea that I wanted to be a trucker, and got me a truck and spent six or seven years out on the road. Anita, she made pottery while I was gone.

Meaders pottery is what was done before me, by Cheever and Lanier and Granny [Arie]. A lot of people give Lanier credit: "There wouldn't be no Meaders pottery if it wasn't for Lanier." I'm going to tell you something, fella: if it wasn't for Cheever Meaders, wouldn't none of us be making pottery. He plugged on during the depression and all; when everybody else quit, he kept making pottery, sell churns for three or four cents a gallon. It was what *they* done that makes Meaders pottery what it is today. And it was the way they made the pottery. You know, Granddaddy used an old mule to grind his clay with. He fired with wood. He used an old treadle wheel. He ground his own glazes with his rock [mill]. But times got a little easier for him when patent glaze [ingredients] came along; they modified it and it turned out to be this "Mossy Creek green."

[On face jugs:] I never seen none of those things at Granddaddy's when I was a little boy. I bet there ain't never been a potter that hasn't put a face on a pot of some kind; it was just the opportunity, and everything was just right when it happened. [The real interest in Meaders face jugs] came about when the Smithsonian came down here in '67, when Lanier carried all of them up there to that [first Festival of American Folklife on the Mall in Washington, D.C.]. And he made face jugs the best of anybody. Granddaddy made a few, but you don't see many of them. He said it was foolishness; he made stuff you could use: churns, pitchers, and jugs.

[On David's favorite thing to make:] I like to make that [tree] stump; I like making that. But you know, I'd probably get burned

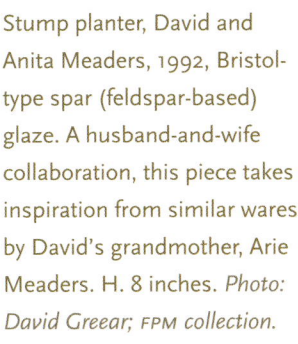

Stump planter, David and Anita Meaders, 1992, Bristol-type spar (feldspar-based) glaze. A husband-and-wife collaboration, this piece takes inspiration from similar wares by David's grandmother, Arie Meaders. H. 8 inches. *Photo: David Greear; FPM collection.*

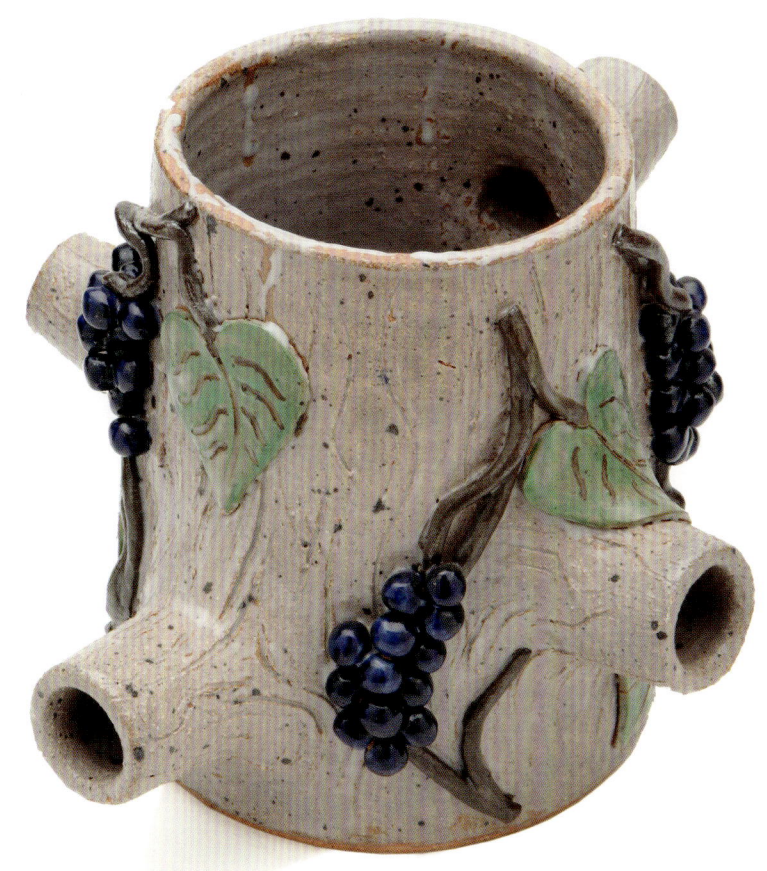

out on that if I *just* made *them*. The way it is, though, you got to make what people want; you'd go out of business if you made what *you* wanted all the time. I've made nothing but face jugs day in and day out; I'll make 75 or 100 of them. And I'll get to thinking, "What in the world does anybody see in those things?" 'Cause they're not pretty.

There's places all over White County to get clay. Frank Miller's place has some of the best clay I've used; it's a real light-firing clay. I've been in there and dug a couple or three times; in '92 and '93 I took a backhoe in there, and that lasted us 'til about '97. What we used for a long time was in the Shoal Creek District of White County; I've got a friend over there who's got a big farm, he gets me a little bit of good clay. But the clay we're using now comes out of Madison County; I really don't like it but it's what we can get. You know, the clay determines the color of your pottery, it's not so much the glazing. Now, one of the glazes I like the best is one of Tarp Dorsey's old glazes: flint glaze. That [commercial] stuff out of the bag won't work right; you [have to] pick up some flint rocks, put 'em in the kiln and burn 'em; softens 'em up. Beat 'em up, mix everything together, and run 'em through the [mill] rocks. Anybody with one eye and half a brain can figure out a glaze; ain't nothing to it!

[Anita is] the talent; I'm the PR [public relations] man! Some people may disagree with me, but she's better than my granny [Arie] was. As far as [Anita's] decorative [work], I'd say she's the best in the family. When we're all dead and gone and they've forgotten about us, they'll remember her. She wanted to learn how to turn, but I'm not much of a teacher. So she'd run me out of the shop and told me to leave her alone. She watched me for five or six months and figured out how to do it on her own. Now, her great-granddaddy, Wiley Asbury Warwick, was making pottery [at Mossy Creek] in the 1850s, about the time the Meaders family came to White County. She's the talent; I take a back seat to her. About the only thing she can't do is dig clay. She can make glazes; she'll fire the wood kiln.

[What David would tell a young family member considering going into pottery:] I'd tell them it's a hard row to hoe; this thing ain't "get rich quick." It took me and Anita twenty years to get to where we can kind of throw down a living at it. But there's a lot of heritage to this. You know, if we ain't real careful, the chain is going to be broke. Lanier said one time that he was going to be the last; I understand now what he was saying. He was the last link between Cheever and [great-]Grandpa John; now, I'm the link to them. And we don't have any children. There's a lot of the old stuff that will be gone; it's gonna happen one day, you know it's gonna happen.

Stanley and Jamie Ferguson, Gillsville

The Ferguson home and pottery shop are located just east of town, set back from Old Gillsville Road, which branches across the railroad tracks from Highway 52; a hand-lettered sign, "Bobby Ferguson Traditional Folk Pottery," points the way. Stanley represents the sixth generation of this third important family of north Georgia folk potters. Born in 1956, he is the son of Bobby, who died in 2005. Before returning to pottery more or less full time, both father and son drove trucks, hauling garden wares for other local shops. Stanley's daughter, Jamie, is the next generation to carry on a tradition that harks back to antebellum Edgefield District, South Carolina. The brightly colored glazes they use are in sharp contrast to the more organic alkaline glazes used by some of the other folk potters but are an extension of glazes developed in the 1930s by Bobby's father, Pat Ferguson, to keep up with changing times.[8]

STANLEY

They's seven generations of us, and we can document it to 1793, when Charles H. Ferguson was born. He was in Edgefield, South Carolina, and actually worked at the same pottery where Dave the slave was at [Abner Landrum's Pottersville Stoneware Manufactory]. He eventually came to down around Statham [Georgia], and [his grandson] Charlie [Charles P. Ferguson] came to Gillsville from Statham in the 1890s and went to work for Addington until 1903.

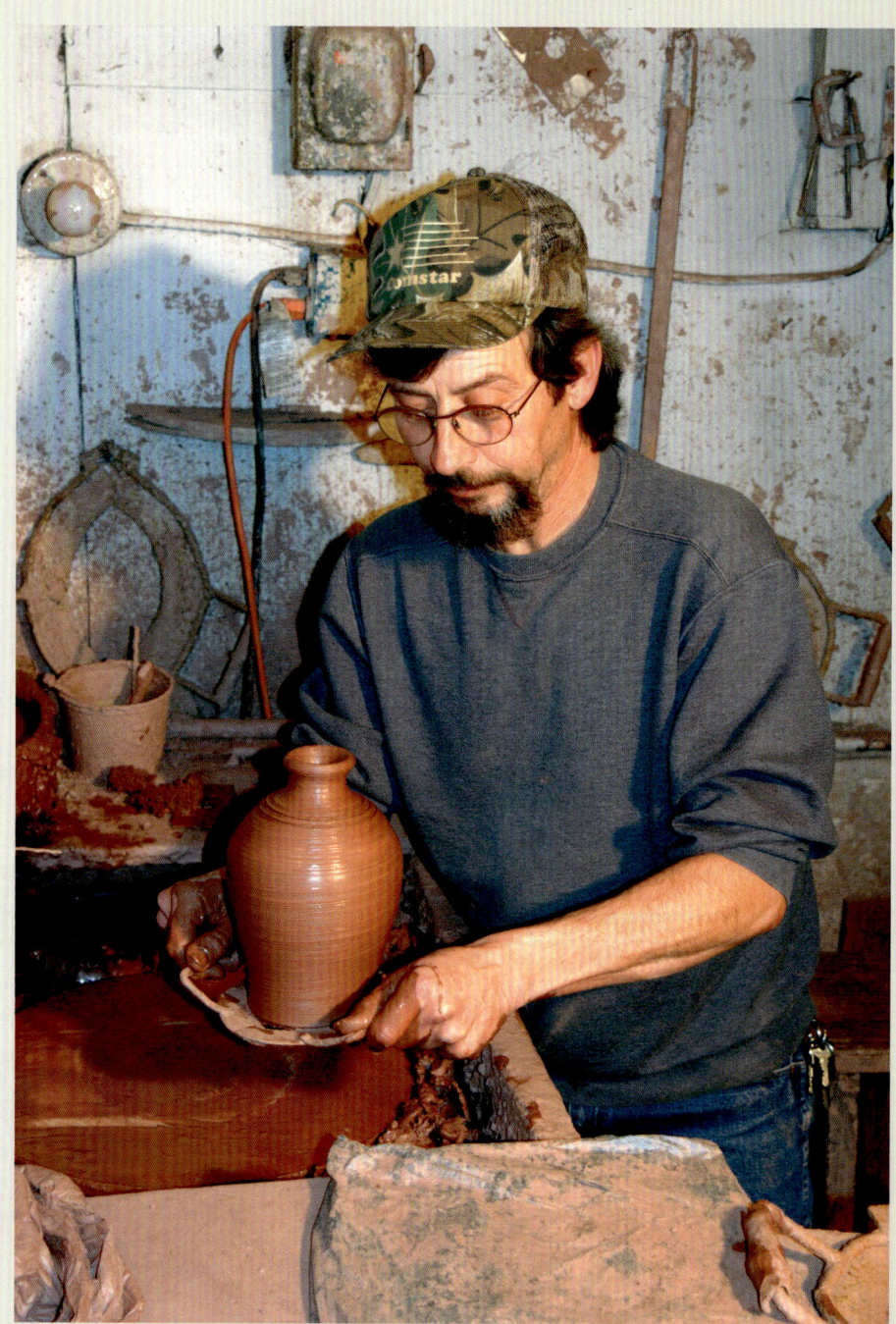

Stanley Ferguson removing a small jug from his wheel with hinged metal "lifters," 2005. *Photo: Emory Jones.*

Then he went to White County and worked some with the Dorseys, and eventually came back to Gillsville before he died in 1917.

[The first Ferguson face jugs] that we know of is Charlie's. We always thought very few were made, but they've started turning up lately, in the last year or so. Most of 'em was probably made for gifts or trading; they would have more time in one of them than they could possibly get out of it, 'cause [pottery] was so cheap then; glazed ware was going for eight to ten cents a gallon. [Charlie's "monkey"-form face jugs] were more of a round, ball-type shape, instead of [Stanley's and Bobby's] upright jug. No piece [of Charlie's] we've ever saw with a face on it had a handle. And where we've got the spout at an angle, every one Charlie made was down on the side and stood straight up, didn't have any tilt to it at all. We don't know why he done 'em like that. [Charlie made two types of face jugs, the first, as Stanley describes, a variation of the monkey form with the neck coming straight up from the side and, instead of a stirrup handle across the top, holes in the ears meant to accept a wire bail handle, and the second, a standard jug form with the neck centered at the top and a vertical loop handle like that shown earlier in this book.]

His son, William Patrick ["Pat"], continued as soon as he was old enough, 'cause he was so young [nine] when Charlie died. He was more or less just left with his mom. But as he got on up in age, he became a potter and turned for many years. I don't know for sure, but I'm sure he was around Eli Hewell, because they worked in and out with the Hewells all the time. And Eli was his grandfather. In his younger life, [Pat] done a little bit of carpentry work but mainly pottery. And then as he got older he got away from the pottery and got into the construction business totally.

Daddy [Robert Franklin, "Bobby"] learned everything from him, worked right along with him. They built a pottery kinda in behind Gillsville, then they sold it to Hallie Wilson. And then they built a pottery right outside our building here now, had it going during the late forties and into the sixties. Daddy worked strictly in pottery until around 1955, and then he started driving a truck and got into the

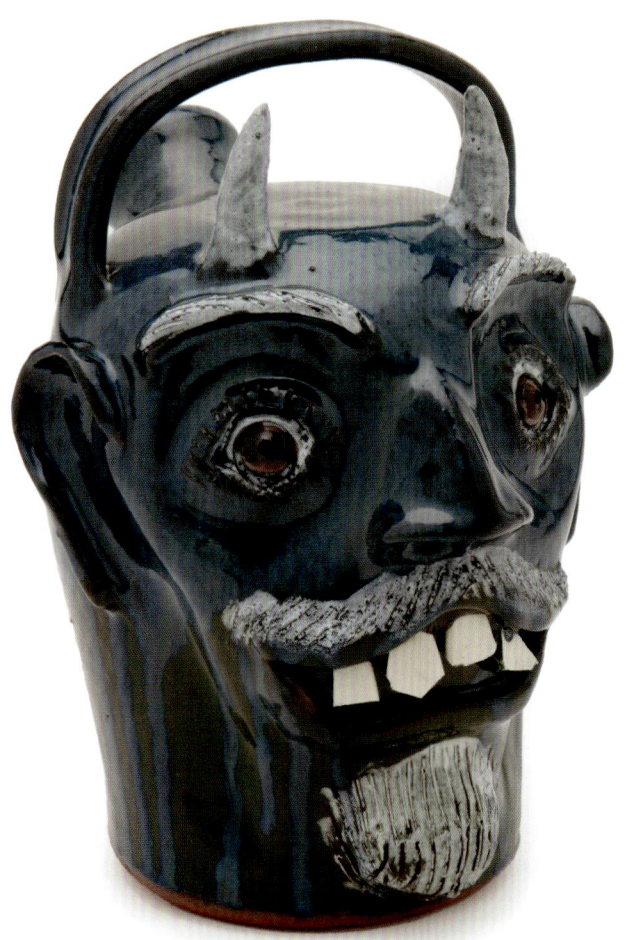

Devil face jug, Stanley Ferguson, 2005, colored glazes. As did his father Bobby, Stanley makes some face jugs in the monkey form. H. 9 inches. *Photo: David Greear;* FPM *collection.*

trucking business. But he always had some form of pottery here, at first in the basement [of their home].

Then in the seventies he started working back here at the shop making mostly garden ware. He did make a few churns and whiskey jugs, and he made a few face jugs; in the late eighties he got to making a lot of face jugs. He was using white stoneware [clay] and making white garden ware; a lot if it was decorated with colors. Nobody in Gillsville made white pottery, so it caught on good; he done real well with it. And he done that at a production rate until his health failed in late '93, and then he switched over to strictly glazed ware. He got back into the red clay with his glazed ware around 1990, but he was still making the white garden ware until probably '94; it was being made by my brother [Danny, who died in 1998], and Roger Corn, and my cousin, Harold Ferguson. . . . Years ago, Daddy started getting this clay out of Ohio that was already air-floated and hammered and cleaned—red and white both. Then we found out that if you combine them, it turns out to be a good red clay with a good temperature range on it. And we mix that with a little Lizella [middle Georgia] clay that's got a lot of sand in it, so it doesn't shrink so bad.

I made pottery in the basement [at home] when I was a teenager; made garden ware, little [tree] stumps and things. I never did do it like [other family members] did; I didn't like it, rather drive the truck. Then in the mid-'80s I started hanging out [in the shop] more and more, got to making a few pieces, just more or less playing. And then around '90 I started making it for sale. I still kept another job, though, driving a truck, until '95; then I went full time here. The thing was, I broke my back and had to give up the truck. And getting over that, I got to where I really enjoyed this and wanted to do it all the time. . . . You can be having a bad day and come in and go to turning, and you just feel better. It's just relaxing; it's good therapy.

I turned and finished all my stuff, and Mom and Dad done stuff together. Dad and I done a double face [jug] together, where I done one side and he done the other. And we were doing some three-face jugs the year he died [with faces by Stanley, his mother Mary, and his daughter Jamie]. All of my stuff, pretty much, is copied from Daddy's stuff. My earlier stuff was really bad looking, didn't resemble nobody's! And then, over the years, I got to where it was more and more like Daddy's. But I won't never be able to turn like he did. . . . [On what makes a good potter:] I think it's uniform, that you can make more than one piece just alike. That you can turn stuff that's pretty much identical, that you can make uniform pottery. That's what Daddy used to say: "Make it the same size every time," to where you can tell that the same person made all of it.

[On what Stanley would like to do in the future:] Make a Rebekah pitcher that looks like Daddy's; mine don't have the right shape. He could make the big round belly on it with a very small stem at the bottom and top. Daddy said that's the hardest thing he ever made was the Rebekahs, took longer and was harder than [other forms]. . . . We fired for probably twenty-five years with gas, until the early nineties when Daddy's health went down. When we went completely to the glazed folk pottery, we went to electric. But I'm converting the gas kiln into a wood burner. Some people, they like the wood-fired; to me it looks better, it looks more traditional. [Stanley plans to use the wood-fired kiln for ash- and slip-glazed wares and to keep the electric kiln for more vivid-colored wares.] We're going to start making more pieces that you can use, like churns in different sizes. I want to start making a canister set; Daddy made some, but I never made any. It's a straight cylinder with a flat lid on it, in a three- or four-piece set of different sizes, that you'd put your flour or your coffee in.

[On Stanley's daughter, Jamie:] She was born in '87; it probably was around '92 when she started hanging out a lot, playing in it. She's got pieces that's dated when she was six years old, and she's been selling pottery since she was nine years old. She got her first article in the paper when she was ten, and she's done shows with me ever since. She's really improved a lot over the years. To start with, it was just something she could play in, but now she really enjoys it, and she wants to keep doing it. She likes the face jugs best; she can play with the expression: the mouth different, with a cigar, or decorated up. She likes to do them crazy expressions on 'em. She also does a chicken jug, a pig jug, a dog jug. And she decorates with grapes. I'm proud of her. We sold two jugs for the same price to a lady; she carried 'em home and run 'em on eBay [Internet auction], and mine sold for $48 and [Jamie's] sold for $79. She rubbed that in for a long time!

I don't see how long we're gonna continue, because me and my daughter are the only two [in the family] now that's doing it. I've got a brother that can do it, and several nephews, but they don't care much for it. And if some of them don't get into it, it may be the end of the line when me and Jamie's done.

JAMIE

Dad can make three pieces to, like, every one of mine. If you ever watched me turn, and then him turn, [you'd see that] we turn completely different. He tells me that if I don't learn to turn the way he

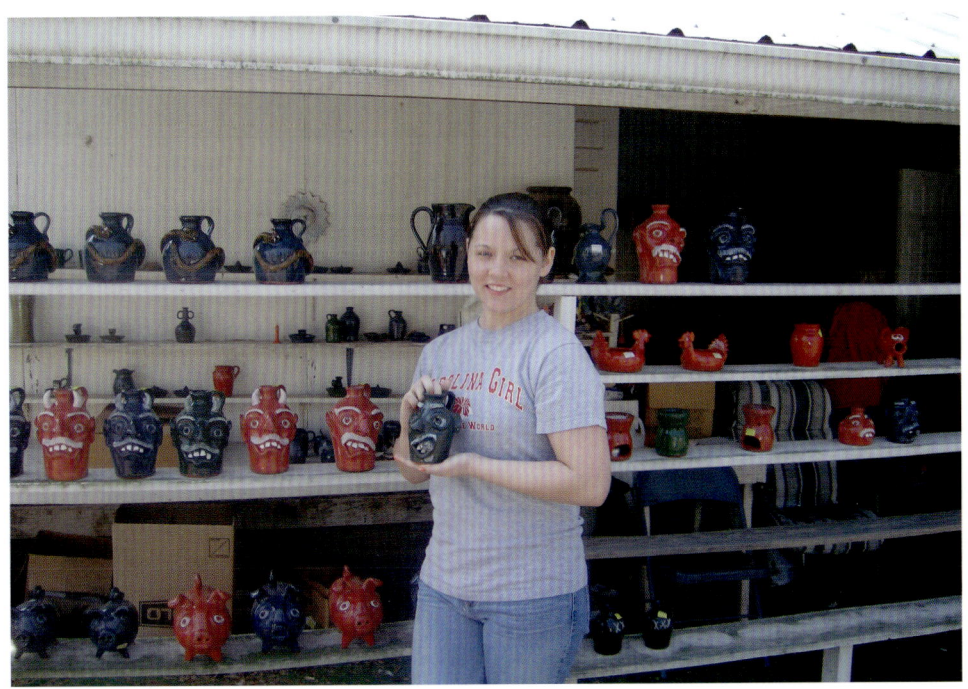

Jamie Ferguson with face jug she made in the style of her father, Stanley, but with her own twist, 2007. *Photo: Anthony Souther.*

does, that I am never going to be able to make anything. Just the way he uses his fingers and stuff; I can't do that, it just don't work for me. He says I ain't never gonna be able to make big stuff. And I am like, well, I will just keep making small!

[On why someone should buy Jamie's work rather than pottery sold at Wal-Mart for half the price:] Folk pottery, one thing about it is that it has a history behind it. When I was in school I always liked history; I mean, I like things that have a background to it. And also, when you get factory-made stuff, that means you are gonna have several that are exactly alike. With folk pottery, you have one of a kind. I would be willing to bet anything that you cannot make two pieces exactly alike by hand; there is always that one little hair of difference to it.

In '05 was when my grandfather [Bobby] passed away, and that got me to thinking about, hey: this is a family tradition. You know, I am a seventh-generation folk potter, and I don't want it to come down to me and then end with me. You know, I want to keep it going, and maybe one day pass it on to more generations.

With the crazy way the economy has been lately, I see me having, like, a main job [as a dental technician], but I never see me leaving *this*, never. I mean, even if it is just once a month I make a piece of pottery. I am never going to leave this completely, never! Right now, yes, it is part-time. But one day I would like to do this full time.

Dwayne Crocker, Gillsville

Dwayne represents those potters who were trained in the area's garden pottery tradition and then graduated to glazed wares. Born in 1958, he is a brother of Michael and Melvin and, like them, began work in his teens at Wilson's, near their family home at Lula. He then refined his throwing skills at Craven's for more than two decades. In 1999 Dwayne built a neat metal workshop behind his house on Diamond Hill Road, east of town off Highway 52, announced by a large sign seen from the highway, "Crocker Folk Pottery." The rooster logo on his shop and pickup truck announces his specialty, as do his live poultry "models" in a pen in his back yard. He and his two brothers are all gifted with artistic talent.[9]

[On getting started at H. A. Wilson's in Lula:] We were always real good friends with the Wilsons, and I always walked by the shop and caught the bus right beside it when I went to school. I enjoyed the clay operation they had, and the wood kiln. And I just got to talking to them; before I knowed it I was working there! I started when I was fifteen or sixteen, 1974 or '75. When I started, I made balls in the clay shop, beating them balls on the wire. They were making strawberry jars, washpots, Rebekahs, things like that. I'd always watch [Hallie Wilson and his sons] Jimmy, Wayne, Jackie, and Ricky [at their wheels]. They'd give me tips [on turning]; I'd watch 'em real close while I was making the clay for them to turn. I did get on the wheel and start playing around a bit. I worked under them a long time and just kinda fell in love with it.

Then I worked at Craven's for twenty-four years. When I started there I was just turning strawberry jars and washpots—garden ware. But I always wanted to do [glazed ware], which I did on the side

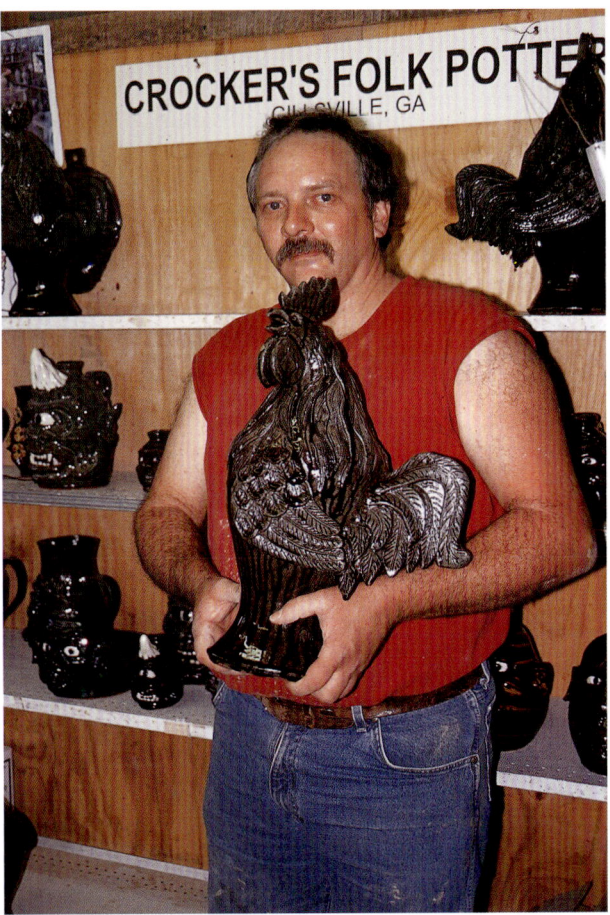

Dwayne Crocker presenting ash-glazed rooster to author, 2001. Dwayne describes his roosters as "a symbol of folkinism," referring to the north Georgia decorative tradition begun by Arie Meaders. Dwayne has been making glazed wares since 1990 at his shop behind his home. *Photo: author.*

anyway, kinda played around with it. When I built me a shop and got my kiln, at first I'd turn at Craven's—go in real early, 'bout 3:00 a.m., stop at 11:30 or 12:00—and come to my shop and work until bedtime. I done that for several years, then I just hung Craven's up and took up my shop full time. One of the scary things about wanting to do mine full time and quitting the other place was, I didn't know how it was gonna work out. But it's worked out great; if I'd knowed that, I'd have done it several years before.

When I was growing up we always had yard birds around the house. Chickens would peck at the snakes in the back yard; I was just interested in them. When I started making my own pottery I wanted to show it through roosters and snakes; I even put snakes

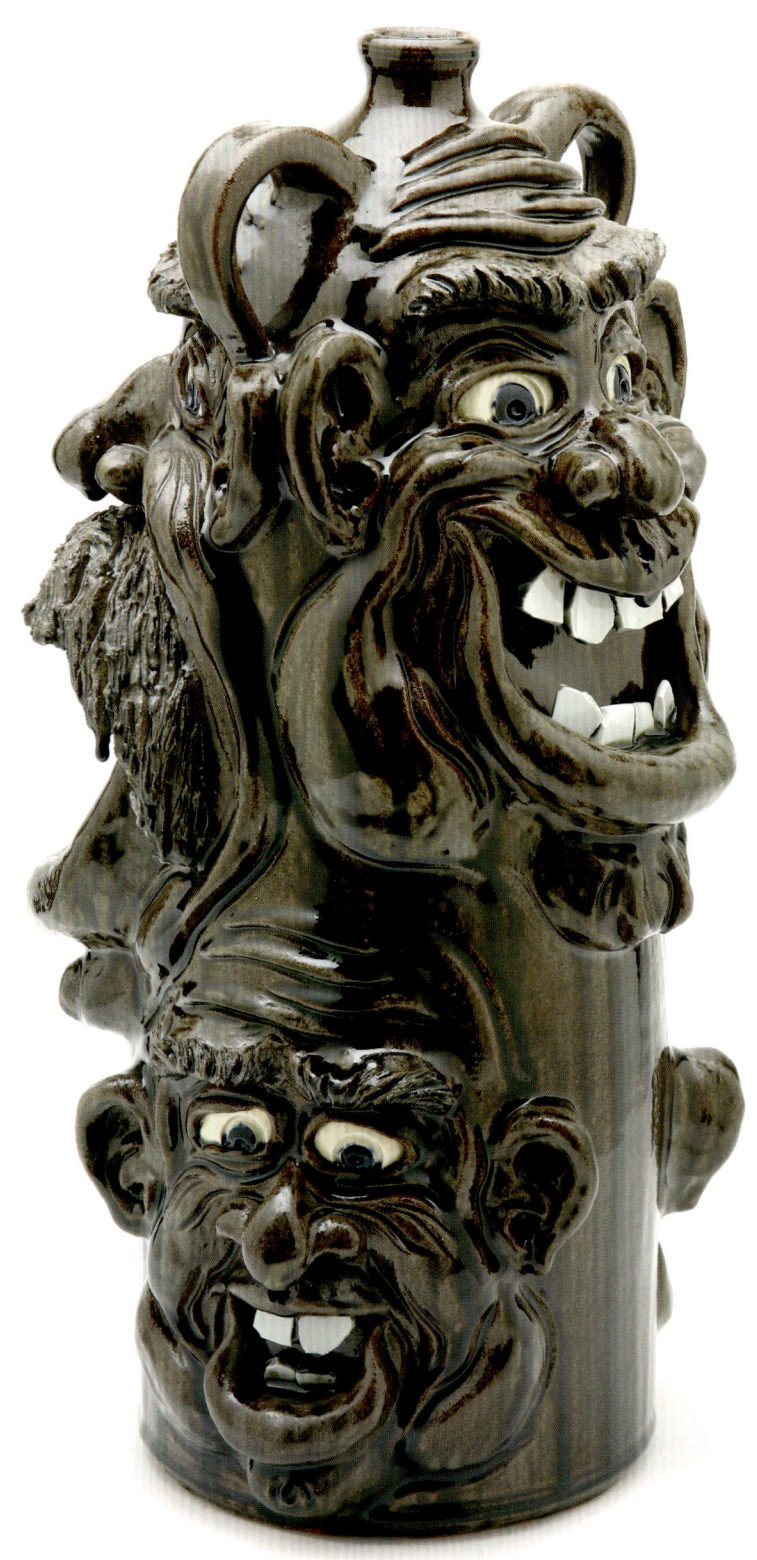

"Totem Pole" jug, Dwayne Crocker, 2004, alkaline (ash) glaze. This five-face jug shows Dwayne's sculptural talent, sense of humor, and popular culture influences (including cartoons). It is displayed on a turntable as a touchable in the Folk Pottery Museum. H. 22½ inches. *Photo: David Greear; FPM collection.*

on roosters sometimes! I may have seen a few [of Arie Meaders's and her son Edwin's roosters], but I wanted to come up with my own style and do something different, the way it was in my head. [On the sources of his ideas, such as the horned, one-eyed cyclops:] It goes back to what I remember from when I was growing up; some is from dreams, some is from pictures I've seen in books, and cartoon characters. I just kinda take it to another level and put my own twist on it.

[On the Catawba Valley Pottery Festival in Hickory, North Carolina:] I was talking to someone who mentioned it, and I got the address and phone number and called them, and they welcomed me in, and I've been going nine or ten years now. That's one of the best shows [sales-wise] I do each year. I also do the Banks County show, Gillsville [in town] on Turning and Burning day, the Mossy Creek show, and the Meaders Homeplace show. I'm thinking about trying Folk Fest in Atlanta. Between the shows and selling out of my shop, it's kinda fifty-fifty. And the big orders that I get [such as the University of Georgia's order for fifty-one mascot bulldog heads] play a big part, 'cause when the shows are slow, the orders carry you through. I enjoy people coming by the shop and really like talking to them.

I love working with clay, and I like the way the old-timers done it before me. I try to stick with some of their roots—which it ain't exactly, 'cause you've got to go with the modern things. But I mix my own glazes [including a runny ash glaze]. To me, that's where it all started, and we shouldn't forget that.

Lin Craven, Cleveland

Born in 1946, Lin represents those north Georgia potters who have undertaken a one-on-one apprenticeship, however informal, with an experienced traditional potter. Although she is from one of the oldest White County (and southern) pottery families, her grandfather and father left the craft, so as an adult, once her children were grown, she apprenticed with Bobby Ferguson at Gillsville. She uses the commercial white stoneware clay and some of the glaze colors that Bobby had used. I first learned about Lin while visiting Betty Jean Meaders, Lanier's widow; I saw on her mantel a group of tiny face jugs Lin had made, and Betty Jean insisted on introducing me to her. That first visit to Lin's home and basement studio on Jenny's Cove Road, out in the country west of Cleveland, convinced me of her talent as an artist in clay.[10]

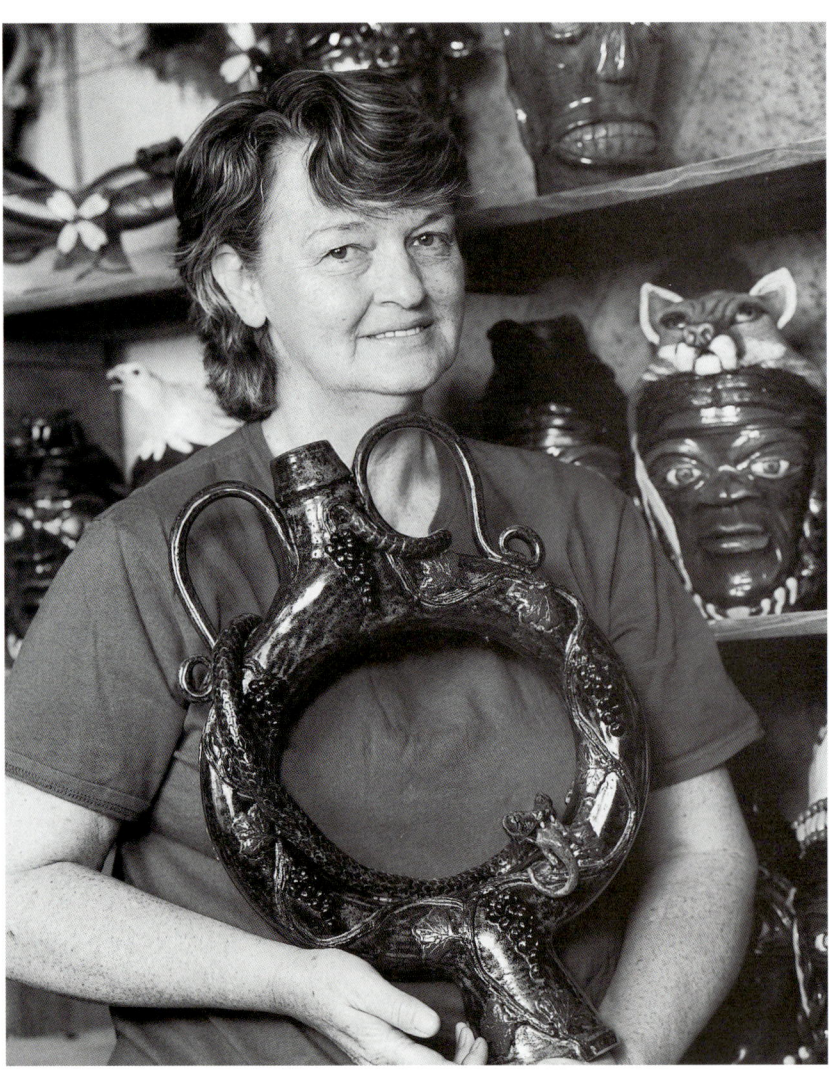

Lin Craven with snake-and-grape ring jug (note rat's hind end in snake's mouth), 2001. *Photo: Chris Swanson.*

Well, I started in pottery about '92 getting serious. But I think it went back to my childhood when my granny taught me how to make mud pies! I always appreciated pottery, and I've been around potters all my life. Not to work with them, but like Lanier, I saw him a lot. We run a grocery store—my mama did—down on Mossy Creek, and every evening when he'd leave his shop to go to Betty Jean's house—that was his girlfriend then—he'd stop by the store to get gas or a Coke or something, and he'd aggravate the fire out of me, what he thought was funny. But he encouraged me a lot when I got started. He couldn't help me [Lanier was quite ill then], but I took him a ring jug and he said, "Girl, if you can do this, you'd better stay in it."

I've always done something with my hands. At first, my kids needed clothes. We really couldn't afford them, so I learned to make clothes. Well, I didn't want to throw their old clothes away, either, so I started making patchwork quilts [from the old clothes]. The more different kinds of fabric it's got in it, the better I like it. I knew [the Cravens] had pottery in our background, but I wasn't interested in it until the kids took genealogy in school, had to know their roots. That's what got me started on my family history. The more I found out about my family, I said, "Hey, this is real interesting; I just wonder if I have that talent, too."

For the last, say, six or seven years I've been hanging out in Gillsville with the Fergusons; I'd go down there two or three days a week and spend the day with them. They finally got tired of me getting in the way and put me to work! And that's what I wanted them to do anyway. So Mary [Bobby's wife] says, "Come on, let's put grapes on these jugs," and so that's kinda how it started. I did do some faces for his face jugs, smiley ones. And he would let me turn at their wheel a little bit. And when I needed a question answered, they were there for me.

My dad [a welder and inventor] built me a wheel. Bobby told me to go home and pick out [a particular pottery form] and stick with it until I learned how to make it: make at least a hundred of them. And so, next time I went down there he asked me what I picked out and I told him, "Ring jugs" [a hollow, donut-shaped jug, difficult to

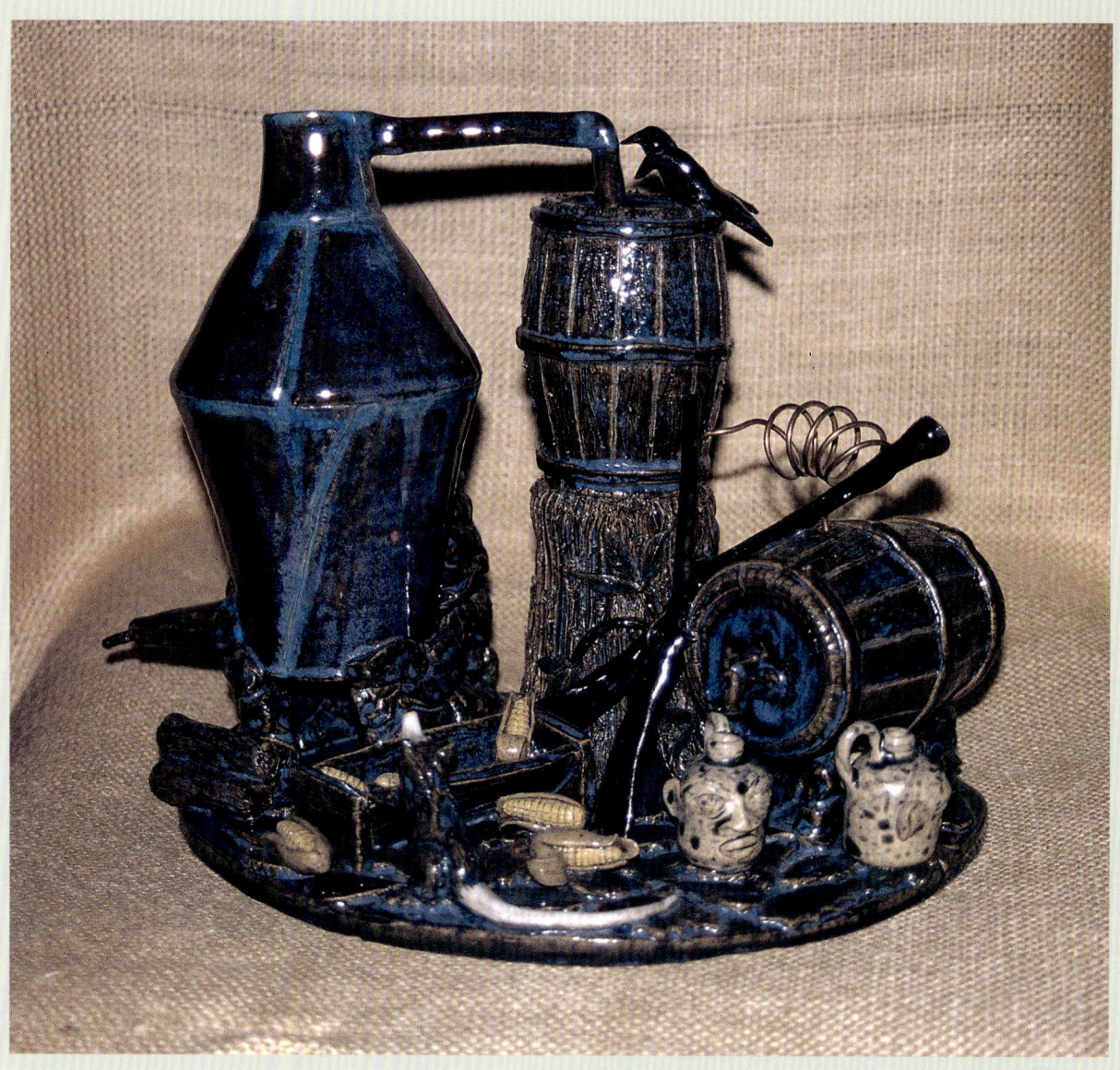

Moonshine still, Lin Craven, 2001, colored glazes. This is the first
detailed still sculpture Lin made; she turned the round parts on her
potter's wheel. The thumper keg between pot and condenser would
be filled with "beer" through which steam bubbles to increase alcohol
content, making a second run unnecessary. H. 9¼ inches.
Photo: author; author's collection, gift of maker.

learn to throw on the wheel]. I just like the looks of them, and I like the challenge.

And he said [sarcastically], "Girl, couldn't you have picked out something harder to do?!" Of course, a year later I could do it! But I really enjoy the ring jugs because there is so much you can do with them [by adding decoration].

I don't do pottery like my family used to. 'Course, they had to have churns and syrup jugs and stuff like that; they didn't need this decorated stuff. My pottery comes from inside, and I don't like to copy other people's work. In fact, something I come up with, like my chicken ring jugs or she-devils, if somebody else starts making them, I'd probably quit, go to something else. [On her ring jugs with a snake swallowing a rat:] The two things that I'm most afraid of are snakes and rats. And everybody was wanting me to do a snake, so I decided to get 'em both out of my system! And now I'm not as afraid of snakes—but I still don't like rats! Everything I do is fairly small; so when I got down there [at the Fergusons' show on Turning and Burning day] with all these potters that can turn these humongous things, I thought, "I'm gonna do a barnyard stack" [column of animals], because I wanted something big on my table; "I can't turn big, so I'll just put it together big."

Things come to my head. I have been down here [in the garage studio] at three in the morning 'cause I couldn't sleep and I had an idea and I couldn't wait. It's a release for me. I can come down and do this, and I'm lost. I'm in my pottery and I can lose the whole world. It's therapy!

Notes

Preface

1. University of Georgia Press, 1983. More recent discoveries about early wares and makers can be found in my 1995 preface to *Brothers*, included in the 2008 edition. For north Georgia's place in the ceramics history of the Southern Appalachian region, see John A. Burrison, "Pottery," in Rudy Abramson and Jean Haskell, eds., *Encyclopedia of Appalachia* (Knoxville: University of Tennessee Press, 2006), 818–21.

CHAPTER 3. From Near and Far

1. Mark Hewitt and Nancy Sweezy, *The Potter's Eye: Art and Tradition in North Carolina Pottery* (Chapel Hill: University of North Carolina Press for North Carolina Museum of Art, 2005), 106–7.

2. For more on alkaline glazes, see John A. Burrison, *Roots of a Region: Southern Folk Culture* (Jackson: University Press of Mississippi, 2007), 60–61, 191n50. Ash-glazed stoneware was made in France (at centers in Puisaye, Haut-Berry, and Martincamp) as early as the 1500s, but I have yet to find any connection to the southern tradition.

3. For further comparisons of southern stoneware forms with British counterparts, see Burrison, *Roots of a Region*, 94, 123–24.

4. For further discussion of face jugs, see Burrison, *Roots of a Region*, 128–33.

5. Wilhelm Elling, *Steinzeug aus Stadtlohn und Vreden* [Stoneware from Stadtlohn and Vreden] (Vreden, Germany: Hamaland-Museum, 1994), 316. For more on kiln origins, see Burrison, *Roots of a Region*, 61, 191n51.

CHAPTER 9. A Home for North Georgia Folk Pottery

1. John A. Burrison, *Brothers in Clay: The Story of Georgia Folk Pottery*, rev. ed. (Athens: University of Georgia Press, 2008), 259. The museum's Web site, which includes a reproduction of the Folk Potters Trail brochure, is at <http://www.folkpotterymuseum.com/>; the museum's 2008 promotional video is at <http://www.youtube.com/watch?v=B3itAd5TMII>.

CHAPTER 10. The Living Tradition

1. Davidson-Terry family letters, Kenan Research Center, Atlanta History Center. James Gunter, son of Edgefield-trained potter Allen Gunter, learned the craft in Elbert County, Georgia, and continued to practice it after moving to Arkansas in the 1870s. See C. Scott Butler, "The Gunters: Migration of a Georgia Pottery Family," *Early Georgia* 30 (October 2002): 171–82.

2. Interviews with Michael and Melvin Crocker are included in George P. Reynolds et al., eds., *Foxfire 10* (New York: Doubleday, 1993), 438–56, and with Steve Turpin in Kaye Carver Collins et al., eds., *Foxfire 12* (New York: Anchor Books, 2004), 199–217.

3. Interviewed by the author in July 2008, except for parts of the Grace Hewell section from a 2004 interview by Laura M. Drummond and a small portion of the Henry Hewell section from a 2008 video interview by Chris Brooks and David Greear for the Folk Pottery Museum.

4. Slip trailing involves controlling the flow of liquid clay from a container through a narrow tube onto a pot's surface in lines or dots of contrasting color.

5. See Leonard Todd, *Carolina Clay: The Life and Legend of the Slave Potter Dave* (New York: W. W. Norton, 2008). For Thomas Chandler, see Cinda K. Baldwin, *Great and Noble Jar: Traditional Stoneware of South Carolina* (Athens: University of Georgia Press, 1993).

6. Interviewed by the author in 2005.

7. Interviewed by Tyrie J. Smith in 2002.

8. Stanley was interviewed by Anthony Souther in 2007; Jamie was interviewed by Jennifer Corcoran in 2008.

9. Interviewed by the author in 2008.

10. Interviewed by the author in 1999 and by Leslie Gordon in 2000. The video clip, "Lin Craven: Making a Ring Jug," can be seen in the "Folk Pottery" entry of the online *New Georgia Encyclopedia* <http://www.georgiaencyclopedia.org/nge/Multimedia.jsp?id=m-1594>.

Books on Southern Folk Pottery

A few items in this list include nonfolk, as well as traditional, potters and wares, or folk ceramics beyond (but including) the South. Earlier works are omitted when their contents were improved or expanded in those listed. Out-of-print titles may be available at local libraries or from used-book sellers.

Baldwin, Cinda K. *Great and Noble Jar: Traditional Stoneware of South Carolina.* Athens: University of Georgia Press, 1993.

Beam, Bill, Jason Harpe, Scott Smith, and David Springs, eds. *Two Centuries of Potters: A Catawba Valley Tradition.* Lincolnton, N.C.: Lincoln County History Association, 1999.

Bivins, John, Jr. *The Moravian Potters in North Carolina.* Chapel Hill: University of North Carolina Press for Old Salem, 1972.

Blumer, Thomas John. *Catawba Indian Pottery: The Survival of a Folk Tradition.* Tuscaloosa: University of Alabama Press, 2004.

Brackner, Joey. *Alabama Folk Pottery.* Tuscaloosa: University of Alabama Press with Birmingham Museum of Art, 2006.

Bridges, Daisy Wade. *Ash Glaze Traditions in Ancient China and the American South.* Charlotte, N.C.: Ceramic Circle of Charlotte Journal of Studies 6 and Southern Folk Pottery Collectors Society, 1997.

Brown, Charlotte Vestal. T*he Remarkable Potters of Seagrove: The Folk Pottery of a Legendary North Carolina Community.* New York: Lark Books, 2006.

Brown, Michael K. *The Wilson Potters: An African-American Enterprise in 19th-Century Texas.* Houston: Museum of Fine Arts, Bayou Bend Collection and Gardens, 2002.

Burrison, John A. *Brothers in Clay: The Story of Georgia Folk Pottery.* Athens: University of Georgia Press, rev. ed., 2008.

———. *Roots of a Region: Southern Folk Culture.* Jackson: University Press of Mississippi, 2007.

Burrison, John A., and Suzanne Harper. *Georgia Clay: Pottery of the Folk Tradition*. Macon, Ga.: Museum of Arts and Sciences, 1989.

Carnes-McNaughton, Linda F. *The Mountain Potters of Buncombe County, North Carolina: An Archaeological and Historical Study*. Raleigh: North Carolina Archaeological Council, publication 26, 1995.

Comstock, H. E. *The Pottery of the Shenandoah Valley Region*. Chapel Hill: University of North Carolina Press for Museum of Early Southern Decorative Arts, 1994.

Cormany, James R. *The Potteries of Itawamba and Monroe County, Mississippi: Churn Suppliers to the Mid South*. Homewood, Ala.: privately printed, 2001.

Counts, Charles. *Common Clay*. Indiana, Pa.: A. G. Halldin, rev. ed., 1977.

Crocker, Michael A., and W. Newton Crouch Jr. *The Folk Pottery of Cheever, Arie, and Lanier Meaders: A Pictorial Legacy*. Griffin, Ga.: C&C Productions, 1994.

DeNatale, Douglas, Jane Przybysz, and Jill R. Severn, eds. *New Ways for Old Jugs: Tradition and Innovation at the Jugtown Pottery*. Columbia: McKissick Museum, University of South Carolina, 1994.

Eaton, Allen H. *Handicrafts of the Southern Highlands*. New York: Dover Publications, rev. ed., 1973.

Frankel, Alfred R. *Potters in Paradise: A Collector's Guide to Makers, Marks and History of Old Florida Pottery 1859–1966*. St. Pete Beach, Fla.: Blue Dome Press, 1999.

Gilreath, Ed, and Bob Conway. *Traditional Pottery in North Carolina: A Pictorial Publication*. Waynesville, N.C.: Mountaineer, 1974.

Glassie, Henry. *The Potter's Art*. Bloomington and Philadelphia: Indiana University Press and Material Culture, 1999.

Greer, Georgeanna H. *American Stonewares: The Art and Craft of Utilitarian Potters*. Exton, Pa.: Schiffer, 1981.

Hewitt, Mark, and Nancy Sweezy. *The Potter's Eye: Art and Tradition in North Carolina Pottery*. Chapel Hill: University of North Carolina Press for North Carolina Museum of Art, 2005.

Huffman, Barry. *Catawba Clay: Contemporary Southern Face Jug Makers*. Hickory, N.C.: Hickory Museum of Art, 1997.

Hussey, Billy Ray, ed. *Women Folk Potters: The Southern Pottery Heritage*. Robbins, N.C.: Southern Folk Pottery Collectors Society, 1998.

Koverman, Jill Beute. *Making Faces: Southern Face Vessels from 1840–1990*. Columbia: McKissick Museum, University of South Carolina, 2000.

Laub, Lindsey King. *Evolution of a Potter: Conversations with Bill Gordy*. Cartersville, Ga.: Bartow History Center, 1992.

Leftwich, Rodney. *From Mountain Clay: The Folk Pottery Traditions of Buncombe County, North Carolina*. Cullowhee, N.C.: Western Carolina University, 1989.

Lock, Robert C., with Yvonne Hancock Teague, Archie Teague, and Kit Vanderwal. *The Traditional Potters of Seagrove, North Carolina, and Surrounding Areas from the 1800s to the Present*. Greensboro, N.C.: Antiques and Collectibles Press, 1994.

Mack, Charles R. *Talking with the Turners: Conversations with Southern Folk Potters*. Columbia: University of South Carolina Press, 2006.

Malone, James M., Georgeanna H. Greer, and Helen Simons. *Kirbee Kiln: A Mid-19th-Century Texas Stoneware Pottery*. Austin: Texas Historical Commission, Office of the State Archeologist report 31, 1979.

McLaurin, Arthur Porter, and Harvey Stuart Teal. *"Just Mud": Kershaw County, South Carolina, Pottery to 1980*. Camden, S.C.: Kershaw County Historical Society, 2002.

Mecham, Denny Hubbard, ed. *The Living Tradition: North Carolina Potters Speak*. Seagrove, N.C.: North Carolina Pottery Center, 2009.

Perry, Barbara Stone, ed. *North Carolina Pottery: The Collection of the Mint Museums*. Chapel Hill: University of North Carolina Press for Mint Museums, 2004.

Rinzler, Ralph, and Robert Sayers. *The Meaders Family: North Georgia Potters*. Washington, D.C.: Smithsonian Institution Press, Folklife Studies 1, 1980.

Scarborough, Quincy J., Jr. *The Craven Family of Southern Folk Potters: North Carolina, Georgia, Tennessee, Arkansas and Missouri*. Fayetteville, N.C.: Quincy Scarborough Companies, 2005.

————. *North Carolina Decorated Stoneware: The Webster School of Folk Potters*. Fayetteville, N.C.: Scarborough Press, 1986.

Smith, Howard A. *Index of Southern Potters*. Mayodan, N.C.: Old America, rev. ed., 1986.

Smith, Samuel D., and Stephen T. Rogers. *A Survey of Historic Pottery Making in Tennessee*. Nashville: Tennessee Department of Conservation, Division of Archaeology, research series 3, 1979.

Sweezy, Nancy. *Raised in Clay: The Southern Pottery Tradition*. Chapel Hill: University of North Carolina Press, rev. ed., 1994.

Todd, Leonard. *Carolina Clay: The Life and Legend of the Slave Potter Dave*. New York: W. W. Norton, 2008.

Tomko, Carolyn, et al., eds. *The Pottery of Charles F. Decker: A Life Well Made*. Jonesborough, Tenn.: Jonesborough/Washington County History Museum and Historic Jonesborough Visitors Center, 2004.

White, Betsy K. *Great Road Style: The Decorative Arts Legacy of Southwest Virginia and Northeast Tennessee.* Charlottesville: University of Virginia Press, 2006.

Wigginton, Eliot, and Margie Bennett, eds. *Foxfire 8.* Garden City, N.Y.: Anchor Press/Doubleday, 1984.

Zug, Charles G., III. *Burlon Craig: An Open Window into the Past.* Raleigh: Visual Arts Center, North Carolina State University, 1994.

———. *Turners and Burners: The Folk Potters of North Carolina.* Chapel Hill: University of North Carolina Press, 1986.

Index of Potters

This list of potters mentioned in the text includes a few beyond northeast Georgia; page numbers in italics refer to illustrations of the potters or their work.

Addington, William R., *16*, *50*, 120, 137

Alderman, Clint, *xvii*, 52, *81*, 102

Archer, Marcus J., *16*

Boswell, Annette Meaders, 100, 103

Brown, Horace V., 108

Brown, James Otto, Jr. ("Jimmy"), 108

Brown, James Otto, Sr., 108

Brown, Jerry (Ala.), xiii, 103, 108

Chandler, Clemonds Q., 16, *21*, 23

Chandler, Hezekiah, 23

Chandler, Thomas W. (S.C.), 26, *29*, 118–20

Colbert, Barney, 97

Corn, Roger, *xvii*, 102, 140

Craig, Burlon B. (N.C.), xii, 96, 114

Craven, Billy Joe, 101, 121

Craven, Isaac H., *11*, *24*, 26, *49*

Craven, Isaac N., 23

Craven, John V., 23

Craven, Lin (Linda Craven Tolbert), xi, *74*, *80*, 95, 97, 102, 147, *148*, 149, *150*, 151

Craven, Mike, 101

Craven, Peter (N.C.), 23

Craven, Thomas W., 23

Crocker, Dwayne, xi, *xvii*, *75*, 79, 95–96, 101, 144, *145*, *146*, 147

Crocker, Melvin, *73*, 79, 101

Crocker, Michael, *i*, xi, *xvii*, 79, *85*, 86, 95, 101–2

Davidson, Abraham B., 96

Davidson, Azel W., 96

Davidson, D. Marion, 30

Davidson, Frederick, 9, 23

Davies, Thomas (shop owner; S.C.), 26

DeLay, Russell Van, *15*

Dillard, George W., 18

Dodd, Eugene, *17*

Dorsey, Basil, 23

Dorsey, David L. ("Davey"), *3*, 23

Dorsey, Joseph Tarplin ("Tarp"), *12*, 136